SCANDAL ON STAGE:
EUROPEAN THEATER AS MORAL TRIAL

New plays and operas have often tried to upset the status quo or disturb the assumptions of theater audiences. Yet, as this study explores, the reactions of the audience or of the authorities are often more extreme than the creators had envisaged, to include outrage, riots, protests, or censorship. *Scandal on Stage* looks at ten famous theater scandals of the past two centuries in Germany and France as symptoms of contemporary social, political, ethical, and aesthetic upheavals. The writers and composers concerned, including Schiller, Stravinsky, Strauss, Brecht, and Weill, portrayed new artistic and ideological ideas that came into conflict with the expectations of their audiences. In a comparative perspective, Theodore Ziolkowski shows how theatrical scandals reflect or challenge cultural and ethical assumptions and asks whether theater can still be, as Schiller wrote, a moral institution—one that successfully makes its audience think differently about social, political, and ethical questions.

THEODORE ZIOLKOWSKI is Class of 1900 Professor (Emeritus) of German and Comparative Literature at Princeton University, Princeton, NJ.

Band XXXI — Nr. 804   Wien, am 3. März 1921   Preis K 6.—, Kč 2.50, M 1.50

DIE MUSKETE

Der gesprengte »Reigen«

(Willy Stieborsky)

In der Ausnützung unserer Wasserkräfte sind überraschende Fortschritte
zu verzeichnen.

SCANDAL ON STAGE: EUROPEAN THEATER AS MORAL TRIAL

THEODORE ZIOLKOWSKI

CAMBRIDGE
UNIVERSITY PRESS

CAMBRIDGE UNIVERSITY PRESS

Cambridge, New York, Melbourne, Madrid, Cape Town, Singapore, São Paulo, Delhi

Cambridge University Press
The Edinburgh Building, Cambridge CB2 8RU, UK

Published in the United States of America by Cambridge University Press, New York

www.cambridge.org
Information on this title: www.cambridge.org/9780521112604

First published 2009

Printed in the United Kingdom at the University Press, Cambridge

A catalogue record for this publication is available from the British Library

Library of Congress Cataloguing in Publication data
Ziolkowski, Theodore.
Scandal on stage : European theater as moral trial / Theodore Ziolkowski.
p.   cm.
Includes bibliographical references and index.
ISBN 978-0-521-11260-4 (hardback)   1. Theater–Moral and ethical
aspects–Europe.   2. Theater and society–Europe.   3. Theater–Political
aspects–Europe.   I. Title.
PN2051.Z56 2009
306.4'8094–dc22
2009023521

ISBN 978-0-521-11260-4 hardback

For Fran Benson and George Cody
Friends, neighbors, theater devotees

Contents

Preface

The organization of this book reflects its genesis. My thoughts on theatrical scandals were initially triggered by the public uproar in the fall of 2006 occasioned by the cancellation of Mozart's *Idomeneo* at the Deutsche Oper in Berlin. As I followed the controversy during a stay in that city, my thoughts led me in several directions. I began to ruminate on the emergence and dominant, even domineering, role of *Regietheater* ("director's theater") in the late twentieth century and to wonder whether its justification on the basis of the venerable principle of "freedom of art" was real or imagined, logical or spurious. At the same time I was wondering about the historical and social conditions necessary before scandal on stage could occur. Why do we hear so rarely of "scandal"—at least in the modern sense of the outcry emerging from the aesthetic conflict between tradition and innovation or from the ethical clash between competing systems of belief and value—before the eighteenth century? Those speculations led me, finally, to ask if "scandal" in those senses could perhaps mask a deeper intention on the part of the author and signal a socially revealing reaction on the part of the audience. Could scandal in fact be a response to the effective use of the theater as a moral institution in Schiller's famous sense of the term? And if so, is that function still valid today?

At that point my theoretical reflections prompted me, as theory always should, to test them against the praxis of history. Within a few minutes I came up with an obvious list of ten renowned theatrical scandals over the course of some two centuries and not limited to drama but also embracing opera, ballet, and oratorio. I confess at the outset that my list comprises in most cases works of literature and music I have long cherished and gave me the perfect excuse to re-read old favorites and to spend happy hours listening to music I love. Was it possible to detect common denominators underlying and linking the scandals that accompanied their premieres?

My list of course makes no claim to completeness: this book is not a catalogue or survey but a study of representative cases from various periods and genres. The list consists of works renowned in their respective contexts—works that have received a considerable amount of attention from specialists. While the interpretation in each case is my own, I have not sought primarily to add yet further work-analyses to that already vast corpus. Instead, I set out to consider the biographical circumstances surrounding their composition and the social conditions surrounding their premieres, to ask within those contexts why a particular work aroused a particular response, and to test on these ten specific examples Schiller's notion of theater as a site of moral trial. I would like to believe that the comparative study of works from different countries, periods, and genres puts them into new perspectives that expose fresh aspects for their understanding and appreciation. I hope, too, that the method used here may be applied illuminatingly to other examples that occur to readers from different areas of expertise.

I should stress at the outset that this is a work of literary and cultural history and that my approach as a literary historian/critic differs distinctly from those of theater historians or students of performance art. I have perused a number of those studies with attention and appreciation although few of them deal with the periods or works that concern me here. Susan Bennett's fundamental examination of *Theatre Audiences*, through its "theorization of audience," offers valuable insights into the production and reception of stage works but cites specific examples only briefly in passing.[1] Similarly, Daphna Ben Chaim's *Distance in the Theatre* develops an "aesthetics of audience response" but considers primarily theoretical works and few actual performances.[2] While both works heightened my sensitivity to aspects of audience response generally, they had little relevance for the history and analysis of the specific works that concern me here. James H. Johnson's *Listening in Paris* constitutes a fascinating cultural history of listening and sharply characterizes shifts in public response to, and behavior at, musical performances in France between 1750 and 1850, arriving at conclusions that are often applicable, *mutatis mutandis*, to theatrical as well as musical performances and to Germany as well as France.[3] Neil Blackadder's brilliant *Performing Opposition: Modern Theater and the Scandalized Audience*, which takes up three of the ten works that I consider, focuses on the dynamics of scandal during the period from 1889 to 1931—that is, the complex choreography of interaction between theater and audience and within the audience itself, based on theoretical models involving audience sociology, reception theory, theater design, and norms of social behavior, but leaving aside the intention of the author.[4] I have gratefully acknowledged his contributions to my understanding in the appropriate places. Anya Peterson Royce's *Anthropology of the Performing Arts* takes an approach that is quite remote from my own but provides through its cross-cultural perspective certain basic insights: for instance, that such diverse forms as *commedia dell'arte*, kabuki theater, and classical ballet all depend on a consensus between audience and performers on certain conventions of genre that must be honored.[5]

My own work, in contrast, is based on a conception that is at once comparative, that extends historically from 1782 to 1968, and that embraces musical compositions as well as drama. My approach is aesthetic and ethical, emphasizing in each case the work as art and the artist's expressed intention in creating it. Within those specific contexts I examine the extent to which those intentions were fulfilled or lost in the audience's and critics' response to the premiere performance. I am fully aware of the central theory governing studies in reception aesthetics: that any work consists of the accumulated readings and/or performances it has undergone since its inception and that the author's original "intention" becomes irrelevant. However one may regard that theory, it can be plausibly argued on the basis of biographical evidence that artists often express an explicit intention with respect to their work and that at least the premiere performance during the artist's own lifetime fulfills as effectively as possible that intention—or not, as the creator's occasional first-night indignation suggests. Throughout I have been guided by Schiller's conception of the theater as a moral institution, which I propose as a theoretical tool with which to explore larger issues exposed by the initial scandal on stage. I hope that readers from theater history and performance studies will find my work as complementarily useful to their own as I have done with theirs.

Finally, I should make it clear that my unhappiness with the extremes to which *Regietheater* of recent decades, and notably in Germany, has all too frequently allowed itself to be carried is a matter of personal taste and judgment. This is an issue on which opinions are strongly divided, as was evident already in the fundamental 1993 essays by Thomas Zabka and Adolf Dresen in *Dichter und Regisseure* and more recently in the conference papers in *OperMachtTheaterBilder* as well as Johanna Dombois and Richard Klein's article on *Regietheater* in opera.[6] If a director wishes to add through gesture, gaze, and rhetorical emphasis a Freudian slant to his production of *Hamlet*, that is a legitimate interpretative approach. But if he has his Hamlet exclaim, "I want to fuck my mother," as was the case in a production in Bochum (cited by Zabka), he is doing violence to Shakespeare's text and its subtlety of meaning.[7] However, it is not my bias that matters here. What matters is simply the fact that *Regietheater* represents in today's discourse about theater and opera one of the more radical positions regarding "freedom of art" and "scandal" and must therefore be taken into account in that context (in my Introduction and Conclusion). For the history of the ten actual scandals treated in Chapters 2–6, "*Regietheater*," as a late-twentieth-century phenomenon, is irrelevant.

I am grateful to Linda Bree at Cambridge University Press for her encouragement and support as she shepherded my manuscript through the editorial process. Thanks to her resourcefulness I gained the benefit of two knowledgeable and perspicacious readers, whose perspectives, insights, and suggestions have appreciably improved my text. Also at Cambridge, Maartje Scheltens guided me patiently and skillfully through the publication procedures. Michael Assmann of the Deutsche Akademie für Sprache und Dichtung came to my assistance quickly and generously with bibliographical references, and music critic Wolfgang Stähr kindly sent me copies of his helpful essays on the premieres of *Das Floß der Medusa* and of Bartók's *Der wunderbare Mandarin*. My friends and colleagues, Professor Jürger Kohler of Greifswald and Professor Harold James here at Princeton University, easily solved a couple of legal and historical riddles that had puzzled me. Finally, I could not have carried out this research without the rich resources of Princeton University's Firestone Library, including its Interlibrary Loan department, and the splendid Mendel Music Library. Peter Harrington at Brown University Library generously provided the digital image of *Die Muskete* for the cover and frontispiece from the Anne S.K. Brown Military Collection. My daughter, Professor Margaret Ziolkowski, offered valuable references for the historical background to Stravinsky's *Le Sacre du printemps* my son, Professor Jan Ziolkowski, alerted me to the scandal surrounding Mary Garden's *Salome* in New York; and my son, Professor Eric Ziolkowski, contributed insights into the differences between scandal and blasphemy. Since theater is by definition a collaborative event, I am again indebted to my wife Yetta, who has shared with me various performances—though not the scandalous premieres!—of many of the works here considered and offered me her invariably frank and penetrating responses.

CHAPTER I

Introduction

SCANDAL AS A NON-EVENT?

The most sensational theatrical scandal of the year 2006, in Germany and internationally, turned out to be a non-event. On September 26, the General Manager of the Deutsche Oper Berlin announced that, as a precaution against possible Islamic protests, she had cancelled the scheduled performance of Mozart's *Idomeneo*.[1] Kirsten Harms explained that she had been alerted by the Berlin office of criminal investigations (Landeskriminalamt) regarding a phone call from a concerned opera-subscriber, who wondered if the programmed production of the opera, which had been performed without incident in 2003, would under current political conditions cause disturbances by Muslim extremists. Following a police assessment of the situation, the Manager was notified by Berlin Senator Ehrhart Körting, Berlin's chief security official, that his office feared a "security risk of incalculable dimensions" ("Sicherheitsrisiko von unkalkulierbarem Ausmaß") if the performance should be mounted. In view of the months of tension in Europe following the publication in September 2005 in a Danish newspaper of cartoons depicting Muhammad,[2] a bombing attempt by young Islamic terrorists on a German train, and the reaction to Pope Benedict XVI's September speech at the University of Regensburg, which cited a quotation that infuriated many Muslims, Ms. Harms cancelled the performance.

Mozart and Muslims? The opera was commissioned in 1780 for the Residenztheater in Munich by Prince Karl Theodor, Elector of the Palatinate, who specified the subject: the legend of the Homeric hero Idomeneus. According to ancient sources—notably Servius's fifth-century commentary on *Aeneid* 3.121[3]—Idomeneus, the King of Crete and a hero of the Trojan War, was caught with his fleet of eighty ships in a great storm on the voyage back to his home-island.[4] In his appeal to Poseidon, the God of the Seas, Idomeneus vowed—alluding implicitly to a common cultural theme also evident, for instance, in the story of Jephthah (Judges 11–12)—to sacrifice the first living creature he should encounter upon reaching Crete. This turned out to be his son, who had come down to the shore to welcome his returning father. When Idomeneus carried out his horrendous vow—or, according to another version, failed to do so, causing the land to be afflicted by a terrible plague—the King was driven into exile by the offended citizens of Crete (to the land of the Sallentines in Italian Calabria, where he established a new kingdom). Servius's account, repeated in such widely consulted eighteenth-century handbooks as Benjamin Hederich's *Gründliches Mythologisches Lexikon* (1724) and John Lemprière's *Classical Dictionary* (1788), was first popularized by François de Fénelon in his political-pedagogical romance *Télémaque* (1699), in which the young hero, in the course of his travels, visits Crete and learns there of Idomenée's tragic fate (Book 5), which Fénelon recounts at leisurely length. Fénelon's version was dramatized by Prosper de Crébillon ("Crébillon *père*") in his tragedy *Idomenée* (1705), which complicated the plot with a love intrigue, having father and son fall in love with the same woman. The son, learning of his father's unfulfilled vow, sacrifices himself in the last scene in an act of suicide. A few years later, Antoine Danchet took Crébillon's version as the basis for the libretto he wrote for André Campra's *tragédie lyrique, Idomenée*, which had its premiere at the Paris Opéra in 1712 and was successfully revived, with minor changes, in 1731. Danchet entangled the traditional tale further by introducing Electra as Ilione's jealous rival for the affection of the King's son Idamante. Idomenée, torn between love and jealousy, decides to save his son and keep Ilione for himself by sending Idamante to escort Electra back to Argos. But another frightful storm prevents their trip, and the god Proteus threatens that a dreadful sea-monster will devastate Crete if Idomenée fails to keep his vow. Idamante slays the monster, brings peace to Crete, and Idomenée renounces both throne and Ilione in favor of his son. But in the last act, just as the young couple are celebrating their marriage, Nemesis appears to warn that the gods are still not appeased. Idomenée is struck with madness and in a seizure kills his son. When he recovers his sanity, his attempted suicide is prevented by the people: it is his punishment to go on living.

Mozart engaged Abbate Gianbattista Varesco, the court chaplain in his hometown of Salzburg, to prepare an Italian-language libretto based on Danchet/Campra's *Idomenée*. But the cleric softened the ending, giving it a Judeo-Christian twist by analogy with Abraham's intended sacrifice of Isaac (Genesis 22) and an entirely un-Homeric and non-tragic ending. Although he omits the jealousy motif and the figure of Electra, he follows *Idomenée* up to the moment when a storm prevents the son's departure. At that point, Varesco departs dramatically from his French source. Idomeneo confesses his sin of omission to the High Priest, whereupon Idamante volunteers himself as a sacrifice. When Trojan princess Ilia offers to take his place, the gods proclaim through an oracle that they will forgive all if Idomeneo abdicates in favor of his son and if Ilia marries the new king. By omitting Danchet's tragic finale, Varesco succeeds in providing a happy ending to the originally, and traditionally, tragic episode. Composed in less than two months, Mozart's first major opera (K. 366) had its premiere on January 29, 1781, to the great satisfaction of the elector, who pronounced it "magnificent."[5]

The action, which takes place in Homeric Greece almost 2,000 years before Muhammad's time, obviously has nothing to do with Islam. The potentially offensive scene does not occur at all in Mozart's libretto but was added by the opera's director, Hans Neuenfels, who took a number of other liberties with the text. He cut the libretto extensively and added a group of zombie-like figures, Ilia's dead relatives, who follow the princess and, gesturing toward their war wounds, silently reproach her for falling in love with an enemy; the oracle announcing the gods' forgiveness is broadcast through a loudspeaker; two figures, in the illusion-shattering manner of Brecht, hold up a banner bearing the famous quotation from Sophocles' *Antigone*: "Wonders are many, and nothing more wonderful than man." At the end, as the final strains of Mozart's music die away, Neuenfels tacks on an epilogue that is anticipated or suggested by nothing in the text. Idomeneo comes back onstage alone, carrying a blood-soaked bag on his shoulder. Opening it with almost hysterical laughter, he takes out one by one the decapitated heads of Poseidon and three other founders of world religions—Buddha, Jesus, and Muhammad—who were all hovering in the background during Act III. Displaying them in triumph, he places them on chairs, a man who has liberated himself at last from the cruel demands of the gods. Neuenfels called the scene his personal protest against organized religions.[6] As his lawyer explained, the severed heads were meant to make the point that "all the founders of religions were figures that didn't bring peace to the world."[7] (The irony is delicious because Varesco/Mozart, first among the various versions since antiquity, specifically added the implicitly Judeo-Christian dimension of forgiveness.)

Think what one may about directorial liberties and the merits of this particular production, the cancellation of the opera produced a flood of criticism in Europe and around the world. In Germany figures ranging from Chancellor Angela Merkel and her Interior Minister Wolfgang

Schäuble, to Mayor Klaus Wowereit of Berlin and Michael Naumann, the former German Minister of Culture and current publisher of the national newspaper *Die Zeit*, expressed their dismay. "If we're weighing security questions against artistic freedom," said Monika Griefahn, the cultural spokeswoman for the Social Democrat Party, "I have to ask myself if the fundamentalists haven't already won."[8] Editorial voices from New York to England and Italy protested the decision in similar terms.[9] The day following the announcement, Minister Schäuble, a prominent advocate of ethnic and religious harmony, sponsored a conference of German political personalities and leaders of the Muslim community in Germany, at which the conferees unanimously voiced their hope of seeing the opera rescheduled.[10] On October 1, the opera company hosted a panel discussion of the incident featuring prominent figures from politics and culture.[11]

As it happens, the opera was subsequently reinstated in the schedule. A month after his initial phone call, Senator Körting informed Ms. Harms by fax that the Landeskriminalamt, judging by the indifferent response in the Muslim world, found no further cause for alarm. (Aktham Suliman, the German correspondent for Al Jazeera television, explained that "Opera is a Western institution, which scarcely plays a role in the Arabic world."[12]) The director himself acknowledged that the only threats he had received, despite his avowed polemical intention in the added scene, were neither religious nor political but entirely aesthetic in nature.[13] In fact, the only act of protest appears to have been the loss, or theft, of the four decapitated heads, which disappeared from the props room and had to be fashioned anew.

The performance on December 18, attended by many political figures including Minister Schäuble, Mayor Wowereit, and the head of the Turkish community (though boycotted by the Muslim Council), took place under heightened security measures, with uniformed police officers along with television crews stationed outside in the broad Bismarck Strasse, while riot vans parked at the ready in the side streets. The whole affair presented a rather farcical and anticlimactic spectacle. Few opera-lovers bothered to attend; some 100 tickets remained unsold. The vast auditorium of the Deutsche Oper was largely filled by politicians and their bodyguards, by police in plainclothes, and by celebrities and journalists, all of whom had to enter through airport metal detectors and present their handbags for inspection. The critic for the Berlin *Tagesspiegel* (December 12) noted wryly that never before had the house been filled with so many people who were now attending an opera for the first time. If anything was scandalous, it was the performance itself, which was unanimously savaged in the reviews. The taste of the production was questionable, the singing was weak, and the conductor succeeded in making Mozart's revolutionary music with its powerful orchestral storm and emotional arias, which shattered the traditional form of *opera seria*, lethargic and even boring.[14] (The police turned out in full force again for the second presentation of the opera on December 29, which was boycotted by a small group of silent Muslim protestors outside and also failed to sell some 400 tickets.)

ART AS PROVOCATION?

Neuenfels protested the cancellation of his production, reasoning that "it's a question of defending our Western understanding of culture" ("*unseres abendländischen Kulturverständnisses*").[15] Neuenfels has reveled in and indeed furthered his career as a director through controversy. Simultaneously with *Idomeneo*, for instance, he staged a production of Mozart's *The Magic Flute* at Berlin's Komische Oper, featuring a Papageno sporting one hand and one predatory claw and a Papagena from whose womb dry sand flows during the famous love duet, and in which a troupe of actors carry on a cynical running commentary on Tamino's progress through fire and water to enlightenment. It should be stressed that it was not the display of decapitated heads per se that was offensive—think of the bloody heads that are routinely featured at the end of Richard Strauss's *Salome* or Hans Werner Henze's *Bassariden*—but the fact that they are the heads of venerated religious founders.

The so-called *Regietheater*, in which the director feels free, indeed obliged, to tamper with the production, whether Aeschylus or Shakespeare or Mozart, and to adapt it to his own political or other views, has dominated the German theater for several decades. Like Neuenfels, Frank Castorf, since 1992 Managing Director of Berlin's prizewinning Volksbühne, achieved his controversial acclaim with often outrageous productions of classical works, in which the actors appear naked and even drunk on stage, omit large chunks of the text, abuse the audience, and generally politicize their plays. This attitude had reached such a point by 1993 that the German Academy for Language and Literature sponsored an essay contest to consider whether "the director's theater is pursuing the execution of the classics" ("*Betreibt das Regie-theater die Hinrichtung der Klassiker?*").[16]

The attitude is by no means unknown in the USA. Almost simultaneously with the Berlin scandal (on October 10, 2006), the American entertainer Barbra Streisand, a self-proclaimed professional liberal, took advantage of her captive audience of 20,000 in New York's Madison

Square Garden to lampoon the then administration in an onstage skit
involving what was supposed to be a comic duet with an impersonator of
President Bush. When one concertgoer yelled out an objection, the aging
diva replied with an obscenity, outraging many members of the audience.
Later Streisand apologized for her outburst but sought to justify the par-
odic sketch by stating that "The artist's role is to disturb."[17] This phrase—
actually cribbed from the painter Georges Braque, who famously stated
in his illustrated *cahiers* that "it is the function of art to disturb" ("*L'Art
est fait pour troubler, la Science rassure*")[18]—is common among present-
day performers in the various media. Ulrich Khuon, Managing Director
of Hamburg's Thalia Theater, which in the fall of 2006 produced a play
depicting Osama Bin Laden as a comical drunken marionette, participated
in the October podium discussion at the Deutsche Oper and used virtually the same words, insisting that art, by its very nature, "must disturb."[19]
It should be stressed that this view goes well beyond Diaghilev's oft-quoted
advice to the young Jean Cocteau—"Surprise me" ("Etonne-moi")—or
what Susan Sontag in a well-known essay calls art's "capacity to make us
nervous" or to "induce contemplation, a dynamic contemplation."[20]

Such opinions have been expressed so frequently and so routinely in
recent decades by practitioners of every medium that they have become
almost wearyingly commonplace—and unthinkingly accepted.[21] Pop artist Roy Lichtenstein told an interviewer that "the problem for a hopeful
scene-making artist in the early sixties was how best to be disagreeable.
What he needed was to find a body of subject matter sufficiently odious
to offend even lovers of art."[22] Robert Rauschenberg coined the familiar
phrase that justified the provocations of Pop Art: "If the painting doesn't
upset you, it probably wasn't a good painting to begin with." The abstract
sculptor George Sugarman, who aroused bitter opposition from federal
judges with his design for the courthouse in Baltimore, Maryland, wondered: "Isn't controversy part of what modern art is all about?"[23] The performance artist Karen Finley, who gained notoriety by smearing her nude
body with chocolate syrup while screaming her political opinions at the
audience, claims that art depends upon "its shock value."[24] Products of
this conviction have been labeled "disturbatory art [...] objects intended
to bruise sensibilities, to offend good taste, to jeer and sneer and trash the
consciousness of viewers."[25] The view received academic validation when
the Curtin University of Technology in Australia proclaimed November 11,
2006 a "Humanities Day of Provocation," including an exhibition at
which five artists "embraced the ethos of the day" in their displays.[26] We
have come a long way from the Romantic conception of the museum as a

"temple of art."[27] The fact that such "art" has lost its ability any longer to shock anyone has struck some observers as a symptom of the "brutalization" of what in Germany is sometimes called our contemporary "nonsense society" ("Blödsinn-Gesellschaft"), which complacently accepts any idiocy, any perversion, any vulgarity that invades our television screens.[28] This almost indifferent acceptance, in turn, drives performers intent on celebrity to more and more radical extremes.

But is provocation truly the function of art?[29] Kant in his *Critique of Judgment* (1790) famously defined beauty as "a form of purposefulness [...] without the idea of a purpose" (Book 1, §17].) In fact, the notion is a relatively recent development in the history of aesthetics and essentially a product of the nineteenth century. For at least two millennia it was held to be the "function" of art, insofar as it can be said to have one, to please its public. Horace in his *Ars poetica* coined the phrase that long defined the poles of the discussion. "Poets," he opined, "wish either to benefit or to amuse or to speak words that are at once both pleasing and appropriate to life" (*"aut prodesse volunt aut delectare poetae / aut simul et iucunda et idonea dicere vitae"*) (vv. 333–334). He summed up his aesthetic creed in the oft-quoted phrase: "He who has blended the useful with the pleasant will carry off every vote, at once delighting and teaching the reader" (*omne tulit punctum qui miscuit utile dulci, / lectorem delectando pariter et monendo"*) (vv. 343–344).

For centuries, writers and artists sought to achieve the Horatian synthesis: to create a beauty at once instructive (*utile*) and lovely (*dulce*), as in Greek drama and Roman epic, in Dante's *Divine Comedy*, in Gothic architecture, in the hundreds of Renaissance paintings and sculptures with religious subjects that fill our museums today, or in the plays and novels of European Baroque classicism. In the mid-eighteenth century, the influential German critic Johann Christoph Gottsched opened his manual of poetics (*Versuch einer critischen Dichtkunst*, 1730) with a translation of Horace's still authoritative *Ars poetica*. Even at the end of that period of idealism Hegel could still maintain in the introduction to his *Lectures on Aesthetics* that art "fulfills its loftiest responsibility when it takes its place in a common union with religion and philosophy and becomes a means of bringing to consciousness and expressing the *divine*, the most profound interests of humankind, the most comprehensive truths of the spirit."[30]

But the nineteenth century, as René Wellek persuasively demonstrated, gradually "lost its grasp on the unity of content and form" and moved toward the opposed poles of didacticism or of "art for art's sake."[31] The Young Hegelians and leftist Marxists, among others, advanced the view that art's essential purpose was propagandistic, provoking Edgar Allan Poe in *The Poetic Principle* (1850) to rail in reaction against "the heresy of 'The Didactic,'" which in his opinion had corrupted poetic literature.[32] At the end of the nineteenth century these opposing views were exemplified in a sublimated form by the pure poetry of Mallarmé and his followers, on the one hand, and the message-novels of Zola on the other[33]—a polarization that we will see illustrated in Chapter 3 in the plays of Alfred Jarry and Gerhart Hauptmann. The situation exemplifies perfectly what Thomas Mann, in his *Doktor Faustus*, diagnosed as "the contrast between aesthetics and morality, which to a great extent dominated the cultural dialectic of that epoch."[34]

While many of the great modern classics again achieved a synthesis of form and content in the works of T. S. Eliot, Paul Valéry, Rainer Maria Rilke, and others, the opposing poles continued to be represented by, say, the so-called "tractor novels," patriotic ballads, and propagandistically representational paintings of fascism in Italy and Nazi Germany as well as socialist realism in Russia and Communist East Germany and, at the other extreme, by the nonsense of Dada, concrete poetry, or the most radical works of abstract expressionism. The artist Ad Reinhardt, despite his leftist-activist ideas, sought to expunge all ideas, emotions, and values "so that his art would have no subject matter and no social or practical value."[35]

The contemporary notion that art, while demanding absolute freedom, has as its principal function to provoke the public, amounts paradoxically to an uneasy and unsynthesized pairing of the two poles. The directors and performers want to impose their religious or political views didactically on their paying audiences. At the same time, they claim an absolute freedom to do so, with none of the controlling restraints of reason or good taste. Ironically, the result is often enough a conspiracy of understanding between the directors and their audiences, which mitigates against any challenging scandal since scandal always arises from a conflict of views.

FREEDOM OF ART?

The controversy surrounding Neuenfels's (*not* Mozart's!) *Idomeneo* raises an interesting question. The immediate discussion revolved almost exclusively around the issue of freedom of art. Although many critics felt that Neuenfels's production was aesthetically indefensible—the reviewer for the national weekly magazine *Der Spiegel* (September 30, 2006) called it "idiotic" and "nonsense" (*Quatsch*)—with one voice they defended the right, indeed the responsibility, of the opera company to proceed with the production in the face of threats: to defend the freedom of art. To be precise, however, the freedom being defended is not of art but of expression, a principle implicit in the First Amendment of the American Constitution and explicit in Article 5, Paragraph 3 of the German *Grundgesetz:* "Art and science, research and teaching, are free."

Historically, the freedom of art has involved its form, not its content. Mozart's *Idomeneo* employs a traditional content and, indeed, one specified by his patron; its revolutionary nature resides wholly in the boldness of the composer's radical transformation of *opera seria* and the librettist's accommodation of the ending to the prevailing Christian ethos. By analogy, Greek tragedy was based in almost every case on traditional mythic themes; its advances involved the gradual addition to the number of actors, the ensuing inversion of importance between choral odes and action, and the emerging centrality of individual psychology versus mythic universality. In fact, it might well be argued that art has never been free in the sense implied by many contemporary statements, always subject as it is to the prevailing social circumstances, whether tribal, imperial, civic, religious, courtly, national, conservative, or liberal. This reality is recognized by the contemporary German composer Siegfried Matthus, who wrote in a piece entitled "Art Has Never been Free" that the mistaken belief stems from a false conception of art, pointing out that it "is always bound to the social circumstances of its immediate present."[36] As Samuel Johnson quipped in a 1747 prologue, "The Stage but echoes back the publick Voice."[37]

A glance at the Old Testament and other ancient religious texts reminds us that literature is closely tied in its origins to religion and social ethics. Think of the Psalms or the Song of Solomon. Ancient Greek drama grew out of ecstatic rituals celebrating the god Dionysus, and theatrical performances in Hellas long retained a pronounced sense of communal celebration—what Thomas Mann called art's "collectivism, its social affect" ("soziale Ergriffenheit")[38]—that still underlay the medieval Christian mystery plays. Virgil's *Aeneid* was composed to commemorate, in all its ambivalence, the founding of Rome and the continuity of its ruling family, from the Trojans down to Augustus. Six of Horace's finest poems are the so-called Roman Odes, which deal with the moral condition of his society. Medieval European literature, architecture, painting, and sculpture are unimaginable without the authority of the Catholic Church and its subject matter (the Bible and Christian legends). Music itself was subordinated to words and the needs of the Church until, in the seventeenth century, the radically new form of the sonata began to emerge—that is, a "pure" music of sound produced for its own sake. It was only around the mid-eighteenth century that art and religion were "functionally differentiated" into independent social partial-systems.[39] It is no accident that the term "aesthetics" to designate the philosophy of art as thus newly conceived was coined in the mid-eighteenth century (by A. G. Baumgarten in his *Aesthetica* of 1750–1758).

From the Renaissance to the late eighteenth century, poets and artists had to satisfy their patrons. During centuries of princely and churchly control, essentially three issues determined the suitability of any stage performance: the interests of the ruling houses; the question of blasphemy; and the text's suitability for viewing by subordinates.[40] Musicians and poets were virtually domestic employees. Claudio Monteverdi composed the first European operas as a servant of the Duke of Mantua, while Torquato Tasso was sequestered by the Duke of Ferrara in punishment for insubordination. Think not just of Mozart's commission for *Idomeneo* but also of Bach in the employ of the Dukes of Sachsen-Weimar and later the City Council of Leipzig; of Handel, who depended on the largesse of the English nobility to subsidize his work; or of Haydn, who for thirty years composed many of his finest works as court musician at the "Hungarian Versailles" of Prince Esterházy. Not until the late eighteenth century did Benjamin West and John Henry Fuseli seek to assert their financial independence as artists by charging admission to see their paintings.[41] As a modern critic has observed, "paintings and sculpture do not become 'art' until they are exhibited in public places. This concept was epoch-making. It changed the past of the arts as well as their future."[42]

It was only in the nineteenth century, when religious and noble patrons gave way first to secular ones and then to paying audiences; when the first public museums were opened in Paris, London, and Berlin; when exhibitions and salons made art available to interested private customers; when notes on art were regularly featured in newspapers and magazines; and when music was liberated from the constraints of church and court, that artists became "free" to do what they wished—as long as their art satisfied their new constituency, the general public, and later, according to the composer Hans Werner Henze, "the masses, the only public that counts."[43] As Walter Panofsky wittily remarked, the concept of *lèse-majesté* no longer existed because "the majesty was now called 'the people.'"[44] Michael Kammen has demonstrated in striking detail how the recent phenomenon of blockbuster shows in museums and galleries resulted from the desire—more, the urgent need!—to attract larger audiences whose steadily increasing fees replace the earlier support of wealthy patrons and donors.[45] The same principle applies in theater and opera. As the traditional opera-going public grays and thins out, managers and directors try frantically, and not only in Germany, to attract newer, younger audiences by offering modernized adaptations of classic works or by providing the celebrity of a few expensive stars. While conductors do not often venture to tamper with the musical scores—although the Metropolitan Opera Company of New York in 2007 felt it necessary to compress even *The Magic Flute* for the supposed benefit of youthful audiences—directors have not hesitated to take liberties with the librettos.[46] The conductor Daniel Barenboim stated the distinction in an article written for a Berlin newspaper apropos the *Idomeneo* affair: "In music the difference between content and perception ["*Inhalt und Wahrnehmung*"] is given by the printed score. The director, in contrast, knows no score."[47] Wagner's and Puccini's and Mozart's music may remain intact, but the figures of *The Ring of the Nibelung* are clad in frock coats to exemplify a critique of capitalism while Lohengrin's swan is replaced by a steam locomotive; the stage action of *Madama Butterfly* is refocused, with gun-toting children, to become an anti-American tirade; *Idomeneo* is butchered to enable the director, in a spirit utterly contrary to the composer's intention, to parade his hostility to religion before his audience. Meanwhile, performance artists smear themselves with blood and feces, photographers reproduce plastic images of the crucified Jesus suspended in urine, painters portray a black Virgin Mary shaped of elephant dung, while sculptors sell to gullible museums and wealthy "art"-lovers sealed cans filled with their own excrement.[48] Freedom? Or the frantic desire to win a new public—that is, to satisfy new patrons—through provocation? "What quite a few American artists clearly *had* learned by the mid-1960s was that provocation helped to build reputations," observes Michael Kammen, "and the more unusual if not outrageous the art, the better."[49] In our civilized society apparently any atrocity or inanity can be justified as entitled to the often misunderstood principle of the freedom of art, although some legislators argue reasonably that it does not follow from that principle that the State has the obligation to support and fund such art, and the public still enjoys the right to stay away.

WHAT IS SCANDAL?

Etymologically "scandal" goes back to the Greek word σκάνδαλον, which originally referred to a trap or snare laid for an enemy and was later adapted metaphorically to designate a moral stumbling block—that is, an offense or, in the modern sense, a scandal. As *scandalum* it was appropriated by the ecclesiastical Latin of the Middle Ages to signify the cause of public offense or of moral delict. (It is worthwhile to distinguish scandal from blasphemy, which has been defined as "an orthodoxy's way of demonizing difference in order to perpetrate violence against it."[50]) Over time, "scandal" has come (according to the *OED*) to embrace a broader spectrum of meanings: from a moral lapse to damage to one's personal reputation; from a grossly discreditable act or person who disgraces his or her class, country, or religion to an offense to the public sense of decency; in a looser sense, gossip or malicious talk; and in the legal sense an injurious report as the foundation for legal action. Recent theoreticians have sought to define scandal in the mass media as violations of norms ("*Normverstösse*")—of the law, of the moral code, of "political correctness"[51]—or, in a more specific literary sense, as arising from "friction surfaces" ("*Reibungsflächen*") between literature and politics specifically or society generally, between freedom of art and other basic rights, and so forth.[52]

In general, and in contrast to such notions as disgrace, shame, dishonor, infamy, and other terms that define personal reputation, "scandal" suggests *public* disapproval in response to improper acts or conduct and, to this extent, presupposes a shared aesthetic or ethical sense in the general public that condemns the act.[53]

The term "scandal," as we have seen, has often been attached to various artistic modes that arouse public disapproval: painting, photography, sculpture, performance art, literature. (Think of Joyce's *Ulysses* or of Nabokov's *Lolita*.) The argument can be made, however, that it is most appropriately applied to theatrical performances since scandal is by definition a *public* issue and theater is a public occasion par excellence. Books are usually read by individuals alone. In the early twentieth century the Futurist theoretician Marinetti called books "wholly passéist" and "the static companion of the sedentary"; he believed that public opinion could be influenced only by theater, and notably by Futurist cinema.[54] Crowds may wander through exhibitions and be shocked or offended successively by something they see, but the setting of the gallery or museum makes it awkward for the public in large crowds to register its outrage all at once, despite the occasional museum-visitor who defaces an objectionable work. Even performance art typically takes place in the restricted venue of small clubs and cabarets, where the paying audience comes precisely because they know what to expect: their reaction is titillation, and even confirmation of their own views, rather than scandal.[55]

Theatrical productions, in contrast, can produce an immediate sensation in a public numbering hundreds or even thousands.[56] The audience at the premiere of a play, an opera, a ballet, or indeed a symphony, often does not know what it is about to experience. (In some cases, of course, as at Berlin's Volksbühne, the audience comes precisely because it confidently anticipates something outrageous from the director.) It has not yet been informed and swayed by the critics of the mass media, who all too often affect the way we later experience the play or artwork we go to see or the book we read. As Thomas F. Kelly points out in his discussion of musical premieres, "Each great work has its infancy, when it is new and fresh, when tradition, admiration, and history have not yet affected its shape, when its audience is unencumbered by previous expectations."[57] Similarly, Neil Blackadder argues in his study of theater audiences that "theater scandals represent a distinct category of event [...] a collective demonstration during a theater production."[58] The theater auditorium is, in sum, the ideal venue for scandal. Indeed, to the extent that theater originated as a place for communal celebration and semi-religious ritual, theatrical scandal is doubly scandalous: it not only flouts morality publicly; it does so in a place initially and long consecrated to shared communal values and beliefs.

If we now consider this view of the theater as the site of public consciousness in light of the earlier discussion of the freedom of art, we realize that scandal in the modern sense is a phenomenon of fairly recent date. Jürgen Habermas, in an influential book entitled *The Structural Transformation of the Public Sphere* (1962) traced the process through which "public opinion" ("*öffentliche Meinung*") as we know it—that is, the collective views of a public of rational private citizens—first arose. It happened when public opinion, still regulated in the Renaissance and Baroque by the authoritarian State, was gradually appropriated by "reasoning private citizens" ("*räsonierende Privatleute*") who had at their disposal a newly created sphere of criticism—in newspapers, salons, coffee houses—vis-à-vis the might of public authority.[59] That Habermas's view has come to govern much modern thought concerning literary scandals is suggested by the assumption underlying a recent volume of essays that "a literary scandal in the contemporary understanding presupposes public opinion."[60]

It was this new public consciousness that was susceptible to scandal when audiences, and increasingly the professional critics, assembled in the larger arena of theaters liberated from the constraints of earlier ages. Ancient theater and medieval mystery plays, like Noh drama and kabuki theater, benefited from a common sense of communal celebration or ritual; the creators of the performed works sought to express the shared values of their public. The emotions of pity and fear, whose arousal Aristotle in his *Poetics* (§13) called the purpose of tragedy, depended on the ethical values he shared with his audience in Athens and set down in his *Nicomachean Ethics*. Audiences may react to such performances in a variety of ways, ranging from incomprehension, consternation, bemusement, and boredom by way of amusement, enthusiasm, excitement, to horror and disgust—but still not be scandalized by an offense to the shared moral sense. The grand festivals of the Baroque were not public occasions but courtly celebrations: they did not serve the pleasure of the participants but demonstrated the grandeur of their sponsors.[61] The theater of that era, as we know from the "quarrel" surrounding Corneille's *Le Cid*, the furor accompanying Racine's *Phèdre*, and the suppression of Molière's *Tartuffe*, was subject to strict authoritarian control.

This is not to suggest, of course, that theater audiences of the past were quiet and restrained: since antiquity, they have always felt free to express approval or disapproval and, especially since the Renaissance, regarded theatrical performances as social occasions at which to see and be seen.[62] This situation changed gradually during the nineteenth century as improved lighting made it possible to darken theaters and thereby to shift the attention away from the audience and to the stage. Later the traditional proscenium stage gave way to innovative designs that involved the audience more directly in the performance.[63]

In the late eighteenth century, as the lower classes gravitated toward such popular venues as music halls, puppet shows, and fairground performances, the new "reasoning" public began to attend theatrical performances, and the theater became one of the most important centers of social activism: a veritable *politikon*.[64] At the same time, as we noted above, artists in their new-found independence began to renounce the venerable Horatian precept of *delectare* and *prodesse*, of synthesized pleasure and edification, in favor of the political/social instrumentalization of art or the opposite extreme of art for art's sake. At this point for the first time conflict began to arise between the artists and their public, between convention and innovation. The new bourgeois audiences and critics arriving in the theater with the moral or aesthetic views of their class could now be scandalized morally or aesthetically, if the artist so desired.

Leaving aside the relatively straightforward issue of freedom of expression, which every civilized society properly regards as sacrosanct and protects through its constitutions, I would like to ask whether scandal in this specifically modern sense exposes any more serious response or purpose.

A MORAL INSTITUTION?

We can approach the answer by reconsidering an influential statement on theater written over two centuries ago and delivered in June 1784 as a lecture before the Kurpfälzische Deutsche Gelehrte Gesellschaft (the

Palatinate German Learned Society)—a statement that the prominent modern dramatist Rolf Hochhuth has called "the authoritative Magna Charta of drama,"[65] comparable as a deed to Martin Luther's posting of his ninety-five theses on the church door in Wittenberg. In an altogether different context, the historian Reinhart Koselleck, in his magisterial study of the "pathogenesis of the bourgeois world," discussed Schiller's essay as an early landmark in the critical and antiauthoritarian movement of the Enlightenment, paralleled by developments in such eighteenth-century secret societies as the Freemasons and Illuminati and culminating in Kant's critiques, that for the first time made a sharp distinction between ethics and politics.[66]

Friedrich Schiller (1759–1805) had a noble conception of dramatic art, claiming that "the supreme product of this genre is *perhaps* also the supreme one of the human mind."[67] In his essay, which has entered cultural history under the title "The Theater Considered as a Moral Institution" (1784),[68] the twenty-five-year-old prodigy of the German *Sturm und Drang*, who had recently achieved national fame with his drama *Die Räuber* (1782, *The Robbers*), opened with general "anthropological" reflections on society as a whole. (It should be noted that, according to the standard eighteenth-century German dictionary, the adjective "*moralisch*" had not only the more specific sense of "moral"—that is, pertaining to good and evil—but also the broader implications of "social" ["*gesellschaftlich*"] and "ethical" ["*sittlich*"].)[69] Religion, he began, is widely regarded as the most steadfast pillar of the State because it provides the State with moral stability. Laws deal with negative duties—what we must not do—whereas religion extends its demands to positive acts. Laws concern deeds and external expressions of the will while religion thrusts its jurisdiction into the most remote recesses of the heart. The theater is necessary to both because it provides presence and vividness for the abstractions of law and religion. "The jurisdiction of the theater begins where the realm of worldly laws ends."[70] When justice is blinded by gold and fear binds the arm of authority, drama takes sword and scales in hand and drags depravity before a terrible seat of judgment. To achieve this goal drama has both past and present as well as history and literature at its disposal. "Everyone treasures his clear conscience when Lady Macbeth, a terrible somnabulist, washes her hands and summons all the fragrances of Arabia to eradicate the hateful stench of murder."[71] Such vivid images, Schiller claims, people the imagination of all men and women and affect us more profoundly and lastingly than do the abstract precepts of morality and laws.

Drama can also go beyond moral exhortation and prohibitive law to reward virtues and punish vices that are not subject to normal discipline.

When Lear knocks in vain at the house of his daughters and tears his white hair in despair, we feel disgust at the sight of flagrant ingratitude. More than any other public institution of the State, Schiller continues, the theater is "a school of practical wisdom, a guide through the life of the average citizen [*"das bürgerliche Leben"*], an infallible key to the most remote accesses of the human soul."[72] Even if drama cannot eradicate or diminish the sum of vices in the world, it acquaints us with them and prepares us to deal with them when we encounter them. Moreover, drama alerts us not simply to other men and women and to human character. "It also draws our attention to destiny and teaches us the great art of bearing it," encouraging us to be just to the unfortunate and to pass judgment with forbearance.[73] "The theater is the common channel through which the light of wisdom streams down from the thinking segment of the people and from there spreads in milder rays through the entire state."[74] If mankind in the eighteenth century has become more religiously tolerant, he suggests, it is because Lessing's *Nathan der Weise* (*Nathan the Wise*, 1779) and other dramas have planted humanity and gentleness in our hearts. "Only the theater is able to achieve this agreement to a high degree because it permeates the entire realm of human knowledge, draws from all situations of life, and illuminates all corners of the heart; because it unites all estates and classes and shows the clearest path to reason and the heart."[75]

Schiller concludes his lofty paean to drama by appealing for a national theater in Germany, at that time still a loose confederation of some 300 different principalities. "If we should live to have a national theater, we would also become a nation."[76] The theater is the institution where pleasure is coupled with instruction, tranquility with exertion, and—in a Horatian turn—amusement with education (*Bildung*).[77] "In the theater misery can share its grief with that of others; the happy are sobered, and the secure feel concern."[78] In the theater the individual is filled with a single sensation, he ends: the desire to be a complete human being. Schiller's essay constitutes a summation of Enlightenment views of the theater as represented by such works as Johann Georg Sulzer's *Philosophische Beiträge über die Nützlichkeit der dramatischen Dichtkunst* (1760; *Philosophical Contributions on the Usefulness of Dramatic Poetry*), Gotthold Ephraim Lessing's *Hamburgische Dramaturgie* (1767–1768), and Louis-Sébastien Mercier's *Nouvel Essai sur l'art dramatique* (1771; *New Essay on Dramatic Art*). As such it voiced a powerful response to Rousseau's attack on the theater in his *Lettre à d'Alembert sur les spectacles* (1758; *Letter to d'Alembert on Performances*). But if we look beyond what is specific to his own time, the thrust of Schiller's argument remains valid for future ages. Repeatedly dramatists and critics of the twentieth century pick up Schiller's notion regarding the higher and independent "jurisdiction" of the stage and his view of the theater as a site of moral trial where those in power—whether eighteenth-century aristocracy, late nineteenth-century *beau monde*, or twentieth-century theatergoers along with the professional critics—are confronted with uncomfortable realities and truths.

If we apply Schiller's conception of the theater as a moral institution—in his large sense of "moral" as a spiritual and intellectual dimension transcending both law and religion—to the issues outlined above, we see that scandal, understood in its most profound significance, can be regarded as a symptom of ethical concern—as an occasion when convention, irritated by innovation, is challenged to reflect on its values and meaning.[79] Thus, the scandal of *Idomeneo*, as ill conceived as the director's appended conclusion may have been, aroused a widespread debate in Germany and the world at large on such grave issues as the existence of God, the role of religion, the rights of minorities, and freedom of speech. Here, as in all such cases, the answer we give is less important than the fact that we are awakened to the problem and compelled to take it seriously.

In the following chapters I propose to examine notable cases of theatrical scandal in the course of two centuries in order to test Schiller's thesis of the theater as a moral institution, bearing in mind Thomas Mann's admonition that only in Germany, where "veneration of the theater" is inherent as in no other nation, could his essay have been written.[80] This does not mean that every scandal raises profound ethical issues or that every theatrical performance that raises such issues must result in scandal. But scandal may be regarded as a red flag waved by premiere audiences, including critics, to the world at large, suggesting that accepted views have been challenged and that momentous matters of public concern are at stake.

CHAPTER 2

Overtures

THE MORALITY OF ROBBERS (SCHILLER'S DIE RÄUBER)

For reasons that will become apparent, we may appropriately begin our survey of theatrical scandals with the 1782 premiere of Friedrich Schiller's *Die Räuber* (*The Robbers*).

A Franconian count, Maximilian von Moor, has two sons, Karl and Franz. Karl, the fundamentally decent older son, goes off to the university in Leipzig, where he falls in with a group of reprobates, becomes involved in scandal and burdened with debt, and is forced to flee the city. Overcome by remorse, he writes to his father and promises, in a genuine conversion, to return home and settle down to a decent life. Franz, feeling cursed by nature for his ugliness and consumed by envy and malice, conceals Karl's letters and, by bearing false reports, succeeds in turning his father against his brother. He writes to Karl with the news that their father has cursed and disinherited him. Karl, completely undone by this unexpected turn of events, flees with his companions to the Bohemian forests, where he soon becomes leader of a notorious band of brigands.

Back in Franconia, meanwhile, Franz tries to win Karl's beloved Amalia, who steadfastly maintains Karl's innocence to his father. Unsuccessful in his machinations, Franz persuades a henchman to appear before the father with a false report of Karl's death. Shattered by the news, Maximilian falls into a deathlike coma. Franz, proclaiming publicly that his father has died, hides him away in a dungeon to die of starvation and assumes title to the family estate, which he rules in absolute despotism. Meanwhile Karl, a German Robin Hood, has become renowned for his extraordinary deeds of brigandry, punishing the tyrannical rich and helping the deserving poor. Pursued by the law, his small but heroic band rejects the offers of surrender conveyed by a priest in the service of the secular powers and defeats a much larger army.

At this point, reminded by a friend's story of his own love for Amalia, he resolves to see his homeland and his beloved once more. He returns to

Franconia and, unrecognizable now, presents himself under a false name. Amalia is attracted to the unknown stranger, but Franz suspects his true identity and resolves to have him poisoned. When Amalia finally recognizes him, Karl—out of sworn loyalty to his fellows—returns to his band of brigands, who are encamped nearby. That evening, as he sits near the castle's tower, he observes a servant who is secretly nourishing his imprisoned father. He frees Maximilian and, enraged at his brother's heinous behavior, sends his most trusted companions to bring him to justice. The previously nonbelieving Franz, overcome by a sudden fit of religious guilt, strangles himself in despair. When Karl reveals his identity to his father and confesses that he is actually the leader of a notorious gang of robbers, the already debilitated old man dies of shock. Amalia is still in love with Karl, and he is tempted to stay with her; but his band sternly reminds him of his solemn oath to remain their leader. Amalia, saying she can no longer live without him, begs Karl to kill her. He does so and, having thus fulfilled his oath to his fellow brigands, goes off to surrender himself to justice (and, in the process, to enable a miserable working man with many children to collect the reward for his capture).

This melodramatic tale of two brothers who go to opposite moral extremes in their monstrous ambitions, constitutes an epitome of the literary, intellectual, and historical trends of the age.[1] The titanism of egos feeling justified to go to any lengths to satisfy their desires characterized the early *Sturm und Drang* poems of Goethe ("Prometheus," "Mahomets Gesang," and others), while the powerful emotional outpourings of both brothers were anticipated in the letters of the hero of Goethe's *Die Leiden des jungen Werther* (*The Sorrows of Young Werther*, 1774). The theme of hostile brothers was treated in several popular works of the 1770s, notably C. F. D. Schubart's "Zur Geschichte des menschlichen Herzens" (1775; "On the History of the Human Heart") and Johann Anton Leisewitz's drama *Julius von Tarent* (1775). In the characterization of the brothers Schiller acknowledged the literary influence of two writers who enjoyed enormous popularity among his contemporaries: Cervantes for his portrayal of the noble brigand with a thirst for vengeance in the figure of Roque in *Don Quixote* (which had only recently appeared in a complete German translation); and Shakespeare's depiction of evil genius in *Richard III* and in the figure of Edmund in *King Lear*.[2]

The powerful moral sense that leads Karl to question the existing social and intellectual order of his world reflects the Enlightenment ideas that characterized Schiller's education and which reached its culmination with Kant's three critiques, the first of which appeared in 1781, the year that saw the publication of Schiller's play. The theme of revolution against despotism, stated explicitly in the title-vignette of the book's second edition in 1782—*in Tirannos*—had recently been manifested in the American Revolution. Dire social circumstances, which had reached an extreme in late-eighteenth-century absolutist society, producing jobless students and impoverished workers, led to the formation of actual bands of robbers and highwaymen in Schiller's Württemberg (including the notorious "Sonnenwirt," who was captured and executed in 1761).[3] The theological debates over the existence and role of God that punctuate scenes with both brothers betray the pervasive influence of the pietistic Protestantism that colored Schiller's youth in the principality of Württemberg. And the Baroque drama and opera that dominated the stages of the royal theaters in dozens of German petty principalities, including the Hoftheater in Stuttgart, which Schiller frequently attended in his youth, accounts for the flamboyant rhetorical prose that characterizes the piece.

It was Schiller's brilliant dramatic sense that led him to orchestrate his work as a counterpoint of contrasting sections built around the two brothers: interior scenes dominated by few persons in the Franconian castle, and outdoor scenes populated by many figures in the Bohemian Forests. Moreover, his dramatic instinct led him to realize that "a man who is wholly evil is simply not an object for art and exudes a repulsive power instead of seizing the attention of readers."[4] Citing Milton's Satan, Euripides' Medea, and Shakespeare's Richard, he points out that they fascinate us precisely because they are *whole* figures, who display good qualities that even the most evil persons cannot lack. So his Franz, who with Karl shares the focus of interest, is a spirit attracted to extreme villainy because of the sheer grandeur attached to it, the power that it requires, the dangers that accompany it—an implicit critique of rationalism without any controlling moral virtue. By analogy, Karl, in his ambition to overcome social evil and religious hypocrisy and to avenge morality and bourgeois laws against their enemies, is sometimes forced into deeds whose unnaturalness offends his soul. In both brothers, who represent respectively feudal despotism and revolutionary fervor, Schiller seeks to show—an endeavor startlingly new on the German stage—how monstrous behavior is balanced by positive characteristics and how, ultimately, the individual must re-enter the realm of divine and human law and submit to its authority. "Because of its remarkable catastrophe," Schiller concludes his preface, "I may rightfully claim for my writing a place among the moral books."[5] Schiller's complex view of human character, utterly at odds with the classicistic ideal of fixed representative figures, reflects the new Enlightenment theories of anthropology and psychology.[6]

Schiller (1759–1805) wrote his play over the course of several years (1773–1780) while he was still a student of law, then medicine, in the so-called Karlsschule, the military academy established by Duke Karl Eugen of Württemberg to train future soldiers and government officials for his duchy, and Karl's longing for freedom from the restraints of absolutism reflects Schiller's own adolescent feelings of frustration at the severe restrictions of his military education and his forced employment as a regimental doctor. Realistically anticipating that despite its lofty and proclaimed moral intentions a drama directed so explicitly against private and public tyranny could never be performed in the court theaters of the era, he described it as a "dramatic novel, and not a theatrical drama."[7] "The reader should take this play for nothing other than a dramatic story, which exploits the advantages of the dramatic method to expose the soul in its most secret operations, without otherwise limiting itself within the constraints of a piece written for the theater."[8]

Because no publisher was willing to risk it, Schiller borrowed money in June 1780 to print 800 copies of the work at his own expense—anonymously and with a false place of publication (outside Württemberg)—under the title *Die Räuber: Ein Schauspiel* (*The Robbers: A Drama*). Apart from the predictable enthusiasm among his friends in Stuttgart, who shared his feelings of restriction in their lives, the work enjoyed little public success and received only two reviews, one of which generously predicted that, "if we ever expect a German Shakespeare, it will be this one."[9] However, the publisher with whom Schiller was negotiating cannily brought the work to the attention of Baron Wolfgang Heribert von Dalberg, who had recently become Director of the National Theater of Mannheim.

Theater and opera in the German-speaking lands were at the time still largely under the strict control of the nobility and their values. Only in the free Hanseatic city of Hamburg, where Lessing as house critic was advocating in his *Hamburgische Dramaturgie* (1767–1768) a free public or "national" theater, had a Nationaltheater emerged during the past twelve years. (In Vienna a popular Volkstheater, established in 1776 alongside the Hoftheater, fulfilled that role.) Mannheim, as the residence of Carl Theodor, Electoral Prince of the Palatinate, had for some thirty-five years been a traditional court theater with its French plays, Italian opera, and ballet.[10] But when Carl Theodor in 1777 ascended to the throne of Bavaria, he moved his theater, opera, and ballet to Munich, leaving behind in Mannheim a vastly impoverished theater, which now for the first time

needed to support itself by attracting a new and largely bourgeois subscription audience.[11] The newly appointed director, Dalberg, went about his
business energetically and with enormous acumen. Thanks to various factors—notably the death of Konrad Ekhof, the famous actor and director
of the court theater at Gotha—Dalberg was able to attract to Mannheim
the finest theatrical troupe in Germany, including notably August
Wilhelm Iffland (1759–1814), who became for two decades the principal
actor and occasional director of the new Nationaltheater. Abandoning
the almost exclusively French repertory of the former Hoftheater, Dalberg
and Iffland created in Mannheim the finest theater ensemble in Germany,
adding Shakespeare's works as well as German plays, notably bourgeois dramas such as Lessing's *Minna von Barnhelm* and *Emilia Galotti*,
Goethe's *Clavigo*, and works from the popular genre of sentimental drama
(*Rührstücke*).

Dalberg sensed the popular appeal of this first play by the unknown
young regimental physician in Württemberg and immediately approached
Schiller to cut and revise his "dramatic novel" for the stage. But Dalberg
was also shrewd enough to recognize problems even with the abbreviated
stage version that Schiller submitted in October 1781. He made a number
of further changes that are evident in the prompter's notebook used for the
performance,[12] notably, and without Schiller's knowledge, he shifted the
time from the mid-eighteenth century back to the late fifteenth century
in order to avoid any accusations of political intent; he modified Karl's
killing of Amalia into a suicide; to appease the Catholic Rhineland he
altered the figure of the toadying priest who tries to persuade the brigands
to surrender into that of a civil magistrate; he changed Franz's death from
suicide into judgment and condemnation by the brigands; and to accommodate the scene changes he expanded Schiller's five acts into seven.

The premiere of *Die Räuber* was "one of the very great, epoch-making
events in German theater history," according to a modern authority.[13] "No
stage incident—not even in modern times—is so deeply rooted in the consciousness of the people as is that Sunday premiere on January 13, 1782."
Schiller attended the performance incognito (because he crossed the bor-
der into the Palatinate without the permission of the Duke), and the "sensation" of his work, which for the first time portrayed on the German
stage such a socially marginalized group as robbers, exceeded even his
expectations.[14] Schiller's advertisement for the premiere warned spectators
of what they were going to witness:

The portrait of a great soul gone astray—equipped with all the gifts for excellence, and lost with all his gifts. Unrestrained fire and bad companionship ruined

his heart—tore him from vice to vice—until finally he stood at the head of a gang of murderous arsonists, heaped horror upon horror, plunged from abyss to abyss, into all the depths of despair.[15]

In the figure of Franz one will

see unmasked a hypocritical, malicious sneak who is hoist by his own petard. [...] Here one will cast one's gaze, not without horror, into the inner economics of vice and be instructed from the stage how all gildings of happiness do not kill the inner serpent, und how fear, anxiety, regret, despair are hard on his heals. Let the spectator weep today before our stage—and tremble—und learn to bend his passions beneath the laws of religion and reason.[16]

To see this notorious play, which had benefited from extraordinary advance publicity, reported Schiller's friend Andreas Streicher, people flocked to the theater in Mannheim, which seated an audience of 1,200, from the entire region: from Heidelberg, Darmstadt, Frankfurt, Mainz, Worms, Speyer, and elsewhere.[17] Of the few firsthand reports of the occasion, one is repeated in every biography of Schiller: "The theater resembled a madhouse: eyes rolling, fists clenched, feet stamping, hoarse screams in the auditorium! Strangers fell sobbing into one another's arms, women close to fainting staggered to the door. It was a general dissolution as though in chaos, from whose mists a new creation bursts forth!"[18]

Immediately following the premiere the theater physician Franz Anton May reported to a friend that

I am just coming full of melancholy from the theater, where the innermost folds of the passionate human heart are dissected three times a week for the improvement of morals, for the entertainment and edification of my fellow citizens. The ghastly masterpiece, *Die Räuber*, was presented, my friend—a play that causes human blood to freeze and the nerves of actors and spectators alike to be paralyzed, unless their ancestors were made of cheap timber.[19]

Enlightenment critics with traditional views of classical theater and morality could not be expected to appreciate this utterly new phenomenon. An anonymous review in the journal *Allgemeine Deutsche Bibliothek* called it "a terrible portrait of the most lamentable human misery, the most profound aberration, the most dreadful vice." People born with the power to achieve finer things, he continues, "sunk to the point where they no longer believe in the dignity of humankind, pressed by a series of seductions, alas, and by unhappy destinies to the point of rashing boldly and desperately toward the abyss." And yet, he continues,

as shattering as this portrait is, blow for blow, horror upon horror; as undesirable as it may be that one's heart become accustomed to the view of these horrible scenes; as unsuitable as this play perhaps is for performance in the theater—at the same time (we must confess) it is drawn, painted out so powerfully, the coloring is so lively, the extremely finely worked out and nuanced. Certainly the author is no common mind.[20]

The success of the evening was widely attributed, also by Schiller in his self-review, to the brilliant performance in the role of Franz by Iffland, who—following his own mentor Ekhof—was the leading advocate of the new style of natural acting in Germany, which no longer clung to the strict rules and gestures governing traditional acting.[21] According to Streicher's report, the first three acts did not have the effect that might have been anticipated from a reading of the play—in part, no doubt, because the action was no longer set in the contemporary present. The role of Karl Moor was played beautifully by one of the best actors in Germany, as well as the parts of his two closest friends.

By the manner in which Iffland not only had understood but also assimilated the role of Franz Moor so that it seemed to be one and the same with his own person, he rose above all others and produced an indescribable effect, in that none of the roles that he had played earlier and subsequently offered him the opportunity to shake our souls into their innermost depths, as was possible by the representation of Franz Moor.[22]

If the explosive premiere of *Die Räuber* was not a scandal by twentieth-century standards—a riot with chairs thrown, with placard-waving protestors outside, and with police summoned—it was a scandalous success of a sort not possible earlier on European stages. The renowned "quarrel" triggered by Corneille's drama *Le Cid* (1936) was not a stage scandal but a purely literary, critical, and theoretical dispute in the Académie Française and the journals that succeeded, and in part responded to, the fabulous popular success of the work.[23] A mid-eighteenth-century French survey of literary quarrels from Homer to the present discusses some forty cases, but they deal almost exclusively with poetic and not theatrical works. Only in the chapter on Racine and his contemporary Nicolas Pradon does the author note that "every new play that announces itself with a certain éclat excites a civil war."[24] This is how, he continues, one "arrests the flights of genius and how those that it inspires are constrained to sacrifice sublime and true beauty to the beauties of convention and caprice."[25] But the civil wars of which he speaks are not scandals in the theater but literary disputes—disputes, to be sure, driven by cabals that could spoil the immediate success even of plays subsequently regarded as masterpieces. In traditional court theaters any threats to accepted conventions and to public order were carefully monitored, as in the representative case of Molière's satirical attack on religious hypocrisy, *Tartuffe* (1664). Despite the approval of King Louis XIV and the Papal Legate, the Compagnie du Saint-Sacrement, a powerful cabal founded to protect religion against its detractors and reformers, succeeded for five years (until "la Paix de l'Eglise" was reached between the King and Pope Clement IX) in preventing performances of the comedy and, accordingly, in avoiding any public demonstrations of agreement or disagreement.[26] The situation in Germany was essentially the same.

In fact, *Die Räuber* was widely performed in German-speaking lands over the next three years—but almost exclusively by troupes of traveling players or by private theater groups.[27] It was prohibited at the court theaters—for instance, Stralsund, Danzig, and Leipzig—and elsewhere it had to be drastically revised in order to be acceptable. For the 1784 performance of the severely revised version at Stuttgart, Schiller's name as author was replaced by that of the adaptor because Schiller, who had deserted his regiment and fled from the duchy, was by then persona non grata in Württemberg.

The premiere of *Die Räuber* illustrates perfectly the theory advanced in Chapter 1, to the effect that theatrical scandal could begin to occur only when the theater was opened to a middle-class public and no longer restricted to and controlled by an exclusively noble court audience. Moreover, Schiller's repeated protestations that his play—in which the villainous Franz is punished by judgment of God (in the first version) or by the judgment of his peers (in the stage version) and Karl chooses to submit to secular punishment for his crimes—was a lesson in moral judgment provides an early illustration of the ideas that he was to outline theoretically two years later in his now renowned talk before the Learned Society in Mannheim. There, as we recall, he argued that only the stage "draws from all situations of life, and illuminates all corners of the heart"—notably in the figures of Karl, Franz, Amalie, and their aged father. Moreover, it "draws our attention to destiny and teaches us the great art of bearing it." Schiller's first drama fully exemplifies the principles enunciated in his essay, confronting his audience for the first time in a public forum with the discomforting ideas of the Enlightenment about virtue, politics, and social conventions and challenging the old order that was soon to be unsettled by the revolution in neighboring France.

It should be added that the play also marked a significant turning point in Schiller's own life. When he went secretly to Mannheim for a second time in May, his unauthorized trip was discovered and he was sentenced

to two weeks of arrest. In addition, and more seriously, the Duke forbade him to continue his literary efforts or to engage in correspondence with persons outside Württemberg—in other words, with the theater and publishers in Mannheim. Unwilling to accept these restrictions, on September 22, while the Duke and his court were distracted by festivities surrounding the visit of Prince Paul of Russia, Schiller fled to Mannheim with his friend Andreas Streicher, leaving behind his career as a military doctor in order to devote himself henceforth to his writing.

For these reasons it was fitting to begin our survey with *Die Räuber*. But it is also appropriate in light of the resonance that the play has continued to enjoy. In 1920 the young Bertolt Brecht twice reviewed performances of the play—once in protest that the director and actors were presenting Schiller to the youth of the present so inadequately. "No style, no spirit, no taste."[28] He gives the performance a vote of no confidence. A few weeks later he provided a capsule sketch of the plot to advertise a union production, explaining that

Schiller's youthful work shows in colorful, wild images the poignant story of the suffering of a promising youth who, cast under suspicion in the eyes of his father by the criminal machinations of his own brother Franz, a villainous canaille, in wild defiance errs onto the wrong track, moves to the Bohemian Forests as leader of a band of brigands, there carries out noble deeds, returns home, finds his father in the hunger tower (after his noble beloved or fiancée Amalia has failed to recognize him, frees him, and as avenger has his brother killed, whereupon he surrenders to the police.[29]

The greatest contemporary advocate of Schiller's play is beyond any doubt the dramatist Rolf Hochhuth, who maintained in 1982 that

Die Räuber after two hundred years is still as alive as on the first day, still has so much dynamite that one today doesn't risk performing it.[30] [...] This drama is also the drama of *our* youth, insofar as it doesn't arrive in the world with a clean part in its hair from sheer good breeding.[...] Of all Schiller's dramas this first one is less capable than any other of being grasped, neutralized, explained by clever explications.[31]

Hochhuth ends his talk, written at a time when the murderous terrorism of radical leftist groups in Germany was still fresh in the public mind, with the claim that "the spirit of rebellion that makes *Die Räuber* still today into the most compelling drama that any young man ever wrote— this spirit is not identical with terrorism but only with a radicalism that alone can *perhaps* save Europe."[32] Stressing that Karl Moor sought to eliminate the extremists from his band of brigands, Hochhuth argues that the play is not exhausted with the theme of terrorism. "It is a task for those excluded against their will by the parliamentarians, those who are contemptuously called fringe groups."[33] Schiller's brigands "wanted to harm no one but simply to remind the powerful that they were misusing the power given to them by election ballots for other purposes and responsibilities."[34]

We shall see in Chapter 6 how Hochhuth sought in his own dramatic writings to apply this same lesson to his own generation. For the present we can move beyond Schiller's *Die Räuber*, having explored it from three perspectives: as one of the earliest works offering the possibility for scandal on stage; as an example of Schiller's understanding of theater as a moral institution; and as a model emulated 200 years later by twentieth-century dramatists.

THE BATTLE OF HERNANI (HUGO'S HERNANI)

The premiere of *Die Räuber* on January 13, 1782, "deeply rooted in the consciousness" of the German people, as we have seen, was paralleled by a happening that took place in Paris almost half a century later. The opening of Victor Hugo's *Hernani* on February 25, 1830 was called by a contemporary "the greatest event of the century" and "a date inscribed in the foundation of our past in flaming characters."[35] The two works display striking similarities due in no small measure to the fact that Schiller was "the writer to whom Hugo always gives the first place in his modest pantheon of German writers."[36] Both were first dramas by young writers: Schiller was twenty-two when *Die Räuber* was performed; Hugo (1802–1885), already famed for his *Odes et ballades* (1826) and his virtuosic *Orientales* (1829), celebrated his twenty-eighth birthday on the day following the premiere of *Hernani*, the first of his plays to see the stage.[37] Both dramas were written during revolutionary periods of considerable social and political tension: Schiller's in the years of exuberation among young Europeans following the American Revolution and the atmosphere of progress proclaimed by the Enlightenment, Hugo's in the months preceding the July Revolution of 1830, at a moment when Charles X and his ultraroyalist government headed by the Prince de Polignac were being vigorously opposed by a new liberal and essentially bourgeois majority in the parliament. Both plays were premiered at a time when theaters in Germany and France were still largely under strict government supervision: *Die Räuber* at the historical juncture when the first "national" theaters were beginning to emerge as competition to the conservative Hoftheater, *Hernani* in a France where theaters—not counting the freer *théâtres de foire* and boulevard theaters with their pantomimes, puppet plays, and vaudeville—were still licensed, restricted, and censored according to principles inherited (via Napoleon's 1806–1807 decrees) from the *ancien régime*. The heroes of both plays are robbers of upstanding character—men of noble descent who, for different reasons, rebel in one case against the feudal aristocracy and in the other against the king. Both are in love with young noblewomen who are desired by powerful competitors. Both works end tragically with the deaths of the two lovers. Both plays set the radical youth of the day, respectively the *Sturm und Drang* and *Les Jeunes-France*, against the conservative defenders of the literary, social, and political conventions. And both, finally, precipitated scandalous *causes célèbres*.

We have detailed descriptions of the evening in Paris from two sources close to the author: his wife Adèle and his acolyte Théophile Gautier. Hugo's play, though potentially controversial, had been approved by the powerful commission of censorship because that office hoped to avoid an uproar similar to the one caused a year earlier when it prohibited Hugo's play *Marion de Lorme* (1829) on the grounds that its portrayal of Louis XIII was considered to be a threat to the monarchy. Hugo was justifiably concerned about the response to his work. "Without puffers [*prôneurs*]," he wrote during the rehearsals, "without a coterie, without external support" no work can enjoy the success it deserves. "The most certain means of being right is to be dead."[38] A widespread "Hugophobia"[39] had been spread among traditionalists by his extensive preface to *Cromwell* (1827), which amounted to a manifesto challenging the principles of conventional French drama as formulated by Boileau in his *Art poétique* (1674): notably the unities of time and place (which Hugo rejected for unity of action); the rigorous separation of the comic and the tragic, the grotesque and the sublime; and precise rules governing Alexandrine verse.[40] In their place Hugo demanded, and practiced, realism of scene, action, and language.

Before the premiere, even though the text of the play (written in the remarkably short time from August 29 to September 25, 1829) had not been published, critiques and parodies had already appeared in several journals, reports of the plot having leaked out through spies in the theater. Many of the actors at the Théâtre-Français disliked this challenge to the style in which they had been trained and to which they had become accustomed. Hugo and his wife learned that the woman in charge of renting loges was giving preference to theater habitués opposed to the new school of writers. Hugo was even apprehensive about using any of the claques routinely hired to applaud new productions, believing that they too, favoring such works as the "well-made" plays of Eugène Scribe and the chauvinistic tragedies of Casimir Delavigne, might well turn against him.

Instead, he demanded a great number of free tickets (1,500!)—actually squares of red paper signed with the word "Hierro" ("steel," from a Spanish watchword of liberation)—which were distributed through Gérard de Nerval in groups of six to members of the *cénacle* that met at Hugo's apartment. These friends in turn shared them with like-minded comrades from the various arts: writers, critics, painters, sculptors, architects, and others. "The battle that's going to take place around *Hernani*," Hugo exhorted them, "is a battle of ideas, of progress. It is our common struggle. We're going to combat this old, crenelated and tightly shuttered literature."[41] One of these followers was the eighteen-year-old Gautier, who regarded Hugo with a fawning adulation, arguing that the preface to *Cromwell* was like "the Tables of Law on Sinai," saying that "God was never adored more fervently than Hugo," calling him a "Genghis Khan of the mind," and confessing that "to attend this battle, to fight obscurely in a corner for the good cause, was our dearest desire, our loftiest ambition."[42] In contrast to "the Hydra of wigs" ("l'hydre du *perruquinisme*") Gautier and his fellows wore their hair long in emulation of Albrecht Dürer and dressed outlandishly: Gautier himself in a red silk vest that was notorious even forty years later. "If one pronounces the name of Théophile Gautier before a philistine, even if he has never read two of our verses or a single line, he knows us at least for the red vest that we wore to the premiere performance of *Hernani*." (Gautier the dandy takes ten pages to describe his costume that day and the significance of the color "red" in contrast to the greyishness that dominated the dress of the era.)

To ensure their places Gautier and his comrade defenders of free art ("brigands of the mind")[43]—not, he protested, "Attila's Huns," as they were represented in the hostile press—entered the theater at two o'clock in the afternoon and spent the long hours before the performance in the still unlighted auditorium talking excitedly about the play, eating the chocolate and sandwiches they had brought along, singing—and relieving themselves in corners because the attendants had not yet opened the restrooms. When at last the lamps were lighted and the bewigged, lorgnetted, and well-dressed audience entered, stupefied at the sight of the unruly auditorium occupied by this bizarrely clad horde of bearded and long-haired young people, the *Jeunes-France* courteously applauded the beautiful ladies and laughed at "the orchestra and balcony paved with academic and classical skulls."[44] (Contemporary cartoons by Grandville depict both the hirsute youths and the agitated bourgeoisie.)[45] The house was packed because "all society wanted to attend this fantastic novelty and to witness its formidable fall,"[46] convinced as they were that there would be no second performance. "Two armies were present," Mme Hugo observed, "the past and the future."[47] As Gautier put it, "two systems, two armies, even two civilizations—that's not saying too much—were present, hating each other cordially, as one hates in literary hatreds, demanding only a battle and ready to pounce on one another."[48] "It was not difficult to see that the young man with long hair found the monsieur with his well-shaved face disastrously cretinous and did not long conceal from him this particular opinion."[49]

Before any quarrels could erupt openly the traditional three raps of the baton signaled the curtain-rise, and the furious "hurricane of words" gave way to silence and an absolute immobility.[50] Nevertheless the battle began as soon as the very first words were spoken because traditionalists were offended by the "audacious enjambement" of the opening line: "*Serait-ce déjà lui? ... c'est bien à l'escalier / Dérobé.*" ("Is it already he? On the secret staircase.") Classical admirers of Voltairean verse objected that "such negligence at the beginning of a play ought to be condemned in a poet, whatever might be his principles, liberal or royalist."[51] Whereupon a young Romantic with a head of long thick red hair explained that it was not a negligence but "a beauty" because the delayed word represented the mystery suspended outside on the staircase. In the course of the first act explosions of applause and objection from both sides punctuated the performance: "the second gallery, the parterre, the orchestra pit applauded in an ensemble of feet, hands, bodies, with flames in their eyes and cries in their mouths."[52] At the end of the first act the cast regarded Hugo with a new respect, while the critics were murmuring in the foyer that the play was not without merit. By the end of the second act the actors were smiling at the author. During the pause following the third act a respected dowager greeted Hugo with the words: "He's Homer, he's the young Cid!"[53] And by the time the fourth act was over the publisher Mame sought out Hugo with the bid to publish the play. "After the first act we thought of offering you two thousand francs. After the third act, we would have gone to four thousand. After the monologue we now offer you six thousand francs, paid in cash. I've got the money in my pocket."[54] He didn't want to wait for the fifth act lest he be obliged to offer ten thousand! Hugo, who was in debt and had only fifty francs to his name, eagerly accepted.

When the play ended, women tossed their bouquets onto the stage, and people, in a paroxysm of acclaim, demanded the author.[55] At the door, as Hugo was leaving, a mass of spectators waited, impatient to express their enthusiasm. But the next day and despite the public adulation all the papers, with the exception of the *Journal des Débats*, rejected the play as "one of the greatest scandals that have taken place within the memory of man."[56] The conservatives were offended by the street bums who had installed themselves in the theater, eating and drinking and allegedly celebrating indecent orgies. The liberal papers stated that the singing of the youths was obscene. The royalist journals claimed that the disturbers had been republicans and that the place consacrated to Racine and Corneille had been soiled. As for the play itself, few disinterested individuals had been able to pass judgment because the room was populated by the author's creatures; the few who had penetrated through to it assured their readers that the play was worthy of its coarse public.

Hugo was alarmed at these developments and, believing that the play was now in greater danger than at the premiere, again distributed the same number of tickets as before. Assembling his captains, he explained the situation to them, whereupon his valiant young supporters were delighted to return to *Hernani* and to fight once more. Rumors spread that a great tumult was going to take place, and a huge crowd appeared in front of the theater to see what might happen. Gautier, who boasted that he eventually attended thirty performances, showed up in an even more outlandish costume: to his red silk vest he had added dove-colored trousers with large stripes of black velvet, and his wavy locks cascaded to the middle of his back. Shortly before the curtain rose a vast quantity of small multicolored bits of paper snowed down from the second galleries onto the décolletage of the ladies, clinging to their hair and irritating the paying public. There was no question this time of literary debate. The battle was engaged openly. The entire play was disrupted; every act, almost every scene critiqued: laughter, shouting, droll buffoonery from the boxes elicited vigorous support from the galleries. The next day the papers reported that the scandal would create a success of curiosity, but that the curiosity was meaningless since the hall was half empty at the second performance. The third performance was even stormier than the second, the laughter more frequent and prolonged. The opposition grew stronger, and by the fourth performance a pattern of uproar had been established that continued throughout all following performances. People hooted, laughed, made jokes, protested by turning their backs to the stage, or opened newspapers in the boxes and read ostentatiously. Dismayed by this reception, the actors conspired actively against the play and worked for its discontinuation. *Hernani* was performed forty-five times successively that year. But the resistance to the play as well as the support that it had gained, the controversial articles generated by the occasion, had turned *Hernani* into "*the* event of Paris and counterbalanced the appeal of the two hundred twenty-one deputies, this preface to the July Revolution."[57] When Hugo ran into a favorably disposed editor of the *Courrier français* and asked him "What's new?" his friend replied: "What's new is that you and Poligny are the two most detested individuals in all France."[58]

The play that caused this uproar resembles a melodramatic synthesis of *Le Cid* and *Die Räuber,* in which Corneille's hero, seeking to avenge his father, becomes the noble leader of bandits against society rather than of an army against the Moors and in which young lovers rebel against the restraints of social convention. The play takes place mostly in Spain in 1519, the year when King Charles of Spain was elected Emperor of the Holy Roman Empire. A masked cavalier arrives at the castle of Don Ruy Gomez de Silva in Saragossa and forces the Duenna to conceal him in a cabinet in the chambers of the young Doña Sol de Silva, the niece and promised bride of the elderly grandee. There he overhears the conversation when the lovely Sol—the "sun" around whom three admirers revolve—receives her secret lover Hernani and agrees to elope with him the next night. When the mysterious cavalier emerges from his hiding place and declares his own love, the two men quarrel and draw their swords. Then Ruy Gomez arrives unexpectedly, and the unknown guest reveals his identity as King Don Carlos, who has come to inform Ruy Gomez of Emperor Maximilian's death. Calling Hernani one of his suite, he allows the brigand to escape, not realizing that Hernani desires revenge against him because Don Carlos's father had put Hernani's father to death.

Having overheard the plan of the two lovers, Don Carlos the next night tries with his courtiers to kidnap Doña Sol when she comes down to meet Hernani, but the attempt is thwarted by Hernani and his brigands. Hernani, in return for the king's generosity in protecting him the night before, shields Don Carlos from his men and allows him in turn to escape. But he refuses to take Doña Sol with him, saying that it is much too dangerous now that so many forces are pursuing him.

Some time later, his band of brigands now destroyed, Hernani disguised as a pilgrim arrives at Ruy Gomez's castle on the day the elderly grandee is to marry Sol. When, in despair, he reveals his identity, Ruy Gomez respects the ancient rule of hospitality and protects his young adversary, even after he surprises the two young lovers professing their enduring love. When the King unexpectedly arrives, Don Ruy refuses to hand over his guest and justifies his behavior by giving the King a guided tour of his distinguished ancestry in the portrait gallery. Angered by the refusal, the

King demands Doña Sol as a hostage in his stead. After their departure Hernani tells Ruy Gomez that the King actually desires Sol for himself and intends to marry her. The two enemies swear a temporary truce until they can avenge themselves on the King. Hernani gives Ruy Gomez his signal horn, swearing that he will kill himself whenever the other sounds the horn.

Act IV takes place in Aix-la-Chapelle, where Don Carlos awaits news of the election of the new emperor, ruminating in a grand monologue on power and empire. When he retreats into the tomb to commune with Charlemagne's spirit, the conspirators, led by Hernani and Ruy Gomez, enter the hall and wait to kill the King. Suddenly three cannon shots announce that Don Carlos has been elected emperor. He emerges; the conspirators are captured and disarmed; but in a major spiritual conversion the new emperor now pardons them all, impressing his former enemies by his sudden imperial grandeur and nobility. When Hernani reveals his true identity as Jean d'Aragon, son of an executed nobleman, the Emperor grandly restores his nobility and gives up Doña Sol to him in marriage. Happy ending!

But in Act V, back at Hernani's castle in Saragossa, where the wedding between the two lovers has just taken place and they stand on the terrace declaring their love, Hernani hears the sound of his horn: Ruy Gomez now demands his death! The jealous old man joins the young couple and hands Hernani a vial of poison. When Sol's entreaties for mercy have no effect, she seizes the vial and drinks half of it; Hernani drains the other half, and the two lovers die in each other's embrace. In horror at the results of his own machinations, Don Ruy Gomez stabs himself to death.

It is difficult today to appreciate the furor that arose around Hugo's play. Hugo's ambitions, to be sure, were wholly consistent with the liberal tendencies that produced the July Revolution, as he clearly stated in his preface (dated March 9, 1830) to the published version of *Hernani*. Romanticism, he declared, is "nothing but *liberalism* in literature."[59] When it is finally achieved, literary liberalism will be no less popular than political liberalism. "Liberty in art, liberty in society—this is the twofold goal toward which all consistent and logical spirits should strive in step."[60] Led by today's youth, the wise elite of the older generation will soon realize, after a moment of defiance and reflection, that their children are merely following out the consequences of what they themselves achieved. "Literary liberty is the daughter of political liberty. This is the principle of the century, and it will prevail!"[61] In a revolution everything should move forward: "For a new people, a new art."[62] While the literature of Louis XIV was well adapted to his monarchy, the France of today, of the nineteenth century, ought to have its own national literature.

Hugo goes on to make an important distinction (as discussed in Chapter 1 above) between "the public of books and the public of theaters."[63] There is a danger, he writes, in risking on the stage ideas hitherto confided only to paper, "which tolerates everything."[64] The theater public, eager for pure emotion, did not until recently fully grasp the principle of literary freedom, which is understood by the reading public. But a new public has now arrived and appreciates that "in letters, as in society, there is no etiquette, no anarchy: only laws."[65] Now that the general public has grasped this idea, the only obstacle remaining to liberty in the theater is professional criticism, still bound by the reactionary standards of the *ancien régime*. Recalling the hostile reviews of the published *Hernani*, Hugo speaks of "the thousand abuses of this minor inquisition of the spirit, which, like the other sacred office, has its secret judges, its masked executioners, its tortures, its mutilations, and its death sentences."[66] Hugo gratefully addresses his thanks to this new public, conscientious and free, and to the modern youth which has favored the work of a young man who is as sincere and independent as they are. He promises that *Hernani* is simply the first stone in the edifice that already exists in his imagination.

But the play performed on February 25, 1830, was hardly revolutionary in any larger social or political sense (although it was radical enough that the notion of staging it that same year in Vienna was considered unthinkable in light of the political climate in the Austro-Hungarian Empire).[67] To be sure, Don Carlos as a young king is shown to be an impetuous seducer intent on exercising his royal authority, but his essential nobility of character, revealed by his spontaneous protection of Hernani, is confirmed by the imperial benevolence with which he pardons the conspirators and surrenders Doña Sol to her true love. Indeed, at the end of the fourth act, in effect, the monarchy has been reestablished in all its glory and Hernani lifted from brigandry and restored to his inherited nobility. So the censors had no cause to be alarmed at this play by the former royalist author. The desire of the old grandee to marry his young niece was standard fare of boulevard comedies of youth versus age. Indeed, as one modern critic puts it, the uproar seems to have been "not a revolt to substitute one political and social regime for another, but the expression of a sort of intellectual anarchism, a protest against a world that bars a place for youth"—even, more cynically, "the solution of problems by evasion, by art."[68]

In fact, Gautier's description is a case in point. What made an impression was the red silk of his vest, not the red of revolution. And all the examples he produces for audience indignation are purely literary—even technical.[69] We have already mentioned the opening line with the daring enjambement ("l'escalier / dérobé") that violated all the rules of classical metrics. Gautier goes on to cite another passage that scandalized the audience: when at the beginning of Act II, Don Carlos, waiting for Doña Sol to appear for her rendezvous with Hernani, asks one of his courtiers if it is yet midnight ("Est-it minuit?" "Minuit bientôt.") These few words aroused a tempest because it was regarded as unseemly for a king to ask the time like any ordinary bourgeois and for his attendant to respond with such boorish abruptness. Rather than considering the utter novelty of the work being performed before their eyes with its vivid action, the audience was obsessed with metrics, with social niceties, and with their fright at the antics of Hugo's supporters. Gautier and his companions, in turn, had little interest in the political implications of the play, rejecting as they did any politicization of *l'art pour l'art*.

While the young Romantics of Hugo's *cénacle*, in their eagerness for a reform of the theater, applauded Hugo's poetic liberties, liberals with less literary inclinations showed an astonishing insensitivity to his hopes—indeed, a direct opposition to his theory that "literary liberty is the daughter of political liberty." Armand Carrel, leader of the liberal party, attacked *Hernani* in four articles in his journal *Le National*. He acknowledges that great social and political advances have been achieved since the revolution of 1789. "But what does liberty in art, the revolution in literary forms, add to the liberty and well-being of all?"[70] The people, he continues, have no need of any theater beyond traditional melodrama. In sum, Hugo's work inflamed the fury of neoclassical aesthetes through its language and metrics, shocked the social conservatives with its seeming anarchy (of plot and of audience!), and offended some liberals with its misbegotten effort to add a wholly unnecessary element to the bourgeois theater. Despite the scandal surrounding its premiere, then, the play did not succeed in fulfilling Hugo's Schillerian ambition of using the stage as a moral institution. His audience insisted on viewing the work as a purely aesthetic insult.

Despite the conspicuous parallels connecting *Die Räuber* and *Hernani*, notable differences are apparent between the two epoch-making works, each representative of its own stage in national development. *Hernani* was written at a point in French history when many of the social and political liberties that were still only an ideal and dream in Schiller's Württemberg had actually been achieved. Accordingly, the audiences responded to wholly different aspects of the two works. Schiller's public was excited by the attack on feudal absolutism, but the language of his work, while rhetorically brilliant, was not essentially different from that of the poems, novels, and plays already familiar in the *Sturm und Drang*. Hugo's audience, in contrast—supporters and opponents alike—was able to take the social and political advances for granted and thus focused on the "literary liberties" of the text—that is, on its aesthetic aspects. In addition, the respective effects of the two works were no doubt qualified by the fact that Schiller's work was performed by a young troupe that believed devoutly in his play, which offered so many opportunities for their new style of acting, while Hugo's play was actually undermined in part by a conservative cast who resented his innovations. The seemingly paradoxical result was that political radicalism produced a more restrained scandal in Mannheim than did the literary radicalism in Paris. While Schiller's audience responded to the "moral" message of *Die Räuber*, Hugo's public was for the time being "morally" content and, accordingly, turned its attention to the play's artistic liberties. These two overtures, in any case, exemplify respectively the two principal aspects that will precipitate scandals on stage in the later nineteenth and early twentieth centuries: sociopolitical and aesthetic.

CHAPTER 3

Scanning the surface

Fin-de-siècle Germany would have been unrecognizable to Schiller. The kaleidoscope of kingdoms and principalities that he knew had been replaced since 1871 by a unified German Empire which, following the Franco-Prussian War of 1870–1871, had become the mightiest industrial and military power in Europe. Rapidly escalating industrialization had radically altered the geographical and sociological landscapes. From the Ruhr to Silesia, coalmines ravaged countrysides formerly devoted to farming, and the proliferating establishment of firms and factories in the cities caused the period to become known in German history as *Gründerzeit* ("founding period"). In this once totally rural country the number of employees in urban factories now equaled that of agricultural workers. The rapid industrialization had also put vast wealth into the hands of an upper middle class that vied with the land-based aristocracy for political power and, in the process, turned away from its formerly liberal values. Conservative capitalists and aristocracy alike were united in their struggle to maintain their power and influence against the growing strength of the urban proletariat and the lower bourgeoisie. The interests of the working classes—riddled by poverty, disease, and alcoholism—were represented by various political groups, which by 1878 constituted such a threat against the status quo that Bismarck's government issued a notorious *Sozialistengesetz* ("socialist law") prohibiting all socialist, social democratic, and communist associations, meetings, and publications. The same conservatism dominated the cultural scene of the *nouveaux riches*, who gloried in the often vulgar extravagance of their luxurious villas[1] while enforcing their conventional standards in the public venue of the theater by rigid censorship. As a result, the German stage of the period following the glories of such theatrical masters as Schiller, Kleist, and Hebbel was dominated by translations of French salon plays of Scribe and Sardou, by routine revivals of classical works, and by epigonal historical plays consistent with the grandiose *Gründerzeit* spirit of aggression and the will to power.[2]

THE DRAMA OF SCHNAPS AND FORCEPS (HAUPTMANN'S VOR SONNENAUFGANG)

It was against this background that in April 1889 a group of leading young Berlin writers, critics, and intellectuals—Maximilian Harden, Otto Brahm, Paul Schlenther, the brothers Heinrich and Julius Hart, Samuel Fischer, and others—established the association Freie Bühne ("free theater") in loose imitation of André Antoine's Théâtre Libre in Paris.[3] This organization had two fundamental purposes: first, to avoid the censorship laws governing public performances by producing "private" stagings of theatrical works—notably works from countries where contemporary theater was more advanced than in Germany; and, second, to provide through subscriptions a steady financial basis that would enable the group to produce controversial works not dependent upon commercial appeal and success. In the words of the founding manager, Otto Brahm, introducing the journal he edited in 1890 to accompany the work of the theater: "We are setting up a free theater for modern life. Art will stand in the center of our efforts: the new art that looks at reality and present-day existence."[4] Looking back two decades later, Brahm grandly proclaimed that "1889 was the year of the German theater revolution, just as 1789 was the year of the revolution of mankind."[5]

The Freie Bühne opened on September 29, 1889, with Ibsen's *Ghosts*, the public performance of which was still prohibited in Berlin although it was freely staged in several other German cities. The third and fourth perform-ances featured *Henriette Maréchal* by the brothers Goncourt and Tolstoy's *The Power of Darkness*. But to avoid the label of "wretched foreignity" ("*traurige Ausländerei*") imposed by its opponents,[6] the theater introduced for its second performance the premiere of the first drama by a twenty-six-year-old German writer known principally for a "novellistic study" that he had published a year earlier in the avant-garde journal *Die Gesellschaft*: "Bahnwärter Thiel," a powerful and sympathetic psychological account of a tragic episode in the life of a simple train-crossing attendant.

Gerhart Hauptmann (1862–1946), the future Nobel Prize-winning dramatist, came to the theater after a long period of intellectual flounder-ing.[7] Hauptmann was the son of a prosperous hotel owner in the Silesian town of Ober-Salzbrunn, which in addition to its spa waters also featured active weaving and mining industries. Following elementary school in Salzbrunn, Hauptmann was sent at age twelve to the Realgymnasium in the nearby city of Breslau, where for the first time he experienced first-rate professional theater—the renowned ensemble from Meiningen with works by Shakespeare, Schiller, and Kleist. But after four years poor grades and inadequate motivation led him to drop out. Because his parents had suffered financially from the economic crises of the 1870s and had given up their hotel, Hauptmann worked for a year as a trainee on his uncle's farm, where he encountered pietist religious fundamentalism of a sometimes hysterical sway. By 1879, having determined that he was too sickly and weak for agricultural work, he returned to Breslau, where he lived with his older brother Carl and wrote his first poems and dramatic fragments. A year later, deciding that his true calling was sculpture, he entered Breslau's Art Academy while continuing to write—notably his (unpublished) dramatic poem "Germanen und Römer."

In 1882, having become engaged to Marie Thienemann, the daughter of a wealthy family (who not incidentally had been educated in a pietist boarding school), he left art school and enrolled briefly as a special student at the University of Jena, where his brother Carl was studying, and heard lectures by such luminaries as the philosopher Rudolf Eucken and zoologist-philosopher Ernst Haeckel and became involved in a "Pacific Society" whose members styled themselves "Icarians" and entertained plans to set up a socialist community in the USA. In less than a year he left the university and, following a trip around the Mediterranean, spent the winter of 1883–1884 in Rome, where he was inspired by the works of Michelangelo to return to his sculptural efforts and had visiting cards printed with the inscription "Gherardo Hauptmann, Scultore." But after his return and another few weeks in drawing classes at the Dresden Academy of the Arts he committed himself finally to literature. He studied for two more semesters at the University of Berlin, where he continued to write—notably the no-longer-extant historical drama *Das Erbe des Tiberius* (*The Heritage of Tiberius*)—attended the theater, and toyed with the idea of becoming an actor.

In spring 1885 he married his fiancée and settled down in Berlin— soon in a stately villa in the eastern suburb of Erkner—where he wrote a number of poems, contemplated a play or novel about Jesus, published his narrative poem *Promethidenlos* (*Fate of the Sons of Prometheus*), and became acquainted with the leading young figures of the literary club Durch! ("Through!"). In Erkner he also wrote his novella *Bahnwärter Thiel* (*Crossing-Keeper Thiel*), which appeared in 1888 along with a volume of poems, legends, and fairy tales under the title *Das Bunte Buch* (1888, *The Colorful Book*). That summer, in the course of a visit with his brother in Zurich, he was persuaded by his schoolfriend Alfred Ploetz, who was studying medicine there, to become—though it only lasted for only two years—a vegetarian and teetotaler. During these years, still knowing nothing of Zola, Ibsen, and other European modernists, he became disenchanted with the theater and usually walked out "after the first or second act of the corrupted play."[8] Then he became acquainted with Ibsen and Tolstoy, who showed him things that he had believed attainable only in a distant future.

> Utterly astonished I let the performances of *Ghosts* take their effect upon and, at home, followed the incomprehensibly fine and natural dialogue. Then came Tolstoy with *The Power of Darkness*. This drama opened the path to life even more widely: under its impact I became aware of my own possessions and began to coin my gold.[9]

Accordingly, Hauptmann set out to write a play focusing on contemporary social problems and based on scenes he knew at firsthand from his childhood and from the varied experiences of his wayward youth.

The immediate result was the "social drama" *Vor Sonnenaufgang* (*Before Sunrise*), which was written in the spring of 1889 and published that summer with a dedication to "Bjarne P. Holmsen, the most consistent realist"—the pen name of Arno Holz and Johannes Schlaf, whose volume of three stories entitled *Papa Hamlet* (1889), a landmark of German literary naturalism, had deeply impressed him for its highly realistic language. Holz was himself the leading theoretician of naturalism, who sought in his manifesto *Die Kunst: Ihr Wesen und ihre Gesetze* (1890, *Art: Its Nature and Its Laws*) to reduce literature to a series of laws, the most fundamental being: "art = nature – x." But Hauptmann was no theoretician and believed that such terms were like signs outside that don't reveal what's inside the store. "When I hear the word Idealism, I imagine artistic dilettantes who walk with crutches and borrow. When I hear the word Realism, I think of a grazing cow. If someone mentions Naturalism, then I see Emile Zola before me with large darkgreen glasses."[10] He was influenced not by the theories of his young friends but by the actual works of such writers as Ibsen, Tolstoy, Zola, and "Bjarne P. Holmsen." As a result, it is not helpful to label Hauptmann as a "naturalistic" writer. Indeed, it is even difficult to define any specific "naturalism" since there were so many competing variations that were linked mainly by their common opposition to the conventional values of the *Gründerzeit*.[11]

Beyond the model of realistic language, what he accepted from Holz was the suggestion to change the heading of his drama from *Der Säemann* (*The Sower*) to its now familiar title *Vor Sonnenaufgang* (*Before Sunrise*). Both titles, to be sure, have a biblical resonance that appealed to Hauptmann's lifelong fascination with religion.[12] But while the first alluded more positively to the play's hero as the disseminator of liberal ideas, the second refers through its reminiscence of a darker passage in Genesis 19:15 to his behavior at the end: "When morning dawned, the angels urged Lot, saying, 'Arise, take your wife and your two daughters who are here, lest you be consumed in the punishment of the city.'"[13]

At first glance, *Vor Sonnenaufgang* resembles nothing more than a synthesis of Ibsen's *Ghosts* with its ravages of alcoholism, set in the corrupt peasant milieu of Tolstoy's *The Power of Darkness* and spiced with details from Hauptmann's own life and those of his friends.[14] The setting of the play, which adheres closely to the Aristotelean unities of time (barely twenty-four hours in September) and place, comprises the main room (Acts I, III, and V) and the barnyard (Acts II and IV) of a peasant establishment in Silesia. Even before the first words are uttered, the scene exemplifies the situation: the low-ceiled room, which cannot conceal its humble beginnings, is now covered with expensive carpets and filled with luxurious, albeit tasteless, furnishings.

The exposition acquaints us with the degenerate family of the fifty-year-old peasant Krause, who has suddenly become wealthy from the coal deposits beneath his land and now spends his days drinking himself into a stupor in the village pub. His much younger second wife, a vain and ignorant parvenue who married him for his money and now feasts on oysters and champagne, is sleeping incestuously with her half-idiotic nephew, whom she is trying for her own sexual convenience to marry to her step-daughter Helene. Helene, the only unspoiled member of the family, was saved when her dying mother insisted that she be sent off for an education at a pietist boarding school, but she must now come to terms with the grotesque conditions to which she has returned at home, including sexual advances from her alcoholic father and her scheming brother-in-law Hoffmann. Hoffmann, a once-idealistic engineer, has made his own fortune through an exploitative deal with the mines to sell their coal. At present he is staying with his in-laws while his alcoholic wife, Helene's sister Marie, awaits the imminent birth of their second child. (The first, we learn, died at age three when the alcoholism inherited from his mother led him to seize and shatter a bottle of vinegar, in the belief it was schnaps, and to cut open with the shards a large vein in his leg.)

It is into this Tolstoyan peasant atmosphere that the Ibsenian "messenger from afar" intrudes as the catalyst: Alfred Loth (= the biblical Lot? based on Hauptmann's friend Alfred Ploetz), who emigrated briefly to America with the hope of founding an ideal state and then on his return, as a Reichstag candidate for a workers' group in Leipzig, was imprisoned

for two years on grounds justified by the Sozialistengesetz that he had mis-
used the association and its funds for purposes of political agitation. Now
editor of an obscure workers' journal, he has come to the Silesian village
to write a socioeconomic report on the conditions of the miners (a timely
topic since the year 1889 witnessed the most widespread wave of strikes to
date among miners across Germany). Having learned that his boyhood
friend Hoffmann, a former fellow member of his idealistic Icarian society,
is also in the vicinity, Loth turns up unexpectedly at the Krause farmstead
and is invited to spend a day or two there. But when Hoffmann hears of
Loth's research plans on the exploitation of the workers, which will expose
his own corrupt business practices, he tries to persuade his friend to go
away again.

Not only a dogmatic socialist, Loth is also a passionate eugenicist and
teetotaler with a firm belief in naturalistic determinism through heredity,
milieu, and education. But he is so utterly limited and self-centered in
and by his idealism—he rejects Goethe's *The Sorrows of Young Werther* as
a book for weaklings and calls the works of Ibsen and Zola "medicine"—
that he is oblivious to all the signs around him, including the drunken
singing of old Krause staggering home at four o'clock in the morning,
that he is in a house almost totally wracked by alcoholism. As a result, he
allows himself, in a convincing and widely praised love scene (Act IV), to
become infatuated with Helene, known in criticism as "the rose on the
dung heap," who in turn looks to him as her only hope for escape from the
hellhole to which she is condemned.

On the second evening (Act V), when the local physician arrives to
await the birth of Marie's child, Loth recognizes in him his close friend
Schimmelpfennnig from university days in Jena. In the course of their
conversation, which is punctuated by the screams of the woman in labor
upstairs, the cynically realistic doctor, who has spent six years in the mining community to earn enough money to enable him to return and work
for his true commitment to women's rights, tells Loth the hard truth about
the family, remarking that his friend must have renounced his former
eugenicist convictions if he now intends to marry a woman from this
family of inherited alcoholism. After a brief struggle with his conscience,
Loth decides to leave the house and Helene straightway. Immediately after
his departure Helene rushes in to tell Hoffmann that the child was still-
born. As her shattered brother-in-law hastens out, Helene looks around for
Loth, desperate for rescue from this doomed house. As she reads the few
words of farewell that Loth has left for her, she hears the drunken singing
of her father returning from the pub. In her despair she seizes a hunting

dagger hanging from the set of antlers above the sofa and rushes out. A few moments later the servant girl comes in looking for Helene. Glancing into the room where Helene disappeared, she comes out screaming. The final words of the play are the father's drunkenly mumbled refrain: "Ain't I got a pair of lovely daughters?"

With *Vor Sonnenaufgang* Hauptmann succeeded in reasserting the place of German literature within *Weltliteratur* and the modern developments represented by Zola, Ibsen, and Tolstoy. In one important respect he advanced the dramatic techniques of realism beyond Ibsen and Tolstoy. Several of the characters speak a pure and natural Silesian dialect, the likes of which had never before been heard on the stages of Germany or elsewhere.[15] This new dimension of realism was further enhanced by several scenes, such as the concluding one, which are communicated almost entirely by gesture or by inarticulate cries and fragmented speech. The elaborate stage directions, specifying the characters' appearance, gestures, movements, and other details, reveal the affinity to epic that is typical of German naturalistic drama. In Hauptmann's hands, finally, the drama surrounding the decline of a single peasant family is used to symbolize the dangers facing Germany as a whole as a result of over-rapid industrialization and capitalism.

The play, which was published in August 1889, was well received by important figures in Hauptmann's cultural world. Arno Holz, who read the work in manuscript, assured him that he and Schlaf "regard it as the best drama that has ever been written in the German language. *Tolstoy included!*"[16] A few weeks later, Julius Hart, a leading critic and theoretician of naturalism, congratulated him on a work that "belongs not only to the most characteristic, but also to the most significant that I have read in recent times."[17] Not all his friends were completely happy with the play. Alfred Ploetz complimented Hauptmann on a plot that was "masterfully dramatic," but he had reservations about the figure of Loth, which he regarded as oversimplified and too free of inner conflict—but in part also because he resented the conspicuous resemblance to his own life and character.[18] Indeed, so general was the criticism of Loth's socialist and eugenic pontifications that Hauptmann was moved to write an (unpublished) rebuttal, pointing out that Loth talks to Hoffmann about matters that would naturally arise when two old friends meet and catch up on their lives and that in his conversations with Helene he is not giving public lectures but talking in simple terms to an intelligent but largely uninformed young woman.[19]

If praise from the "most consequent realist" and from prominent contemporary critics was heartening, even more meaningful was the reaction of two other figures. Theodor Fontane, the grand old man of German literature, who was still refreshingly open to contemporary developments, wrote to Hauptmann's publisher, congratulating him on the publication of such an "outstanding" work and promising, if the author wished, to recommend the work to Otto Brahm for performance in the newly established Freie Bühne.[20] A few days later Fontane notified a grateful Hauptmann that he had indeed written to Brahm. But Brahm, as it turned out, had already read the play and communicated to the author his intention to win the work for his theater.[21] A week later Brahm informed Hauptmann that *Vor Sonnenaufgang* had been accepted for performance and would be presented on October 20 as the second performance of the season. Brahm was so taken by the play that, on the day preceding the premiere, he wrote to Hauptmann, who in the interval had become his "Lieber Freund" ("dear friend"), to assure him of his growing "conviction of its significance and grandeur."[22]

Whatever the culture boors may have in store for you, it will always be for me a matter of pride to have contributed to the presentation of this play; and I trust that you will advance toward these hours of battle with the same feeling as I: that only the public can disgrace itself today—not you and I.[23]

The premiere that Sunday afternoon became one of the greatest scandals in the history of German theater. The subscribers to the Freie Bühne comprised not only the advanced-thinking journalists, musicians, poets, students, and actors of Berlin, who enthusiastically welcomed this bold new undertaking. It also included the fashionable elite—businessmen, lawyers, civil servants, women from the bourgeoisie as well as the demimonde—who were accustomed to the lighthearted fare in the Residenztheater and who joined because it was the latest trend but who lived by the motto: "In the theater I want to be amused; there are tragedies enough at the stockmarket."[24] Because the play had already been published, it was heatedly discussed for days and weeks before the premiere, and "everyone arrived with an opinion, anticipating something unusual."[25] The audience was especially curious to learn whether or not the playwright, director, and actors were actually going to depict some of the more daring scenes. As Hauptmann recalled,

that a play about peasants cannot ignore dung heaps and other agricultural necessities; that a peasant creeps away in the morning from his mistress and not, as in the Residenztheater, a marquis; but mainly, that the birth of a child is reported on stage—all this went well beyond the indecencies that people were prepared to tolerate on the stage.[26]

Anonymous letters were sent to the actors, singling out especially the noted Else Lehmann, who took the role of Helene and was generally regarded as the star of the play, trying to intimidate them in advance. One of the spectators, a certain Dr. Isidor Kastan, even showed up for the premiere with a pair of delivery forceps that he intended to toss onto the stage at the crucial moment. The mood in the audience was so unruly that, waiting for the curtain to rise, one of the actors remarked to Brahm that "you would believe you're standing on a battlefield: you hear the bullets whistle, but unfortunately you can't shoot back!"[27]

During the first act the audience, finding Loth's preaching on abstinence ridiculous but not crude and despicable, remained fairly calm.[28] But they became agitated during the second act, when the drunken Krause tries to grope his daughter and when her fiancé creeps out of her stepmother's bedroom at daybreak. At that point, Dr. Kastan stood up and shouted "Are we in a theater or a brothel?"[29] The outcries intensified in the third act when Hoffmann tries to cuddle up to his sister-in-law and when Loth outlines his socialist ideas for his friend. The love scene of Act IV provided a respite of sorts: people had no reason here for moral indignation, but certain scandalmongers incited by Dr. Kastan wanted to disturb the tranquility of the scene by laughing and making fun of it—an effect helped by the passing appearance in that act of a hopping and skipping epileptic peasant. In Act V, finally, although the director cut out the whimpers and screams of the woman in labor upstairs, Dr. Kastan, who had come prepared, did not let the omission restrain him: he whirled his forceps around his head and hurled them onto the stage all the same. "This act in the action [of the play] was the highpoint of the wildest and most chaotic noisy scenes."[30] The crowd became so wayward that it looked at several points as though the play could not be acted through to the conclusion. "Rarely," wrote the critic Paul Lindau in his review, "have we found the contrasts that are present in every public so sharp, indeed so brutal in their expression."[31] Theodor Fontane, who was as happy with the performance as he had been earlier when he read the play, observed that "in the public, depending on the partisan stand, more or less violent signs of applause or disapproval were heard, approving or mocking laughter, also one of those critical impromptus in which the people of Berlin excel."[32]

Following the "storm of moral outrage" over what the Berliners began to call this "schnaps and forceps drama,"[33] the slender, well-dressed, and modest young playwright himself appeared before the curtain looking so harmless and innocent that the audience, expecting a bearded and broad-shouldered wild man, was astonished, prompting Fontane to conclude his review wittily with a quotation from a book by a renowned forensic physician: "My murderers all looked like young girls."[34]

The battle over *Vor Sonnenaufgang* continued to rage for weeks in the cafés, salons, and newspapers.[35]

Old friends had a falling out, the like-minded came together, and opposition against the innovators or the approval of them became a watchword in the aesthetic campaign: Guelfs here, Ghibellines there. The banner of German Naturalism fluttered in the breeze, was reviled and admired, with varying gestures; but it was not to be lowered again for years to come.[36]

Most of the published reviews, in contrast to the letters from Hauptmann's friends, were negative.

Even other "Naturalists," in this literary movement that was still seeking a common ground, objected to the play. Almost a year after the premiere Conrad Alberti, the leading critic for the Naturalist journal *Die Gesellschaft*, wrote a "necrology" for the detested Freie Bühne, in which he singled out *Vor Sonnenaufgang* for his special contempt. "The action is little more than null, and that little is the purest nonsense that ever dilettantish brazenness dared to offer the public."[37] "Never," he repeats for emphasis, "has such brain-scorched nonsense come to my attention."[38] In order to catch the attention of the public for his "fricassee of nonsense, childishness, and insanity," Hauptmann saturated it "with a mixture of crudities, brutalities, nastinesses, filths as was previously unheard-of in Germany. Manure was carried onto the stage by the bucket, the theater turned into a dungheap."[39] A play of this sort, he sneers, was praised by Otto Brahm and his consorts as *Die Räuber* of our age. With friends like those, who needs enemies?

On the morning after the premiere Karl Frenzel proclaimed in the *National-Zeitung* that "all the indecencies with which the play is richly blessed cannot compensate for its lack of action and the intellectual vacuity."[40] Often Hauptmann was used as a whipping boy through whom to attack the entire Naturalist movement. In the *Berliner Tageblatt* Paul Lindau advised the author:

If Herr G. H. really wants to learn something from yesterday's performance, then it can only be one thing: that he must free himself as much as possible from the teachings of the new school to which he has given his allegiance, that he should create in a literarily independent manner [...] without allowing himself to be befuddled by the incense that has already been sprinkled upon him in a wholly irresponsible manner by his critical partisans.[41]

And in that evening's edition of the same paper Lindau continued his attack: "Yes, repulsive! I can find no gentler expression for what I must regard in this dramatic effort as the product of the new school. What does it actually want? Truth?—'What is truth?' Is only the ugly, the disgusting, true? only filth, muck, the cloaca?'[42] This refrain was widely echoed. "Exaggeration of the ugly and the repulsive is the mistake that G.H. shares with many representatives of realistic art," fumed Raphael Löwenfeld in the *Freisinnige Zeitung* (October 23, 1889).[43] And the anonymous reviewer in the *Volkszeitung* (October 22, 1889) opined that he did not want to deal with the issue of Naturalism versus Idealism or with the justification of the so-called "realistic" school. He simply wanted to raise his objections to "the shamelessness of a literature that degrades our theaters to sailors' dives and, under a false flag, bears contraband that exudes miasmas."[44] The *Norddeutsche Allgemeine Zeitung* (October 22, 1889) hailed "this first child of realistic art," whose father has decked it out "with all the charms that are characteristic of alcoholism, delirium tremens, adultery."[45] Attacks such as these were no doubt outweighed in the young author's mind by the praise of his idol, Henrik Ibsen, who told him, when they met in 1891 on Berlin's Friedrichstrasse, that he found the play "courageous and spirited" ("*tapfer und mutig*").[46]

Following its premiere at the Freie Bühne, the play had a subsequent public performance in Berlin's Belle-Alliance-Theater from November 11 to December 12, 1889, in a form so extensively cut and altered that it could not offend the prevailing moral and political norms[47]—and so remote from the author's original intentions that he could barely bring himself, despite the producers' urging, to attend the performance.[48] Thereafter, the play was not often performed until its revival after World War II. But a further sign of the impression it had made upon the public mind is given by the parodies that soon appeared in Berlin's Parodie-Theater and elsewhere. In one of these—*Nach Sonnenaufgang, Parodie in einem Akt von Erhart Glaubtmann*, which was produced as early as December 1889—Helene doesn't kill herself at the end but marries Loth and lives happily ever after.[49]

Although it was not frequently performed, the play went through many editions during the following years, was extensively discussed, and established its reputation firmly as one of the foundation stones of modern German theater and drama. Through his adaptation of Ibsen's analytic drama, Hauptmann single-handedly created the German social drama. The critic Alfred Kerr claimed that with Hauptmann's play the words spoken after the Berlin premiere of Ibsen's *Ghosts* had been fulfilled: "Pay attention! Today there begins a new epoch of German literature."[50] Ever since that October matinée in 1889, *Vor Sonnenaufgang* has been a touchstone in all discussions of German Naturalism. As Roy Cowen states in the introduction to his authoritative study of Naturalism, "the perform-ance of his drama *Vor Sonnenaufgang* in the year 1889 conquers the stage for the German Naturalists."[51] After Hauptmann, the language of the stage was no longer determined by convention and tradition but by real-ism; and acting—in a manner that Schiller and Iffland would have under-stood and appreciated—was infinitely expanded and enriched by gesture and silences.

Apart from Hauptmann's immeasurable contribution to the develop-ment of German drama, the scandal surrounding the premiere of *Vor Sonnenaufgang* alerts us to the moral and political issues that agitated minds during those years. Bourgeois audiences were offended not sim-ply by the vulgarities of the language or the openness with which the young author treated such down-to-earth realities as birth and barnyard life. A society fearful of socialism was alarmed by the author's boldness in confronting them on the open stage not only with the effects of the *Sozialistengesetz* on a generation of disaffected young German idealists but with such glaring social problems as alcoholism, the often corrupt practices of capitalism in Germany's rapidly industrializing society and their effect on regional agricultural communities, the everyday reality of adultery and sexual aggression, and the constraints placed upon women by social con-vention. In sum, the scandal of the premiere signaled Hauptmann's success in forcing his audience vividly to confront realities recently identified by the socialists—realities that, although initially viewed with indignation, gradually shaped national social policy as they came to be accepted during the following decades—and to make "moral" judgments about them in Schiller's sense. As Brahm assured Hauptmann in his letter immediately before the premiere, "only the public can disgrace itself today, not you and I." While the premiere audience was distracted by the superficialities of "schnaps and forceps," Hauptmann's play rapidly established itself as keystone of Naturalist drama and its social program, thus fulfilling the effect of theater as a moral institution.

THE DRAMA OF THE SAVAGE GOD (JARRY'S UBU ROI)

Apart from the riotous scandals that accompanied them it would be difficult to imagine any two plays more unlike than Hauptmann's *Vor Sonnenaufgang* and Alfred Jarry's *Ubu Roi* (*King Ubu*), which had its premiere (and only performance for the next decade) in Paris's Théâtre de l'Oeuvre on December 10, 1896. The differences were immediately signaled by the sets. In contrast to the detailed *trompe-l'oeil* realism of Hauptmann's Silesian barnyard and peasant house, the curtain in Paris opened on crudely painted scenery depicting blooming apple trees beneath falling snow. On one side was painted a bed with a palm tree at its foot and on the other a skeleton dangling from a gallows. Within this unchanging set, "changes of scene were announced," according to Arthur Symons's firsthand account, "by the simple Elizabethan method of a placard, roughly scrawled with stage directions" and transported by "a venerable gentleman in evening-dress," who trotted in and out on tiptoe between the scenes.[52]

The difference was further emphasized by the contrast between the authors. Hauptmann surprised his audience at the premiere by appearing for curtain calls as a modest, unassuming, and vaguely bemused young man whereas Jarry—"a small, very young man, with a hard, clever face," according to Symons, dressed in an oversized suit, cravated like a clown, with his long hair combed à la Bonaparte and his face painted "like a whore"[53]— seated himself before the curtain rose at a table covered with an old sack-cloth and, in curiously clipped speech patterns, delivered a ten-minute-long "conférence" to the audience in the overheated room on the meaning of his play—a harangue so remarkable that it was reprinted in full in the early biographies. After thanking several reviewers who had given a friendly reception to the previously published text of his play, Jarry explained that the audience was welcome to see in the figure of Ubu "multiple allusions" or "a simple puppet, the deformation by a schoolboy of one of his teachers who represented for him all the grotesqueness of the world."[54] The set, he continued, is intended to situate the play "in eternity" as the background for an action that takes place "in Poland, that is to say, Nowhere."

For the benefit of that majority who were unable to understand his weirdly articulated and mystifying discourse, the printed program contained further clarification. "Nowhere," he elaborated there, "is everywhere."[55] Ubu speaks French, "but his various faults are by no means French vices exclusively [...] Monsieur Ubu is an ignoble being, and that's why he resembles (at his worst) all of us." Ubu, the spectators read, is obsessed with three things: *Physics*, which is nature as compared to art; *Phynance*, or the self-awarded honors (that is, booty or plunder) resulting from one's satisfaction with oneself as opposed to the opinion of others; and *Merdre* (Jarry's own concoction of the unmistakable vulgarism *merde* [shit] with the interpolated letter "r": "shitr" or "shite.")

Who was this strange young man, who, as he confessed to the produc-er, had set out to "make certain people cry out at the scandal"?[56] Alfred

Jarry (1873–1907) was Hauptmann's opposite in almost every conceivable sense.[57] Unlike the Silesian gymnasium dropout, his younger French contemporary was a brilliant if erratic student who acquired a splendid education in ancient and modern literature, as well as science and math, at the lycée in Rennes and later at the renowned Lycée Henri IV in Paris. While Hauptmann's modest manner and attire concealed a fundamental self-confidence, the outlandish dress and weird behavior of the five-foot-tall Jarry masked an underlying insecurity and cynicism. In contrast to the Naturalist apostle of temperance Jarry was an alcoholic who drank himself to an early death. Unlike the young family man in his suburban villa, the acquaintance of Oscar Wilde and André Gide was a basically unloving bisexual who lived in a split-floor garret in which he could barely stand up. Hauptmann was a member of the group of young Naturalists centered around the journal *Die Gesellschaft* in Berlin; Jarry belonged to the cotérie of Symbolists surrounding Mallarmé at his *mardis* (Tuesday soirées) and the journal *Mercure de France*. Hauptmann gave up sculpture to write while Jarry, whose works featured his own drawings and woodcuts, used his small inheritance in 1894 to found a short-lived but luxurious journal dedicated to art history, *L'Ymagier*. While the social dramatist was profoundly influenced by Ibsen's realistic social dramas, the prophet of an antirational view of the world that he called 'Pataphysics was enthusiastic only about Ibsen's fantasy *Peer Gynt*. Above all, Hauptmann's firm belief in social determinism qualified by heredity and milieu was flatly at odds with Jarry's claim on absolute freedom of the individual—freedom from any and all restraints of tradition or society. He was indeed, Roger Shattuck concluded, an "unregenerate misfit."[58]

As Jarry noted in his preliminary remarks, his play was based on material drawn from a cycle of little plays and mock epics that he and his fellow students in Rennes had concocted about their detested teacher of physics, the unfortunate Professor Hébert, who was remarkably fat, pedagogically incompetent, and incessantly tormented by his students, who delighted in asking him questions that he was unable to answer. One of these plays, *Les Polonais*, was actually staged in a friend's attic—performed live by the students themselves and as a puppet show with homemade marionettes.[59] As Jarry became increasingly obsessed with the material, Père Heb gradually developed from a schoolboy caricature into Père Ubu (suggested in part perhaps by Latin *ubique* "everywhere"?) as a symbol for the worst in human character as seen by the sardonic young writer. In April 1896, after it had appeared in several different fragmentary forms—one of which, *Guignol*, won a literary prize—*Ubu Roi ou les Polonais* was published in the monthly review *Livre d'Art* and, two months later, in the now stand-ard text by the Éditions du Mercure de France: *Ubu Roi: Drame en cinq actes en prose; restitué en son intégrité tel qu'il a été représenté par les marionnettes du Théâtre des Phynances en 1888.*[60] At the same time, Jarry was engaged in negotiations with Aurélien Lugné-Poe, Director of the Théâtre de l'Oeuvre, who in February 1896 had produced Oscar Wilde's scandal-ous *Salomé*, for the performance of his play, which—by another curious contrastive parallel to Hauptmann's career—was also preceded in the 1896–1897 season by a work of Ibsen: not *Ghosts* or one of the realistic plays but *Peer Gynt*, the first French performance of which was instigated and largely directed by Jarry.

In September 1896, three months before the premiere of *Ubu Roi*, Jarry published an essay "De l'inutilité du théâtre au théâtre" ("On the uselessness of the theater for the theater"), which begins by asking whether the theater should adapt itself to the wishes of the mob (Jarry regularly refers to the public by the unflattering term "*foule*"), which goes to the theater to see the plays of Molière and Racine performed as they always have been and thus misses their meaning, or vice versa. Two factors, he states, uselessly encumber the contemporary stage: the decor, which is neither wholly natural (that is, real) nor wholly artificial (that is, imagina-tively free); and the actors, who distract from the essential characters they are meant to represent by their attempts at individualization. Instead, the scene should be so unspecific in time and place as to be universal, and the actors should wear masks that exemplify the character they are supposed to represent, showing mood changes solely by different light reflections of the planes of the mask. In effect, Jarry sought to reverse the shift from mythic generalization to psychological individualization that took place in Greek drama of the fifth century BC.

In fact, this is what happens in Jarry's play. We have already heard how the stage was decorated. As for the characters, each figure is dressed differ-ently: Ubu in a gray gown with a bowler hat and a pear-shaped mask that, according to some, anticipated the gas masks worn in World War I;[61] Mère Ubu in a housekeeper's outfit with a red hat; King Vencelas of Poland in a royal cloak and crown and his wife accordingly; their son Bougrelas, acted by a thirteen-year-old boy, who turns out to be the hero of the play, in a child's dress and bonnet; and the other figures in various historically inaccurate "national" outfits—Hungarian, Polish, Russian, and so forth. The crowd scenes and great armies, Jarry explained, should be represented by a single individual, and each figure should speak in a different and characteristic accent or "voice."[62]

The action of these grotesque figures against this weird backdrop and without the least pretense at unity of time or place, is quite simple—like a juvenile hash of motifs from *Macbeth, Hamlet,* and *Julius Caesar* with a title by analogy with *Oedipus Rex* and spiced with images from the popular guignol theater. Père Ubu—the grossly fat former King of Aragon, whose words and actions expose him as sadistic and violent, avaricious and stingy, aggressive and cowardly, gluttonous and treacherous—is urged by his scheming wife to kill the King of Poland, in whose army he serves, and to take over the realm.[63] Persuaded not out of any desire to rule but out of sheer greed for the fortunes involved, Ubu agrees and persuades Bordure and other officers with promises of great rewards to join him in the conspiracy (Act I). Even though he has just been rewarded for service by the noble but unsuspecting King Venceslas, he and his followers assassinate the King, who has ignored his wife's warnings, at a review of troops and kill two of his three sons. The youngest, Bougrelas, escapes to the mountains with his mother, who soon dies, whereupon the ghosts of the family appear to the young prince and incite him to revenge. Bordure and Mère Ubu, who has now become Queen, urge Ubu to celebrate his new kingship with a great public feast. Although he is reluctant to spend any of his newly acquired wealth on food for the masses, Ubu finally does so, having understood that he will more than compensate for any spendings with the heavy new taxes he intends to impose (Act II).

Ubu soon condemns the nobles of the kingdom, along with the judges and the financiers, to a cruel death by "disembraining" and seizes their wealth. He then visits the peasants, demanding double and triple taxes and destroying their homes when they are unable to pay. Despite growing unrest in the populace, Ubu imprisons Bordure for demanding the reward he was initially promised. Bordure escapes and flees to the Czar of Russia, whom he persuades to overthrow Ubu. When Ubu learns that the Russians are approaching, he sets off for war on a wooden horse, leaving behind Mère Ubu, who decides to make off with the treasure they have stolen (Act III). Frightened away from the treasure by a spectral voice from the tomb of a former Polish king, she is pursued by the young prince Bougrelas, who has arrived with his supporters. Meanwhile, Ubu and his men are defeated in the battle with the Czar's troops, and he flees with two of his followers to a cave. When they are attacked by a bear—Bordure costumed in a bear's skin—Ubu clambers cravenly onto a high rock and chants the Lord's Prayer in Latin as his men fight and kill the beast (Act IV). As Ubu lies sleeping and dreaming in the cave, Mère Ubu comes in and, pretending to be the archangel Gabriel, seeks to persuade Ubu of her loyalty and devotion. Suddenly Bougrelas enters with his men; in the ensuing battle Ubu tears some of the enemies into pieces—his favorite tactic!—but is finally defeated by the fierce child-prince and flees with a few of his loyal followers. We last see him on board a ship sailing along the coast of Germany en route to France, where the irrepressible Ubu confidently expects to become "Maître des Finances à Paris" (Act V).

What was it about this adolescent pastiche, lacking all psychological subtlety, that set off one of the most scandalous riots ever seen in a French theater? A scandal often compared to "the battle of *Hernani*" between the young—the Decadents and Symbolists—and the entrenched audience?[64] The Paris theater, like that in Berlin, was still attended largely by a traditional establishment: that *haute bourgeoisie* portrayed by Proust with ironic precision, together with a jaded aristocracy debating whether "the 'fashion' of hearing the beginning of a play was more up to date, was a proof of greater originality and intelligence, than arriving for the last act after a big dinner-party and having put in an appearance at a reception."[65] While it was becoming accustomed to the new realism of André Antoine's Théâtre Libre, learning to accept Ibsen, and "knew more or less which way the wind was blowing," as Rachilde put it in her biography,[66] it was willing to accept the avant-garde only in moderate, fashionable doses.[67] The immediate signal for their uproar was the word "merdre," the first word exclaimed in the play and to which Jarry had added the "r" "in order to confer majesty on it" and render it "at once efficacious and contagious."[68] That "mot de Cambronne," as it was delicately called in the reviews—because it was famously uttered by one of Napoleon's generals at Waterloo—had never before been heard on the stage in France. It introduced a litany of what one reviewer labeled "verbal defecation"[69] throughout the play and that soon came to be known by Jarry's admirers as "le Parler Ubu." The word "merdre" itself was spoken, both by Ubu and his wife, over thirty times in the course of the play, including such combinations as "choux-fleurs à la merdre" on the menu served to the conspirators, "madame de ma merdre" for his wife, "garçon de ma merdre" for one of his retinue, "sac à merdre" for another, and "le sabre à merdre," "ciseau à merdre," and "croc à merdre" for various weapons and implements.[70] Typically, Ubu's shouted "merdre" is the signal for the conspirators' attack on King Venceslas. When the word was distinctly pronounced in a strange staccato by Firmin Gémier (the actor playing Ubu) at the beginning of the play, "such a tumult ensued that Gémier had to remain mute for a quarter of an hour"[71] and finally restored calm by dancing a little jig. The literary figures in the audience laughed, but the "profane" members, especially the ladies, never recovered. People shouted from box to box and railed at one another. "Every time the word was spoken for the rest of the play it got the

same reception: cries of rage, of indignation or mad laughter."[72] Through
it all, Gémier and Mme France (Louise France), who had the role of Mère
Ubu, displaying monumental self-control and talent, played their parts to
the end.

The notorious evening has been often described. Another member
of the audience reported that the first word scandalized the audience.[73]
Francisque Sarcey, the conservative critic who wrote a theatrical column
for *Temps* under the pseudonym "Notre Oncle," and attended the performance as "apparently the official representative of good sense for the
epoch," was so brutally aroused "that one could see him almost leap out
of his seat."[74] The public shouted invectives, laughed, applauded, scarcely
heard the dialogue, which was dominated by the infamous vocable.
Occasionally the management turned up the lights, quietening people
temporarily, while Sarcey, shrugging his heavy shoulders, left the hall after
the first act and did not return. Indeed, in his column a few days later,
Sarcey did not even deign to review the play, which he called "a lewd joke
that merits only the silence of disdain."[75] Some people were madly amused;
others applauded aggressively; the monocled Edmond Rostand smiled
indulgently. People debated, grappled, insulted one another. All evening
long one heard frenetic applause, strident hissing. The fanaticism of half
the audience exasperated the other half. Lugné-Poe, who had been apprehensive about the premiere, was so distressed at the scandal that he refused
to schedule any further performances.

The reviews that appeared in the following days and weeks were similarly divided.[76] Several critics explained apologetically that they had been
unable to hear or understand much of the play because of the deafening
noise in the auditorium. Others simply threw up their hands in despair at
the unintelligible words and actions. One reported that the audience had
been bored to death by a play that lasted too long: "People laughed for ten
minutes; by the end of the first half-hour they yawned; and at the end of
the first hour they hissed."[77] And more than one reviewer felt, like Sarcey,
that the best response to such a hoax would be not a conspiracy but "the
judgment of silence."[78] "It is completely useless to give an account of the
lucubration performed yesterday evening."[79] But the majority reacted with
vituperation.

Robert Vallier in *La Republique Française*, having given an account of
Jarry's preliminary remarks, the stage set, and the plot, reported on the
"formidable tumult of protestations intermingled with shouts, hisses, catcalls, ululations, and barking," summarizing that the whole effort struck
him as "more puerile and pretentious than squalid and shocking."[80] In the

republican journal *La Paix*, one reviewer remarked that, if the word "mer-dre" were removed from the five acts, there would be no play left, while another regretted that so gifted an actor as Gémier had lent his talent to "such a prodigious imbecillity."[81] The reviewer for *L'Événement* complained of a headache and confessed that his first act upon getting home afterward was to take a shower to remove the filth to which he had been exposed.[82] Another critic said that out of respect for his readers he would not even have mentioned the premiere of *Ubu Roi* were it not for the unparalleled uproar that accompanied the performance. "The public protested with an uncommon violence upon hearing this succession of phrases whose coarseness vied with their incoherence."[83] And in *La Laterne* the reviewer reported that "when the curtain rose, the first word that Ubu utters is the celebrated *mot de Cambronne*. So the public was warned. After that, Ubu is able to take any liberties he wishes."[84] These representative examples make it clear that most reviewers were offended, first, by the scatalogi-cal language and, second, by the sense that they were being hoaxed. The analysis rarely goes beyond the linguistic vulgarities or seeks to derive any more meaningful sense out of the "mystification."

But a few of the early critics took the play more seriously, sensing that it amounted to more than a mere lampoon against the bourgeoisie. In the audience that evening was, among other notables, the thirty-year-old William Butler Yeats. Because Yeats did not understand enough French to follow the plot, he simply reported on the action. "The players are sup-posed to be dolls, toys, marionettes, and now they are all hopping like wooden frogs, and I can see for myself that the chief personage, who is some kind of King, carries for Sceptre a brush of the kind that we use to clean a closet."[85] Feeling bound, he says, "to support the most spirited party," he shouted along with the supporters of the play. But afterward he confessed his sadness at the growing influence in art and society of a comic spirit that reduces everything to simple black and white. "After all our subtle colour and nervous rhythm, after the faint mixed tints of Conder, what more is possible? After us the Savage God." It is notable how often the word "savage" occurs in responses to the play.[86] Arthur Symons, who was also in the audience, wrote that the play "has the crudity of a schoolboy or a savage" and that it is "the gesticulation of a young savage of the woods."[87]

What Symons and Yeats sensed, albeit without much appreciation, was the emergence of a new literary type or, more precisely, the acknow-ledgment of a previously repressed aspect of humankind: what more recent critics have labeled, in Freudian terminology, the "universal Id"[88] or a pessimistic version of Everyman.[89] Jarry's advocate, Catulle Mendès, found the play tedious and acknowledged "the hisses, the howls of rage and rattles of malicious laughter, the benches ready to be hurled onto the stage, people in the boxes clamoring and shaking their fists—in a word, a mob, furious at being hoaxed" and at "allusions to the eternal human imbecillity, the eternal lewdness, the eternal gluttony."[90] Nevertheless, he concludes positively, "Père Ubu exists."[91] And despite the silliness of the action "a type has been presented to us, created by the extravagant and brutal imagination of an almost infantile man."[92] A few days later, Mallarmé, who knew Jarry from his soirées, wrote to congratulate him on having created "a prodigious personage" who will "enter the repertoire of high taste and will haunt me."[93] Similarly Romain Coolus (pseudonym for René Weil) noted that within just a few weeks "literature, art, politics are impregnated with Ubu: wherever you turn it smells of Ubu."[94] He lists all of Ubu's bad traits: gluttony, ferocity, cupidity, coarseness, cowardice, and many more. Ubu is "the hero of all the puppet shows ['*guignolades*']," seen many times and recognized. "Here he is particularly brutal and of an exceptional violence because our farce is addressed to somewhat older children who must be jogged out of their digestive apathy."

Ubu's typicality had already been established by Jarry's friends at the *Mercure de France*, whose reviewer noted that Ubu is "the caricatural resumé of everything ignoble, cowardly, contemptible, and disgusting concealed by the human animal living in society" and symbolizes "the apotheosis of the belly and the triumph of the snout in universal history."[95] He continues: "When a type has taken shape like this and at the same time encountered the naturalist predestined perhaps by eternal wisdom to catalogue it and name it, there is a good chance that it will be definitive." In that same journal's subsequent review of the performance, Ferdinand Hérold (who had been responsible for lighting at the premiere) claimed that "M. Alfred Jarry will have had the rare honor of creating a type, that of Ubu."[96]

While some critics were content to identify Ubu as a mythic type, others sought to analyze the figure's components. Catulle Mendès concluded in the review cited above that Ubu was a composite figure made of a wild assortment of literary and contrasting historical types:

of Pucinella and Polichinelle, of Punch and Karageuz, of Mayeux and M. Joseph Prud'homme, of Robert Macaire and M. Thiers, of the Catholic Torquemada and the Jew Deutz, of an agent of the Sûreté and the anarchist Vaillant, an enormous slovenly parody of Macbeth, of Napoleon, and of a pimp become king—he exists all the same, unforgettable.[97]

Henri Bauer, who wrote no fewer than three appreciations of the play for *L'Echo de Paris* (November 23, December 12, and December 19, 1896), continued in much the same tone and using many of the same images. "Ubu is the extreme product of the dynasties of skullduggery, engendered by the French Revolution and the state of civil and military bourgeoisie, which it designates under the names of Caesar, of Bonaparte, of Louis-Philippe, of Joseph Prudhomme, of Chauvin or of Napoleon."[98]

But *Ubu Roi* does not merely set out to shock the bourgeoisie with its scatology, to mystify with its hoaxes, or, in the words of Henry Fouquier, critic for *Le Figaro* (December 13), to function as "an anarchist of art [...] repeating in the world of letters what I saw happening, with my own sorry eyes, at the time of the Commune" and seeking to "exercise over the public a veritable terror"[99]—in sum, to express his contempt for modern civilization and its values. Despite supporters and opponents alike, Jarry's satirical attacks on the bourgeoisie, the State, and religion were not meant as a manifesto of anarchism, a literary terrorism in keeping with the contemporary wave of anarchist bombings. In response to some of the favorable reviews of the published version, Jarry insisted that Ubu represents "not exactly Monsieur Thiers, nor the bourgeois, nor the vulgarian: he would be rather the perfect anarchist, with all that prevents *us* from ever becoming the perfect anarchist."[100] Indeed, among the targets of his satire are not only the obvious ones—the staid bourgeoisie, the conventional critics, and so forth—but also his friends who were searching for deeper political and other symbolic meanings in his fundamentally straightforward text.[101] Hence, no doubt, his ironic warning in his "conférence" preceding the premiere for those who seek "multiple allusions" in his play.

No, for all his outlandish, often juvenile behavior, Jarry—highly educated, brilliantly intelligent—had a serious purpose more in keeping with Schiller's idea of the stage as a moral institution (although he would no doubt have ridiculed the notion). In an article written shortly after the premiere, in which he sought to address some of the misunderstandings of his play, Jarry wrote that it was his intention, once the curtain rose, that

the scene appear before the public like that mirror in the fairy tales of Mme Leprince de Beaumont, in which the vicious man sees himself with the horns of a bull and a dragon's body, according to the exaggeration of his vices; and it is not astonishing that the public should have been stupified at the sight of his ignoble double, which had never yet been wholly presented to it.[102]

He went on to surmise that "the mob was angered precisely because it understood all too well despite its protests." This view was seconded by his lifelong friend Rachilde, who observed in her biography that the audience, which anticipated merely "something new, including absurdity and even the powerlessness of absurdity," understood all too well what Jarry had in mind and therefore made him into "the first victim offered in holocaust to the furious folly of novelty."[103] In sum, a positive moral goal underlies the obscenities, the absurdities, the juvenilities of Jarry's play—the perhaps futile hope that the audience, having seen the deficiencies of its own society exposed, will return to a simpler, more childlike, more innocent vision of wonder and universal types.

Jarry's moral intent was misunderstood by most of his contemporaries, supporters as well as enemies. It was only in later decades that readers, having in the meantime experienced two world wars, began to appreciate the profounder aspects of his superficially simple farce. His play effectively disappeared from the stage following its premiere. With the exception of a single performance in 1908 it lay dormant for three decades. Then, in 1926, Antonin Artaud along with Roger Vitrac founded the Théâtre Alfred Jarry, in which they staged Surrealist plays claiming the heritage of their eponymous predecessor. In the theatrical chaos following World War II, Jarry, who in his early essay on "The uselessness of the theater for the theater" had rejected all modern modes of theater, was claimed as a forerunner, rightly or wrongly, by various new dramatic schools and as the initiator of avant-garde theater.[104] In accord with what Jarry's friend Rachilde Vallette called "*l'école des démons de l'absurde*"[105] he came to be regarded as a precursor of the modern theater of the absurd.[106]

In the century since that legendary premiere other meanings have been attributed to Jarry's unique work. Ubu has been identified, as we have seen, as an exemplification of Freud's universal Id. As the Savage God he has entered the mythic realm of universal types exposed by C. G. Jung's explorations of the collective unconscious. Ubu has been seen as a precursor of the totalitarian dictators of the twentieth century[107] and of the violence that characterized the wars of that century—including, as we noted, even the gas mask. The nonsense of 'Pataphysics has been taken to heart by various schools of anti-rationalism. Because, with his vision of a theater diametrically opposed to that of Ibsen and Hauptmann, he anticipated many developments of the twentieth-century stage in Europe and the USA, the play has enjoyed an astonishingly successful revival on stages across Europe and the USA.[108] Yet, in a larger sense, Jarry regarded his play as the vehicle of a moral vision consisting of universal images and myths—a vehicle that fittingly found its place in the theater as a moral institution.

CHAPTER 4

Sounding the depths

Vor Sonnenaufgang and *Ubu Roi* scandalized their publics because they drew attention with blatantly offensive language to aspects of fin-de-siècle society that, while readily evident, were assiduously ignored by all: the alcoholism, the sexual improprieties, the greed, the violence, and others. Two works of the following decade used, in contrast, the language of music to expose more deeply rooted elements of human nature and culture.

FEMME DE SIÈCLE (WILDE/STRAUSS'S SALOME)

Almost precisely a century before the Berlin *Idomeneo*, another decapitated head on stage aroused worldwide scandal—this time not the imagined indignation of Muslims over the head of Muhammad but the real outrage of Christians over the head of John the Baptist. The affair began auspiciously. The premiere of Richard Strauss's *Salome* in the Dresden Royal Opera on December 9, 1905, which featured that head, was "a sensational success."[1] Following the performance and a stunned silence the applause lasted over a quarter-hour, and the audience, including what a contemporary newspaper report called "the European elite of artistically interested spectators,"[2] such as Serge Rachmaninoff and Arturo Toscanini, summoned the soloists along with Strauss and the conductor, Ernst von Schuch, for curtain calls almost forty times. A day later, the *Dresdner Nachrichten* reported that "our Hofoper has not enjoyed a sensation of similar significance since Wagner's last works."[3] Strauss himself wrote to the conductor that he was hugely pleased with "the colossal success of *Salome*."[4]

During the following weeks and months, *Salome* was performed on many stages in Europe, especially those not dominated by conservative royal families. Within the first three weeks following the Dresden premiere, Strauss recalled, the work had been accepted at ten theaters, including Breslau and Prague. In May, the first Austrian performance with Strauss himself at the podium took place in Graz, despite concerns over possible Christian Socialist demonstrations. In Munich, over strong opposition in the local Catholic press, the opera was performed in November 1906 even though several prima donnas turned down the role on moral grounds.[5] *Salome* was first heard in Paris at the Petit Théâtre on April 30, 1907, with such spectators as Romain Rolland and Maurice Ravel in attendance. In May of that year the opera was finally performed in Vienna—but only at the Volkstheater with the visiting Opera Ensemble from Breslau—and offended the religious feelings of many.

Yet despite the opera's growing popularity with audiences it immediately aroused strong opposition. Gustav Mahler had sought to dissuade Strauss from that particular subject for an opera. "Mahler was violently opposed," his wife recalled. "He had a thousand reasons; there was first of all the moral objection, but also, neither last nor least, that the production might be barred in Catholic countries."[6] Sure enough, the work was promptly condemned by Church officials, both Protestant and Catholic, and formally prohibited in many cities and countries. In England the Lord Chamberlain cited an ancient law prohibiting performances of works based on figures and stories taken from the Bible—including Saint-Saëns's *Samson and Delilah* and Massenet's *Hérodiade*. As Sir Thomas Beecham delightfully relates, the Lord Chamberlain subsequently (1910) relented when the libretto was modified (a) to eliminate the name of John, who was called simply the Prophet; (b) to refine Salome's sexual passion into a desire for spiritual guidance; (c) to transform her line "if you had looked upon me you would have loved me" into "if you had looked upon me you would have blessed me"; and (d) to substitute for the decapitated head a covered platter.[7] (As it happened, in the course of the performance the singers gradually replaced the bowdlerized lines with "the viciousness of the lawful text"—to great success.)[8] The composer Arnold Bax recalled in his memoirs that even English schoolgirls studying in Dresden were not permitted to attend the performances there.[9]

In New York the opera was produced before a sold-out house at the Metropolitan Opera on January 22, 1907, and extra policemen were required to handle the unusual crowd. The performance received a lengthy and glowing review in *The New York Times*. But in the same issue the paper reported that many in the audience were "disgusted by the Dance and the Kissing of the Dead Head."[10] All was calm until Salome began her dance. "Many of the women in the Metropolitan Opera House that night turned away from it" while men twisted in their seats and withdrew to the corridors to smoke. When Salome began to sing to Jochanaan's head, a group of men and women from the front row got up to leave, and other parties "tumbled precipitately into the corridor and called to a waiting employee of the house to get their carriages." The protests were so vehement that following that single performance the board members, including prominently J. Pierpont Morgan, forced General Manager Heinrich Conried to withdraw the work from the repertoire, where it did not appear again for twenty-seven years.[11] (On January 28, 1909, the diva Mary Garden enjoyed a brief triumph with her performance as Salome in New York's Manhattan Opera House, but when she took the same role to Philadelphia the local churches issued formal protests.)[12]

In Vienna, despite Mahler's best efforts, the Imperial Opera House was forced by the morally severe Archduchess Marie Valerie to withdraw the initial approval won by Gustav Mahler and prohibited any performance of *Salome* until 1918, a few months before the collapse of the Habsburg monarchy. As Archbishop Piffl of Vienna explained in a handwritten letter to the composer, he was unable to rid himself of his reservations when he imagined "the person of the Holy Man, before whom even Herodes trembles in veneration, confronted by the love-fury of a raging sadist."[13] Kaiser Wilhelm II of Germany finally acceded to the performance, conducted by Strauss, at the Berlin Royal Opera in December 1906, but only after the director slyly, and wholly anachronistically, introduced the rising Star of Bethlehem at the end of the opera to hint at the Christianity that succeeded the horrors of the action.[14] In Bayreuth, still dominated by a Wagner cult headed by Cosima Wagner, who regarded the opera as the work of a madman, the performance was forbidden. In Riga the censors would be willing to allow the performance, Strauss was informed, only under specific conditions: if the action were moved to another country, if all the names were changed, if all statements referring to the Bible were deleted, and if the decapitated head were not displayed.[15]

Why the controversy? After all, despite her inauspicious beginnings in the Bible, by 1900 Salome had become the celebrated *femme fatale* of the fin-de-siècle. In the brief gospels accounts (Matthew 14:1–12; Mark 6:14–29), she is still the unnamed and obedient daughter of Herodias, whose dance pleases Herod Antipas so greatly that he vows to reward her with whatever she wishes; on the command of her strong-minded mother—because the prophet had loudly criticized Herodias's marriage to Herod as adultery—she requests, and receives, the head of John the Baptist on a platter. (Herodias's first husband, Antipas's brother Philip, was still alive and imprisoned.) It was not until the early fifth century that she got her name from Isidor of Pelusium, who knew (from Josephus's

Jewish Antiquities) that Herodias's daughter from her first marriage was called Salome. The early church fathers used her example, with and without a name, principally to illustrate the temptation of women and the sinfulness of dance, as does Johannes Chrysostomos in his late-fourth-century commentary on the Gospel of Matthew (48th homily): "Wherever there is a dance, the devil is also present. God did not give us our feet for dancing but so that we might walk on the path of righteousness."[16] With relatively few exceptions—several medieval mystery plays and various Reformation dramas, in which Herodias is still the principal villainess— the theme engaged little literary interest until the mid-nineteenth century. In paintings of the Renaissance and Reformation, in contrast, it enjoyed considerable popularity, showing up in works by Botticelli, Ghirlandaio, Veronese, Rubens, Titian, Leonardo da Vinci, and Albrecht Dürer, among many others—paintings that feature Salome as the manifestation of sheer beauty rather than as the symbol of moral delinquency.[17]

Then, inspired principally by Heinrich Heine's ballad *Atta Troll* (1847), which achieved a notable success in France, Salome/Herodias became an increasingly iconic figure in the modern aesthetic consciousness. In Heine's ironic treatment, Herodias, clearly identified as the wife of Herod, still occupies the central role: in the phantasmagoria of the Wild Hunt that the narrator observes on St. John's Eve from the window of a witch's house in the Pyrenees (cantos 18–19) he sees three female figures on horseback: the Greco-Roman goddess Diana, the Celtic fairy Abunda, and the biblical Herodias, carrying in her hands a golden platter with the head of John the Baptist. She is condemned to ride eternally in the Wild Hunt, Heine reports, for her blood-guilt in demanding John's head; but she secretly loved him, according to popular legend, for which reason she passionately kisses his decapitated head and from time to time tosses it up into the air. (This hysterically laughing Herodias clutching the platter with the Baptist's head was taken over by Théodore de Banville in his sonnet *Hérodiade* [1870]).

In Mallarmé's problematic and fragmentary dramatic poem *Hérodiade* the heroine coldly rejects all earthly pleasures and clings almost hysterically to her virginity. The poem, begun in 1863 and not published until 1898 but often recited by the poet to his coterie, brought the story to the forefront of advanced literary thought in France, where the blurred figure of Herodias/Salome became the icon of an elitist Décadence with its belief in an eternal conflict between the virtuous male spirit and an evil female nature and obsessed with violence, madness, and sexuality. With Théodore de Banville's sonnet *La Danseuse* (1870), finally, Salome began to emerge as the embodiment of dance. Flaubert's dazzling novella *Herodias*, the third of his *Trois contes* (1877), provided the classic full narrative of the episode, focusing on the effect that Salome's dance exerted on the indecisive Herod but retaining Herodias as the motivating force behind the decapitation. In Jules Massenet's opera *Hérodiade* (1881), Salome and Jean are in love; having first tried to kill Hérodiade, Salome commits suicide after his death.

These prominent examples, in which Salome gradually emerged from the shadow of her mother, produced a wave of poems, plays, stories, and novels featuring Salome,[18] accompanied by a veritable flood of late-nineteenth-century paintings by such artists as Henri Reynault, Gustave Moreau, Aubrey Beardsley, Gustav Klimt, Franz von Stuck, Max Slevogt, Lovis Corinth, Franz von Lenbach, Arnold Böcklin, and countless others.[19] In Joris-Karl Huysmans's *À rebours* (*Against the Grain*) (1884) the neurotic aesthete Des Esseintes spends hours contemplating the two paintings by Moreau (which he is said to own): *Salomé* and *L'Apparition* (both 1876). This iconic Salome in her role as the personification of pure art through dance, an art opposed to religion embodied by John the Baptist, became so prevalent that Jules Laforgue parodied it bitingly in his *Moralités légendaires* (1887): his Salome is so tediously loquacious and self-centered that the guests at the party begin to wonder when she'll finally be sent to bed. By the last decade of the century, then, Salome had come to combine several of the fin-de-siècle's most compelling interests: the sexuality of the *femme fatale*, the association of love and death, and the power of art (= dance).[20] An additional factor, which we will encounter again in Chapter 5, was the association of sexuality with Jews, a commonplace since the early nineteenth century in Europe, which raises the issue of anti-Semitism.[21]

It was against this feverish background that Oscar Wilde in 1891–1892 wrote—in French—his *Salomé*. (With more than a touch of Romanic loyalty, Mario Praz, having reviewed the preceding French tradition, concluded ironically: "as generally happens with specious second-hand works, it was precisely Wilde's Salome which became popular."[22]) Wilde, who was thoroughly familiar with both the iconographic and literary traditions of Salome, had also been acquainted with Mallarmé's fragmentary *Hérodiade* through a reading at the poet's renowned *mardis*.[23] While his play retains essentially the structure of Flaubert's novella, which Wilde first read in 1877 in a copy lent to him by Walter Pater[24]—notably the setting, the temporal compression, and the focus on the wavering Herod—it borrows many details from other works in the French tradition and shares many of their views.[25] However, Wilde made several distinctive additions to the story whose total effect was a demythification, secularization, and ironization of the traditional Christian version. He attributed Salome's demand for John's head to her scorned love for the prophet, toward whose hair, body, and lips she feels a powerful sexual attraction—a new motif in the long history of the theme. Through her passionate kiss on the lips of the decapitated head Wilde clearly aligned Salome with the *eros/thanatos* association that occupied so central a position in the imagination of Décadence. (The well-known refrain of Wilde's *Ballad of Reading Gaol* states: "All men kill the thing they love.") He intensified the traditional opposition of pure art and religion by associating Salome and John, respectively, with the views of his two teachers, the rarefied aesthetics of Walter Pater and the ethical criticism of John Ruskin.[26] Wilde was the first writer to have Salome killed for her behavior—at least as much on dramatic as moral grounds. Finally, and above all, Wilde invented the Dance of the Seven Veils that Salome's name today inevitably invokes. (Wilde was perhaps influenced by the recent fashion of veils and their complex significations, including outright sexuality, in late-nineteenth-century Paris.[27])

From the gospel accounts down to Banville's poem and Moreau's painting, Salome simply dances—a dance described by Ernest Renan in his *Life of Jesus* (1863) as "one of those dances in character which were not considered in Syria as unbecoming a distinguished person."[28] Even Flaubert's extended portrayal of the dance, as well as Banville's sonnet, makes no mention of veils. Wilde's Salome, in contrast, makes a point of telling Herod that she is waiting to begin until her slaves bring perfumes and "the seven veils." But the veils signify far more than mere apparel. Immediately before Herod first asks Salome to dance for him, Herodias reminds him that he himself stole the veil or curtain (Hebrew *parokhet*) of the sanctuary that has disappeared from the Temple, much to the chagrin of the five Jews present that evening. And, as the final gesture in his appeal to Salome not to demand the head of Jokanaan (Wilde's name for the Baptist), he offers her even the veil of the sanctuary. This blasphemous association of Salome's veils with the veil of the sanctuary implies quite clearly that both veils conceal "the holiest of holies"—in the one case, the Ark that contains the Torah scrolls and symbolizes God's presence in the Temple; in the other, the raw sexuality that for the Décadents of the fin-de-siècle represented the destructive female power.[29] (Wilde's friend, the poet Pierre Louÿs to whom the play was dedicated, picked up the motif of the seven veils immediately, using it in the first line of his sonnet "La Danse" [1891].)

Wilde wrote his play specifically with Sarah Bernhardt in mind for the role. In June 1892 she had already begun rehearsals for a performance in London when the Lord Chamberlain, who licensed all plays, hauled out the old law prohibiting the portrayal of biblical figures on stage and stopped the production.[30] (The play was not performed in England until 1905, when it was done privately.) Wilde was properly indignant and argued the absurdity of laws that censored poets for dealing with precisely the same material conceded to painters. (The situation provides a perfect illustration for the point discussed above in Chapter 1—that the theater offers occasions for scandal that are not present when individuals view a painting or read a book.) Accordingly the play was published (in French) in February 1893, and Wilde distributed many copies, for which he received letters of thanks and praise from Mallarmé, Pierre Loti, Maurice Maeterlinck, Henri Barbusse, and others.[31] The following year, an English edition, translated by Lord Alfred Douglas and illustrated by Aubrey Beardsley, evoked a widespread hostile critical response. According to *The Times* (February 23, 1893) the work is "morbid, *bizarre*, repulsive, and very offensive in its adaptation of scriptural phraseology to situations the reverse of sacred."

The first performance of Wilde's *Salomé* took place on February 11, 1896, at the Théâtre de L'Oeuvre in Paris, where it enjoyed the generally friendly reception anticipated by the letters the author had already received. But Wilde never saw his play on stage. When it had its premiere he was in Reading Gaol. And the next production—following private performances in Munich and Breslau, which elicited no critical resonance—took place in Berlin in Max Reinhardt's Kleines Theater on November 15, 1902, two years after his death. The widely acclaimed production, featuring the actress Gertrud Eysoldt (whose name will return in a later chapter), used the vigorous translation by the poet Hedwig Lachmann,[32] which had been published in the art journal *Wiener Rundschau* in June 1900 and which was itself based not on Wilde's French original but on Douglas's English translation.[33] Thanks to Lachmann's translation and Eysoldt's rhapsodically praised performance, which was repeated for a record 200 times, Wilde's play achieved a sensational success in Germany, making its way gradually to stages in Hamburg (February 1903), Vienna (December 1903), and elsewhere.[34]

Richard Strauss (1864–1949) first saw Wilde's *Salomé*, as he reports in his memoirs, at Reinhardt's Kleines Theater, where he had been invited to see Gertrud Eysoldt in her famous role.[35] The composer was already familiar with the play because the Viennese poet Anton Lindner had sent him a copy of Lachmann's translation, offering to poeticize it as an opera libretto. Dissatisfied with Lindner's sample lines, Strauss began to contemplate the idea of making his own prose libretto directly from Lachmann's version, beginning with the young Syrian's opening exclamation—"How beautiful is the Princess Salome tonight!"—and ending with Herod's command: "Kill that woman!" "From that moment it was not difficult to cleanse the piece of its purely literary effects so that it became a rather nice 'libretto.'"[36] In his effort to adapt the work for the operatic stage—that is, to accommodate it to the slower pace necessitated by the music—Strauss cut Lachmann's text by almost half, eliminating many repetitions, several characters, and minor plot devices.[37] The effect of his changes, although he retained the famous opening and closing lines, was manifold. Strauss shifted the focus of the action from Herod to Salome and, in the process, intensified the almost animal sexuality of the heroine. The dance, which in Wilde's text is indicated only by a simple stage direction ("Salome dances the dance of the seven veils") is expanded musically to a scene lasting almost ten minutes. Salome's final monologue with the fateful kiss of Jochanaan's dead lips, despite Strauss's radical abbreviation of the text, lasts almost three times as long as the spoken text of the play and thereby acquires a particular significance.

Strauss worked on the opera, during a full-time career as conductor, from August 1903 until June 1905. He has written amusingly about the frustrations preceding the premiere in Dresden. Strauss had confidence in Ernst von Schuch because that conductor had successfully premiered his second opera *Feuersnot* in 1901 (and later conducted the premieres of *Elektra* in 1909 and *Rosenkavalier* in 1911). Schuch gladly took on the challenge, despite public murmurs about the unsuitability of the subject matter. He was initially confronted with musical-technical objections from his soloists, all but one of whom proclaimed the parts unsingable. Even after the singers had accepted the roles, his Salome—the redoubtable and acclaimed Marie Wittich, who was also the wife of a prominent Dresden city official—objected to certain of the actions, exclaiming "I am a respectable woman." Since her stately figure was hardly suitable for Salome's sinuous dance, a professional dancer took her place for that great scene, to the vast amusement of the audience, who concluded "that Salome's complicated sexual inhibitions had in a moment caused her to lose several stone in weight."[38] Despite all the difficulties, the premiere took place as scheduled on December 9, 1905, and enjoyed the huge success described above.

What accounted, then, for the ensuing scandal surrounding the work and following most of its performances around the world—what Strauss called "the nonsense of the press, the resistance of the clergy"?[39] We can distinguish two principal reasons: the more obvious moral-ethical-religious objections, which we have already encountered, and the subtler musical-aesthetic ones. The latter problem was recapitulated quite precisely by Thomas Mann in his novel *Doktor Faustus* (1947). His hero, the composer Adrian Leverkühn, having already attended the premiere of *Salome* in Dresden, travels to Graz in May 1906 to hear the performance conducted there by Strauss himself. (Another member of the actual audience—in addition to Gustav and Alma Mahler, Giacomo Puccini, and Arnold Schoenberg—was the sixteen-year-old aspiring artist Adolf Hitler.)[40] Leverkühn's response to the work was ambivalent. "He wanted to hear again on this occasion the happily revolutionary work whose aesthetic sphere in no way attracted him but that naturally interested him in a musical-technical connection and especially as the setting of a prose dialogue."[41] "Never," he felt, "were avant-gardism and the assurance of success more confidently matched. Affronts and dissonances enough—and then the good-natured restraint, reassuring the bourgeoisie and indicating that it wasn't meant in a bad way."[42] Similarly, Leverkühn's fictional contemporary, Romain Rolland's Jean-Christophe, hailed *Salome* as a masterpiece—but "an odious masterpiece" by "the genius of bad taste." "To enjoy the handling of such divine powers and to turn them to such uses!"[43]

This dualism recurs over and again in the contemporary reviews. The prominent Viennese critic Julius Korngold—father of the composer Erich Wolfgang Korngold, who was Strauss's direct competitor—held such conflicting opinions about the work that he published his first long review as a dialogue featuring two interlocutors representing opposite points of view.[44] The skeptic begins by surveying the mountain of contradictory material that has already appeared in print:

Salome is the overcoming of Wagner and his ineffectual distortion, a step forward in art and its hopeless decline, new musical-dramatic territory and the monument of a sick age, a triumph of modern musical power and its declaration of bankruptcy, a creative achievement and a mere juggling act of technique, a revelation and a business gimmick, an inspiration and a calculation, a precious fruit and a rotten ulcer.[45]

But it has enjoyed a worldwide success, the advocate objects. Yes, if you judge by market value alone. But true art requires a longer period to take root. The skeptic stresses that his objections have nothing to do with Wilde's play. Wilde's poetry did not need music; it was the musician who needed the poetry. The final scene, rather than softening Wilde's version, makes it even more revolting—and the fashionable comparison of Salome's death to Isolde's *Liebestod* is far fetched. Turning from the material, the supporter asks what the skeptic thinks about Strauss's music. Even here the critic denies its novelty, arguing that Strauss has his roots in Wagner. While acknowledging the unity of the score and the unprecedented predominance of the orchestra, he believes that it brings about a "degradation of the vocal element" and that the singing is often no more than "organ-grinding, nervous chatter, agitated screaming."[46] He agrees with full conviction only about the orchestral effects: "Here mainly is where you find Strauss's inventiveness."[47] The composer can achieve literally any effect through his sound mixtures, his "mysterious, satanic, orgiastic, bacchantic sounds."[48] But the exposition drags, and Salome's grand crescendo as she kisses Jochanaan's lips is more of a paroxysm. As for the quintet of the disputing Jews, the whole vocal score of the grotesque work strikes the skeptic as *mauschelnd* (a Yiddish term for wheeling and dealing). Moreover, the dance is too long. The discussants reach no agreement. The advocate insists that the lively impression is decisive: *Salome* is gripping, has him in its power. And the skeptic concludes that he doesn't feel the slightest thing once the curtain has fallen.[49] Other Viennese critics treated the work even more harshly.[50]

Similar voices, albeit milder, were heard in Berlin. Hans Warbeck praised the performance in the Royal Opera House even though the orchestra did not have the same "sweet fulsomeness" of the Dresden Royal Orchestra.[51] The critic believed that Strauss "with brutal ruthlessness" subordinated the stage action to the music, restraining the purely vocal element for the sake of an utterly independent orchestra and thereby confusing the listeners, who regarded him sometimes as a dazzling orchestral technician and at other times as a strict thematician, sometimes as a philosopher and sometimes as a naively creative artist. Warbeck posits a dichotomy between "Romanic" and "Germanic-Slavic" music. The one, rather than exposing the depths of character, stays with surface generalizations for which it uses melody. The other investigates the components of which character consists, using harmony to express the result. This analytical "Germanic" aspect explains the often confusing proliferation of themes and motifs that characterizes the music of *Salome*. Hence Strauss's emphasis on and brilliant manipulation of the orchestra. In *Salome* "the orchestra follows clinical paths that have hitherto never been trod."[52] (Warbeck anticipated a critic who maintained decades later that in *Salome* Strauss brought "the psychological orchestra" to a perfection never previously or subsequently achieved.[53]) Accordingly *Salome* develops "truly modern principles from which there can be no retreat."[54] In the process, however, "the mixed mood of cruelty, perversity, and fatalism that Reinhardt was able to charm out of the lustful rhythms of Wilde's poem has here been weakened to a Middle European normal temperature."[55] The review ends by praising the Star of Bethlehem at the end of the Berlin production as "sweet and foreboding."[56]

It was precisely this widespread "redemption hypothesis," adapted in order to make Strauss's work "officially possible" in Berlin, to which Rudolf Louis in Munich objected.[57] It's a matter of moral taste, he argues, whether one finds more satisfaction in a penitent Salome or in a blasphemous heroine slain at the height of her sinfulness. But has Strauss done justice aesthetically to his subject? Convinced (rightly so, according to Strauss's own expressly non-Christian views) that Strauss did not believe in the redemption of Salome, the critic ascertains a profound discrepancy between the subject matter and the means whereby Strauss set it to music. Repeatedly, he charges, but especially in the concluding *caballetta*, Strauss gave way to the need for "pretty" music—or, rather, what the paying theater public expected as such. At the end, in particular, what we see on the stage radically contradicts what we hear in the orchestra. Over and over again, he continues, the composer tires of creating through sound an oriental milieu, decadent neurasthenia, sexual perversity, and all the other effects demanded by "modernitis" and cultural snobbism: all those stretches of musical kitsch, albeit kitsch of the highest order. At such moments he gives way to the temptation simply to make music, not merely pushing the drama into the background but letting it disappear altogether. Louis insists that every work has the right to be judged by its best moments: those passages when Strauss, without thinking of his public, ruthlessly seeks the clearest and most tangible musical illustration of the scenic events. In the last analysis, Salome is "the same capricious and moodily unpredictable, but fundamentally good person" that one knows from Strauss's earlier works: "only her costume is 'Salome.'"[58] Accordingly, he concludes, and apart from the musical characterization that the composer accomplished, "as a work of art one cannot possibly rank his creation highly, or even take it seriously."[59] The musical content is too empty and too greatly oriented toward external sensation and *épater la bourgeoisie*.

We find something similar in the reaction of the young English composer Arnold Bax, who spent the winter of 1906–1907 in Dresden and attended one of the early performances. Bax speaks of "the cerebral lasciviousness of this piece of glorified eighteen-ninetyism," which "disgusted but fascinated" the audience.[60] Aesthetically Bax regards *Salome* as an "unequal work," which contains "echoes of bad Liszt, the altogether atrocious Jochanaan music, and the brain-spun Seven Veils Dance" and, at the same time, in "the theological wrangle amongst the Jews, and the portrayal of Herod's hysteria and neurasthenia, represents the composer at his most astonishingly inventive." Decades later, Bax recalled *Salome* as "the ne plus ultra of the art of music, as far as the possibilities of expressing the inexpressible in sound were concerned."[61]

There were of course reviews that went to positive and negative extremes. On the positive side, J. C. Lusztig believed that a significant event of musical history had occurred on December 9 in Dresden: "the proclamation of a transition to a new developmental stage of musical-dramatic art."[62] Lusztig sets aside the widespread moral and aesthetic concerns and turns to the undeniably musical aspect of the subject. Rarely in the history of musical drama, he says, has there been such a total revaluation of a project as in this case. The human confusion, that in the mind of Wilde's Salome remains an unresolved puzzle, is wholly clarified in Strauss's music. "We gaze through the composer's musical language into the soul of this woman with sharpened eye because the musical unfolding of the events allows us time to concern ourselves more intensively with the psychological problem than is possible in the spoken drama, which rushes past us blow by blow."[63] The most powerful argument for the success of Strauss's undertaking, he maintains, is the overwhelming success of the premiere, despite the colossal difficulties that the score presents to the musicians. All in all, he concludes, "modern music literature has been presented in this *Salome* with a work whose influence will long make itself felt in the modern production of music."[64]

In the eyes of other critics, of course, that very success constituted a mark against the opera. The American critic Henry T. Finck, who attended the one-time American performance in New York, acknowledged that ever since the Dresden premiere the subject "has proved its appeal to the public in the most dazzling manner."[65] Like Korngold, he recognized the conflict aroused by the work: "opinions collided with violence after each first performance in a new place."[66] But why, he wonders, "did Strauss compose a noisy opera on the noisome subject of Salome as treated by Oscar Wilde?"[67] Was it chagrin at the abject failure of his first and still Wagnerian opera *Guntram* (1893) with its renunciative hero that made him "turn from the healthy to the morbid, from physiology to pathology?"[68] He labels Salome's problem "necrophilism" and finds it astonishing that Strauss should have been attracted to such a "repulsive" character. "It is a musical masterpiece," he bristles, "horribly, damnably wasted on the most outrageous scene ever placed before a modern audience."[69] He finds only one consolation: thanks to the prevailing dissonance and cacophony, nobody knows—or cares—whether the artists on the stage sing the right notes—that is, the notes assigned to them—or not."[70] What composer before Strauss, he continues with rhetorical cynicism, "was clever enough to write music in which it makes no difference whether you sing or play correctly?" "No boor ever violated the laws of etiquette as Strauss violates the laws of music."[71] He would have walked out of *Salome* each time he heard it, Finck confesses, "had not my duty as a critic compelled me to submit to the ordeal of such scenes and sounds succeeding one another without a break for nearly two hours."[72]

Finck's indignation was matched by that of many German contemporaries. Thus a certain Professor Krebs in *Der Tag* (Berlin) found that the music achieved no spiritualization of the subject matter but only a "brutalization," no refinement but rather a "coarsening."[73] In the not too distant future, he opines, the world will awaken from its exhilaration and giddiness over Strauss, "whose artistry ever since *Heldenleben* has moved in a rapidly falling trajectory."[74] The critic for the *Kreuz-Zeitung*, noting that "sexual psychiatry is the ideal of all truly modern people," went on to say that the opera dealt with a subject that should properly be left to the gynecologists. "One would think that the Baptist would stand too high to be abused as an object of the randy lusts of a pathologically minded whore." Here again we find the obliquely anti-Semitic reference to the *Mauscheln* of the five Jews.[75]

Dismayed by the popular success of *Salome* in a public "hypnotized by an uncritical press and by the advertising fuss emanating from a certain Berlin press clique" and whose healthy feelings have been corrupted by "press connivance, clique management, and artfully nurtured publicity," the conservative critic Adam Röder gathered the four hostile reviews of the opera that he had published in the *Rheinischer Kurier* into a small brochure in order to present his battle against the opera to a wider audience.[76] He begins by characterizing Wilde as "a decadent, a degenerate, a pervert," whose play is a tedious "excess of cruelty and lust."[77] But when sadists, masochists, lesbians, and homosexuals try to impose their views as art, the public has every right to object. "Art should elevate and ennoble," he opines, but the heroine created by Wilde and appropriated by Strauss, "a small, perverse, disgusting woman," lacks all inner grandeur.[78] The other major figures are equally perverted: Herodias is a vengeful beast, Herod a degenerate, and even Narraboth "a sick brain."[79] Röder contrasts this decadent Salome with such noble operatic heroines as Leonore, Senta, and Brünhilde. Although he deigns to acknowledge Strauss's orchestration, he argues that it should be only the means, not a goal in itself. Today's composers, displaying great technical virtuosity but no new musical ideas, make a virtue of necessity. Music, the loftiest and most profound of the arts, should be the sound of "consolation from the beyond for this world."[80] Röder attributes the entire success of *Salome* to the fact that "the prickling nerve-stimulation with its dominant of perverted sexuality is prolonged through Strauss's music."[81] But he confidently concludes that the success will be brief, for "only what is genuine can be lastingly preserved."[82]

Leaving aside the predictable outpourings of the morally offended parties, serious contemporary musical opinion in Dresden, Vienna, Berlin, Munich, and England seemed to share the verdict uttered by Thomas Mann's Adrian Leverkühn. The critics express great admiration for Strauss's orchestration and brilliant musical effects; but aesthetically they reject the work as self-contradictory (stemming from Strauss's fundamental lack of understanding for the character of Wilde's Salome) and rent by the inner conflict between drama and score. The contentiousness surrounding the work is evidenced by the fact that no fewer than three books had been published on the subject of Salome by 1907 alone: Reimarus's history of the theme, Röder's anthology of negative criticism, and Gilman's reasonably objective effort to analyze the work from a musical-technical standpoint, even though he concluded that Strauss's "harmonic *tour de force*" was "designed quite frankly and obviously as sheer noise, intentional cacophony."[83]

The moral scandal and the more serious musical evaluations following the Dresden premiere set the critical tone for the entire century. "Few operas have provoked more critical discord on their first appearance than *Salome*, and the controversy still persists," wrote John Williamson in 1989.[84] Derrick Puffett shrewdly surmised that "some lingering *moral disapproval* is at the root of *Salome's* critical neglect (there are more books on *Elektra, Der Rosenkavalier* and even *Ariadne*)."[85] Puffett points out that many British critics "seem to feel guilty about enjoying it." As though to prove the point, Norman Del Mar concludes that "the moral issues it raises are ... still as alive as when *Salome* first appeared," despite the irrelevance today of former religious objections.[86]

In German criticism different factors are at work. By Theodor W. Adorno's Marxist criteria Strauss's music was inevitably condemned as kitsch while Schoenberg emerged as the dominant figure in early-twentieth-century German music.[87] So the "scandal" of *Salome* continues into the present. Robin Holloway's questioning investigation "'Salome': Art or Kitsch?" concludes with the paradoxical statement that the *kitsch suprême* of the opera is "the best, by far, of its kind."[88] Yet if the viewer even today feels a *frisson* of fascinated horror when Salome finally kisses the lips of Jochanaan's decapitated head, is it a moral or an aesthetic response? And can such a listener fail to be moved by the sheer splendor of Strauss's powerful score and orchestration? Indeed, it can be maintained that Salome, whose figure utterly lost its iconic appeal to artists, musicians, and writers after World War I, has continued to live as a *femme de siècle* even a century later solely because of the continuing popularity of Strauss's opera with audiences, if not with the critics. At its various world premieres—in Vienna, Munich, Berlin, London, New York, and elsewhere—it was the audience's moral and religious feelings, offended by Salome's raw sexuality, that caused the scandal. It was left to admiring contemporary composers—Busoni, Mahler, Dukas, Ravel—to recognize that Strauss had created with *Salome* "a new orchestra, a new instrument for a new realm of sounds" and thereby a "mutation" in the history of music.[89]

If we look back at the two-stage history of the Wilde/Strauss *Salome* in the light of Schiller's theory, it seems obvious that it was Wilde's intention in secularizing the acclaimed *femme de siècle* to use the figure as a vehicle through which to challenge Victorian views of sexuality and the Christian tradition and that the audience response to premieres in France, Germany, and England demonstrated his success in doing so. In Strauss's revisions of Wilde's text, despite its musical highlighting of Salome's sexuality, the "moral" content became secondary to the desired musical/aesthetic impact, even though the earliest audiences were distracted from the sheer brilliance of his score by what were regarded as the perversions of the story, notably the notorious dance and kiss. We will encounter a similar difference of intention between writer and composer when we reach Bert Brecht and Kurt Weill and their joint production of *Mahagonny*.

SPRING MASSACRE (STRAVINSKY'S SACRE DU PRINTEMPS)

In retrospect it is easy to see the year 1913 as an *annus mirabilis* in the history of European culture—and not only in culture, of course. Niels Bohr's atomic model of that year, based on Ernest Rutherford's theory of atomic structure, sent a shudder through the literary and artistic world. W. B. Yeats announced famously that "Things fall apart; the centre cannot hold" ("The Second Coming," 1916), and Wassily Kandinsky recorded in his memoirs (1913) that "in my soul, the disintegration of the atom equaled the disintegration of the whole world.[90] In the art world, Guillaume Apollinaire's *The Cubist Painters (Les Peintres Cubistes)* heralded the creative spirits, notably Pablo Picasso and Georges Braque, whose "collage cubism" had just introduced the second phase of the movement that ushered in a truly modern art (and shocked American viewers that year in the notorious Armory Show in New York). Gustave Fauré and Manuel de Falla presented music-lovers with new operas (*Pénélope* and *La vida breve*, respectively). Franz Kafka with *The Judgment* (*Das Urteil*) and Roger Martin du Gard with *Jean Barois* published the first of their major works. Marcel Proust opened *Remembrance of Things Past* with *Swann's Way*. Apollinaire in France and Georg Trakl in Austria brought out major collections of poetry. But by any standard the major event of that year was the scandalous premiere in Paris of *Le Sacre du printemps* (*The Rite of Spring*), a joint endeavor by com-poser Igor Stravinsky, choreographer Vaslav Nijinsky, designer Nicholas Roerich, and producer Sergey Diaghilev.

That momentous year is now routinely cited as a turning point whose art, literature, and music marked the climax of prewar European culture and the unconscious cultural projection of social and political forces soon to explode into war and revolution. But the epoch-making significance of Kafka's breakthrough story, where for the first time we recognize the world that we call kafkaesque, was not appreciated for over a decade. Most pre-war readers were still too close and attached to their time to acknowledge the devastating analysis of the dissolution of fin-de-siècle French society presented in the novels of Proust and Martin du Gard. It was only later, after Oswald Spengler's influential theory, that thoughtful people came to understand "the bitter hour of decline" that Georg Trakl had with pro-phetic foresight portrayed in a poem written that year ("Abendländisches Lied"). In contrast to the more leisurely reception of literature, music and art had an instant and immediate impact. The violence of Stravinsky's ballet, which has been called "protorevolutionary,"[91] was matched only by the deformations of Cubism and soon came to be recognized as possibly "the most important single moment in the history of twentieth-century music.[92] In his lively study of "the great war and the birth of the modern age," Modris Eksteins called Stravinsky's ballet "perhaps the emblematic *oeuvre* of a twentieth-century world that, in its pursuit of life has killed off millions of its best human beings."[93]

What could have been the expectations of the Parisian elite who attended the premiere at the newly opened Théâtre des Champs-Elysées on May 29, 1913—that cultural bourgeoisie so mercilessly depicted in volume 5 ("La Foire sur la Place," 1908) of Romain Rolland's *Jean-Christophe*? What associations might have been aroused by a work entitled *Le Sacre du printemps*? The word *sacre* suggests the coronation of a king or the con-secration of a bishop—music such as Mozart's *Coronation Mass* perhaps, or Elgar's *Pomp and Circumstance*. Or even a banquet, which as Roger

Shattuck perceptively suggested, "had become the supreme rite" for the *beau monde* of the French *belle époque*.[94] And what about spring? The first movement of Vivaldi's *Four Seasons* or Haydn's oratorio *The Seasons*? Or, as one listener at that first night cynically opined, "the new fashions promoted by a department store"?[95]

What they got, in fact, was what the announcement that day in *Le Figaro* called "the evocation of the first gestures of pagan Russia," "the strongly characterized attitudes of the Slavic race with an awareness of the beauty of the prehistoric period," "the stammerings of a semi-savage humanity."[96] To this extent, the work with its angular choreography was less in tune with the familiar standard repertoire of Western music and classical ballet than it was with the primitivism, inspired by Gauguin, of Théodore Rousseau and the *Fauves;* with such paintings of pagan scenes as Matisse's *The Joy of Life* (1905/1906); and with the distortions of Picasso's *Les Demoiselles d'Avignon* (1906/1907). During the preceding decade, artists in Europe and Latin America had turned for inspiration to the exciting new findings in ancient archeology and the field of ethnology: as witness José Clemente Orozco and his young contemporaries in post-revolutionary Mexico, who adapted in their work the forms of pre-Columbian art. As for the stammering of semi-savage humanity: just a year earlier, C. G. Jung in his *Wandlungen und Symbole der Libido* (*Transformations and Symbols of the Libido*, 1912) had unearthed sources of the modern consciousness in the primitive myths of Egypt, Assyria, India, Mexico, and other early cultures. In Russia, the spirit of Slavophilic nationalism and the newly awakened interest in medieval Russia produced such works as Vasilii Surikov's acclaimed painting of the seventeenth-century dissident noblewoman Feodosia Morozova (*Boiarynia Morozova*, 1887), Nikolai Leskov's popular adaptations of hagiographical legends, and notably a series of historical operas: Peter Ilych Tchaikovsky's *Eugene Onegin* (1879) and *Mazeppa* (1884), Modest Musorgsky's *Boris Godunov* (1872) and *Khovanshchina* (1886), Aleksandr Borodin's *Prince Igor* (1890), and Nikolai Rimsky-Korsakov's *Sadko* (1898) and *The Legend of the Invisible City of Kitezh* (1907).[97] The neonationalist interest in peasant art was reflected in the journal *Mir iskusstva* (*The World of Art*) published from 1898 to 1904 by the young Sergey Diaghilev.

Given this cultural context, it is not surprising that the idea for the ballet came to Stravinsky in 1910, as he recounted in his autobiography, while he was still working on *The Firebird*. "I saw in my imagination a solemn pagan rite: sage elders, seated in a circle, watched a young girl dance herself to death. They were sacrificing her to propitiate the god of spring."[98] The impresario Diaghilev, by whom he had been commissioned to compose *The Firebird* (1910) and who was himself a talented and fore-sighted dilettante in music and painting, was immediately captivated by the idea and encouraged the composer; but first Stravinsky had to com-plete the second of his Russian ballets, *Petrushka* (1911). In July 1911, finally, on the country estate of the Princess Maria Tenisheva near Smolensk, he met with Nicholas Roerich, the multitalented painter, stage designer, and later mystic/theosopher, to plan their collaborative effort.[99] Stravinsky had admired Roerich's sets for Borodin's *Prince Igor*; moreover, Roerich had achieved a reputation for his (today questionable) knowledge of primitive Slavic culture and ethnic art and architecture. In just a few days they had outlined the scenario and the titles of the dances for the ballet that they called *Vesna Svyashchennaya* ("Sacred Spring" or "Holy Spring"). (The title *Le Sacre du printemps* was coined by the costume designer Léon Bakst; Stravinsky later noted that "The Coronation of Spring" would be closer to his original meaning than "Rite.") As Roerich outlined the action in a letter to Diaghilev:

The first scene should transport us to the foot of a sacred hill, in a fertile plain where Slavonic tribes have gathered to celebrate the spring festivities. An old witch appears who foretells the future: in this scene there is seduction and mar-riage; round dances. Then follows the most solemn moment. The wise ancient is brought from the village to press his sacred kiss on the newly blooming earth. And during this ceremonial act the crowd is overcome by a mystical fervor. After this surge of earthly joy the second scene leads us into a celestial mystery. Virgins dance in a circle on the hill amid enchanted stones before they choose the victim, whom they intend to sacrifice and who immediately will execute her last dance before the ancient elders, who are clad in bearskins. Then the grey-beards conse-crate the victim to the god Jarilo.[100]

Roerich sketched his conception of the backdrops and costumes, based on authentic costumes in the princess's collection of Russian ethnic art—and featuring bearskin in homage to the primitive Russian belief that bear is the ancestor of humanity. On this basis Stravinsky set out to compose his score.

The composer was no wild-eyed bohemian bent on shocking the bour-geoisie. The son of a renowned opera singer, Stravinsky (1882–1971) had a thoroughly bourgeois education, enriched by piano lessons and frequent attendance at concert and opera performances. At his parents' insist-ence, Stravinsky attended and earned a law degree at the University of St. Petersburg, but he spent more time on his private studies in theory and composition than on his legal texts. At the urging of Rimsky-Korsakov, who recognized the young composer's unusual talent, he did not enroll in the St. Petersburg Conservatoire, whose professors still adhered to the tried and trusted methods of the past. Instead, he worked privately with various tutors and notably in weekly supervisions with Rimsky-Korsakov himself. His first major success, the *Scherzo fantastique* (1907/1908), spread his name within Russia's music-loving public, including Diaghilev, who heard it in performance in 1909. The audacious producer gambled on the still-untested young composer by commissioning him with the score for his first ballet, *The Firebird*, which premiered in 1910 before enthusiastic audiences in Paris. When the twenty-nine-year-old family man with three young children, with his spats and cane, his neatly parted hair and owlish glasses, and his aloof manner, began work on *Le Sacre du printemps*, he looked more like a young lawyer or scholar than the most innovative composer of the era.

Returning from his consultation with Roerich to his family now living in Switzerland, Stravinsky set to work on the ballet, which he completed in November 1912, in a state, he recalled for Robert Craft, of "exaltation and exhaustion." Given the circumstances—the general interest in primitive culture and art, his initial vision or dream, and the intense discussions with Roerich—it is hardly surprising that Stravinsky's score displays a conscious effort to adapt primitivism to music, just as his artist-friends in Paris were adapting it to their paintings. (Stravinsky maintained lifelong a serious and informed interest in painting, architecture, and sculpture.) The themes of Stravinsky's first two Russian ballets—the balletomane was admittedly addicted to the genre which, thanks to Diaghilev's Ballets Russes, had recently attained a respectable status in France[101]—were also taken from Russian folklore. *The Firebird* combined two familiar fairy tales: that of the firebird, a symbol of unfulfilled wishes, or the unattainable ideal; and that of the demonic and immortal Kashchey, who can be conquered only when the struggling hero, Ivan Zarevich, discovers (with the firebird's help) and destroys the egg that symbolizes his immortality. (In 1905, Rimsky-Korsakov had produced his own operatic version of *Kashchey the Immortal*.) *Petrushka*, set in the historical past of St. Petersburg in 1830, combines the folklore of a Russian carnival fair with the common Romantic motif (borrowed from German literature, as in Offenbach's *Tales of Hoffmann*) of puppets that come to life. Just as neither scenario moved beyond familiar images of folk and fairy tales, so too Stravinsky's scores for both remained within the bounds of the traditionally recognizable. *The Firebird* is clearly indebted to Rimsky-Korsakov and to the impressionism of a Debussy, while *Petrushka* makes conspicuous use of familiar Russian folk tunes. *Le Sacre du printemps*, completed when the composer was only twenty-nine years old, makes a seven-league leap beyond the first two ballets, both in its story and in its score. Here, as the brilliant young critic Jacques Rivière observed in a thoughtful and lengthy appraisal, we have *"une oeuvre absolument pure,"* divested of all the "sauce"—the shadings, the veils, the poetic sweetenings—that characterize *debussysme*. *"Le sacre de printemps* is the first chef-d'oeuvre that we can oppose to those of impressionism."[102]

A few years later, in connection with his ballet *L'Histoire d'un Soldat* (*The Soldier's Tale*, 1918), Stravinsky observed that "although the character of their subject is specifically Russian, these songs depict situations and sentiments and unfold a moral so common to the human race as to make an international appeal."[103] It is this sense of the larger human meaning of Russian prehistoric myth that motivated both Stravinsky and Roerich in their approach to *Le Sacre du printemps*. Lacking any real "plot" of the sort found in *The Firebird* and *Petrushka*, the ballet revolves instead around the general theme of spiritual rebirth from the sacrifice of the individual for the community—a theme appropriately set in a heathen folk just emerging into humanity from a primal state in which the crowd did not yet exist as individuals. Jacques Rivière even termed the work "un ballet sociologique."[104]

To find the musical correlative for this primitive consciousness Stravinsky resorted to the most elemental component of the musical vocabulary: rhythm.[105] Here, beginning with the bassoon introduction, pitched so weirdly high that even musicians in the audience could not immediately identify the instrument, there was nothing familiar to which the listener could cling. The opening bars sound almost like a direct response to Debussy's *Prélude à l'après-midi d'un faune* (1894), which is introduced by a sweetly pastoral flute solo and which also takes place in a fairy-tale world, albeit in a typically melodic fashion with all the "sauces" of impressionism that Rivière deplored. (In Diaghilev's production of the year before, Nijinsky had shocked the audience with a lewd gesture.) In *Le Sacre du printemps*, rather than melodies or even extended leitmotifs one heard tiny tonal bits, often no more than four notes, repeated with rhythmic insistence and, from time to time, combined by the enormous orchestra of ninety-nine instruments in unresolved dissonances of a sort never sounded before in a concert hall. The compulsive and often complex rhythms hammered out by the five members of the tympani section make the work instantly recognizable. A glance at any page of the score reveals blocks of repetitions that suggest visually the analytic breakdowns of contemporary Cubist paintings. Indeed, Stravinsky initially visualized the choreography as rhythmic movements of groups of dancers—to suggest the still non-individualized community—acting in blocks or clusters.[106] It is this submission of melody to primal rhythm that immediately strikes listeners still today and that startled the first audience. Some proclaimed it noise, and that master of melody Giacomo Puccini called it "the work of a madman."[107] Others heard in it the true sound of modernity, which listeners would begin to appreciate only decades later. It is a tribute to Diaghilev's perceptiveness that he recognized the genius of the score, proclaiming it a masterpiece that would revolutionize music and assuring the astonished conductor of the premiere, Pierre Monteux, that it would make him famous.[108]

When the young Monteux first heard Stravinsky play the score,

> I decided then and there that the symphonies of Beethoven and Brahms were the only music for me, not the music of this crazy Russian. I must admit I did not understand one note of *Le Sacre du Printemps*. My one desire was to flee that room and find a quiet corner in which to rest my aching head.[109]

Even forty years later, although he had conducted the suite many times, he stated emphatically that "I still detest it."[110] Despite his dislike, Monteux studied the score intensively and then rehearsed the orchestra, section by section and in ensemble, until it was capable of giving a creditable premiere of the extraordinarily difficult score, which many of the players initially regarded as unplayable. Thanks to Monteux's ability and persistence, the more perceptive critics, musicians, and artists, many of whom attended the dress rehearsal or one of the subsequent performances rather than the scandalous premiere and were thus able to contemplate the music without distraction, recognized the epoch-making originality of this "music of the future," as one critic heralded it.[111] Louis Vuillemin, while not raising the work quite to the level of genius, announced to readers of *Comoedia* (May 31, 1913) "an admirable force of rhythm and life, of movement, a violence that delights in its magnificent frenzy. A virtuosity in instrumentation which verges on the prodigious."[112] Florent Schmitt, writing in *La France* a few days later (June 4, 1913), had no reservations: he hailed Stravinsky as "the Messiah we have waited for since Wagner" and heralded "the arrival of a new music" characterized by

> frenetic agitation; by the senseless whirl of its hallucinating rhythms; by its aggregations of harmonies beyond any convention or analysis; [...] by the obsessive insistence of its themes [...]; by seeking the most paradoxical sonorities, daring combinations of timbres, systematic use of extreme instrumental ranges; by its tropical orchestration, iridescent and of an unbelievable sumptuosity.[113]

When the music was presented a year later as a concert piece, again conducted by Monteux, it was a huge success. "The audience [...] listened with concentrated attention and applauded with an enthusiasm I had been far from expecting and which greatly moved me," Stravinsky recalled.[114] "Certain critics who had censured the *Sacre* the year before now openly admitted their mistake." (Not all critics agreed, of course; Ernest Newman, reviewing the piece after the war declared that "the bluff has failed" and the "farcical imposture" has finally been exposed.[115])

What, then, if not the music or the generally praised sets and costumes by Roerich, accounted for the scandal on opening night, which Carl Van Vechten recalled in the title chapter of a book entitled *Music and Bad Manners* (1916) and which one reviewer wittily called the *Massacre du Printemps*?[116] The scene, which became so rowdy that Stravinsky left his seat in anger after only a few minutes and went backstage, has been described by a variety of people present that evening and belongs to the folklore of music history. The loges were filled with elegantly dressed snobs of the *beau monde* in pearls and feathers, in ties and tails, most of whom subscribed to the ballet in the expectation of light entertainment and in the hope of catching glimpses of the limbs of young dancers which the Ballets Russes had liberated from the veils and gauzes of classical ballet. Out of disappointed expectations—the dancers were clad in all-concealing peasant-like garments—and a lazy unwillingness to expose themselves to new experiences, these spectators disrupted the performance from the first appearance of the dancers, while elsewhere the young supporters of new music applauded and cried "Bravo!"—all together creating a cacophony so loud that the dancers could not hear the orchestra and had nothing to follow but Nijinsky's frantic gestures offstage as he beat and shouted out the count while Diaghilev flashed the lights on and off in an effort to restore order. As Jean Cocteau described the evening,

The audience behaved as it ought to; it revolted straightway. People laughed, booed, hissed, imitated animal noises, and possibly would have tired themselves out before long, had not the crowd of aesthetes and a handful of musicians, carried away by excessive zeal, insulted and even roughly handled the public in the loges. The uproar degenerated into a free-fight.[117]

Some forty of the protesters had to be removed from the theater.

Much of the fault, apparently, must be attributed to the dances, which were choreographed by Nijinsky (and which, because the choreography was not written down, can be judged only from contemporary accounts of it). Stravinsky admired Nijinsky as a magnificent performer. "To call him a dancer is not enough, for he was an even greater dramatic actor."[118]

But he was fully aware of the personal and professional shortcomings of the young star. While "innocently honest and wholly without guile," Stravinsky also found him "childishly spoiled and impulsive."[119] Above all, the composer lamented the dancer's lack of all musical training and understanding. Not only could he not read music or play any instrument, "he never understood musical metres and did not have a very certain sense of tempo."[120]

At that time, Nijinsky was living in a homosexual relationship with Diaghilev. When Michel Fokine, the great dancer who had choreographed both *The Firebird* and *Petrushka*, had a disagreement with Diaghilev and left the company, the producer decided to charge Nijinsky with the choreography—out of fear of losing Nijinsky both as a lover and as a dancer. By general agreement Nijinsky's choreography was inept. He completely failed to understand Stravinsky's conception of the *Le Sacre du printemps* and the proper relation between music and dance. Stravinsky believed that it was a mistake for the choreographer simply to duplicate the rhythm of the music, which should act as a counterpoint to the dance. Nijinsky, in contrast, "believed that choreography should re-emphasize the musical beat and pattern in constant co-ordination, which, in effect, restrict the dance to rhythmic duplication and an imitation of the music."[121] In one dance, for instance, where the composer imagined "a row of almost motionless dancers," the choreographer made "a big jumping match."[122] The result was predictable.

In the first place, in an effort to convey the untutored condition of primitive Slavonic society, Nijinsky had his dancers assume awkward poses utterly at odds with the graceful positions of classical ballet, which had recently reached its height of perfection with ballet in Russia: the ballerinas stood, knock-kneed with toes pointed inward, in sharp contrast to the first position of conventional ballet; and he trained them to stand with their heads cocked sideways onto their shoulders and resting on their clasped hands—ungainly postures captured in a 1913 studio photograph of the cast and—shades of Hauptmann's Dr. Kastan!—mocked by the crowd with cries for a dentist to assuage their obvious toothache. In the second place, Nijinsky's choreography required the dancers to repeat the same steps over and over and to pound the ground in synchronization with the musical rhythm. As a result, with the brilliant exception of Maria Piltz as the sacrificial maiden—the only solo role in the ballet—the performance was almost unanimously ridiculed. "Imagine people decked out in the most garish colors," wrote one reviewer,

pointed bonnets and bathrobes, animal skins or purple tunics, gesturing like the possessed, who repeat the same gesture a hundred times: they stamp in place,

they stamp, they stamp, they stamp, and they stamp ... Suddenly: they break in two and salute. And they stamp, they stamp, they stamp ... Suddenly: a little old woman falls down headfirst and shows her underskirts ... And they stamp, they stamp ...

And then there are groups that develop close-order drill. The dancers are up against each other, packed like sardines, and all their charming heads fall onto their right shoulders, all congealed in this contorted pose by a unanimous crick in the neck.[123]

The reviewer for *Le Figaro* (May 31, 1913) was equally uncharitable, remarking that Nijinsky sought to realize unknown beauties "by taking the counter-movement of everything that has been done before him and applying himself with a detestable and laughable ingenuity to deforming the human body."[124] The composer Florent Schmitt, proclaiming Stravinsky's genius, was reluctant to qualify his enthusiasm by criticizing the choreography, "which aroused so much disapproval"; he restricted himself to praising the passion and grace of Maria Piltz's dance of religious hysteria, despite "the studied grotesqueries of her movements."[125] Léon Vallas, who applied the punning *massacre* to the ballet rather than its audience, found it "monstrous to celebrate spring with the epileptic convulsions guided by M. Nijinsky and by a painfully discordant music."[126] However, he acknowledges the difference between the music and the dance.

The dance is ridiculous: to prolong a marionette choreography for more than an hour and a half might seem to be a bad joke if we did not know from repeated experience the sincerity and the conviction of M. Nijinsky, the acrobat with incomparable leaps, but a ballet-master incredibly deprived of general ideals and of simply good sense.[127]

Those serious listeners who hated the work as well as those who heralded its genius regretted the appalling discourtesy of the first-night audience—both the elegant subscribers in the box seats and the aesthetes in the less expensive rows who challenged and egged them on. What should have been, according to Carl Van Vechten, "a war over art" and "the principles of free speech"[128] deteriorated into chaos. Clearly the boors who interrupted the work with their jeers were reacting to something so utterly alien to ballet as they knew it—sheer entertainment with its easily accessible music and attractive ballerinas—that it was beyond their comprehension. They do not need to be taken seriously. But Vechten was foresighted in his remark about the "war over art."

What were the elements of this "music of the future" that scandalized, puzzled, fascinated, or delighted the more thoughtful members of the audience that night? First, no doubt, its sheer physical impact, its animal energy, which boldly asserted music's claim to equal standing in ballet vis-à-vis the dance—an aspect stressed by the anonymous reviewer of the London performance, who headed his piece "The Fusion of Music and Dancing."[129] This claim was loudly borne out by an orchestra that was larger and more complex than any previously heard in concert or opera. Within this enormous orchestra the percussions featured instruments rarely sounded in conventional music. Meanwhile, the strings, the brass, the woodwinds competed in insistent dissonances created by unusual polyphonic juxtapositions. All of this "new music," finally, was in the service of a weird "rite" or liturgy that was at once solemn and barbaric—a ritualized killing on stage. In sum, the aesthetic shock at a totally new kind of music was combined with outrage at the violence of the primitivism depicted by the ballet. Yet this very challenge to their accepted values demanded a moral response on the part of thoughtful spectators and auditors to whom, like his Austrian contemporary Sigmund Freud, Stravinsky had exposed the discontents of modern civilization.[130]

Despite his initial wrath at the notorious premiere, Stravinsky displayed remarkable sang-froid that evening. After watching the performance from the wings and coming onstage for curtain calls, he dined with Nijinsky and Diaghilev in a fashionable restaurant. While the composer was initially depressed by the reception of the work, the impresario, foresighted enough to recognize the genius of the music, pronounced the evening a success.

In Schiller's sense the evening amounted to a deferred triumph. Stravinsky was motivated by a genuine and informed interest in prehistoric Slavonic myth and culture, an interest that reflected the more general fascination with primitivism—whether African, Aztec, or Asian—gaining momentum in Europe. It was Stravinsky's attempt to render his enchantment through sound that generated the violent rhythms and dissonances that characterize his score. Ironically, the desired "moral" effect was precluded at the premiere by the tumult that obscured the music and by Nijinsky's counterproductive choreography, all of which distracted the audience from the serious cultural and aesthetic meaning of the primitivism underlying the ballet. But the scandal, as is often the case, was symptomatic. The work's astonishing originality was soon recognized in the concert performances, and it can now be seen as a brilliant musical analogy to similar movements in contemporary art and literature.

As the examples of Strauss and Stravinsky paradigmatically illustrate, the theater may serve as a moral institution for opera and ballet as well as drama. By forcing onto the attention of the public through music and scene new visions, whether of sexuality or religion or musical/aesthetic form, the artist contributes to an intellectual and cultural awakening signaled by the shock of the initial scandal. In this case, the immediate awakening was delayed by the onset of World War I. When it arrived in the 1920s, it came with a bang.

CHAPTER 5

Diagnosing the present

DANCING TOWARD THE ABYSS (SCHNITZLER'S REIGEN)

It has been plausibly suggested that "probably no other dramatic work of world literature has aroused through its scandals such a sensation internationally as Arthur Schnitzler's *Reigen*."[1] Most members of the literary public in Europe and the USA have by now been exposed to the work in one form or another: in its original German; in French films directed by Max Ophüls (*La Ronde*, 1950) or Roger Vadim (*La Ronde*, 1980); on stages or in campus theaters in England and across the USA as *Hands Around* (1920), *La Ronde* (1955), *Rondelay* (1969–1970), and under other titles; or in one of various modernizing adaptations, such as David Hare's *The Blue Room* (1998). All too often overlooked in the controversy over its "pornographic" aspects, however, are the literary qualities of this little dramatic masterpiece, which amounts to a sparkling miniature of fin-de-siècle Vienna at the end of what has been called "Schnitzler's Century."[2]

Arthur Schnitzler (1862–1931) is wholly a product and representative of the Viennese culture that he piercingly and often scathingly, but always insightfully, portrays in his plays, stories, and novels. The son of a successful physician, a laryngologist who founded the *Internationale Medizinische Rundschau*, Schnitzler enjoyed a classical education at Vienna's noted Akademisches Gymnasium and then studied medicine at the University of Vienna. Having interrupted his studies only for a year's service as a volunteer at the Viennese military hospital, he received his degree in 1885 and began specialized training in dermatology with concentration on sexually transmitted diseases—a matter of urgent concern to men and women in turn-of-the-century Europe. Like many other well-to-do young men-about-town he made the usual *Bildungsreisen* and enjoyed an active love life, carrying on successive or simultaneous liaisons of varying intensity with Olga Waissnix, the wife of a hotel owner; the seamstress Jeanette Heeger, prototype of the *süsses Mädel* ("sweet young things" from

85

the suburbs) who play such an important role in many of his works; and the actresses Marie (Mizzi) Glümer, Adele Sandrock, and Marie (Mizzi) Reinhard. In 1903, finally, having long resisted the loss of his bachelorhood, he married the actress Olga Gussmann.

At the same time Schnitzler participated eagerly in the intellectual and cultural life of the city boasting of the thinkers Freud and Wittgenstein, the composers Mahler and Schönberg, the painters Klimt, Schiele, and Kokoschka, as well as the group of writers known as Junges Wien (Young Vienna) and including Hugo von Hofmannsthal and Richard Beer-Hofmann among others. In this heady atmosphere it seemed inevitable that he would himself begin to write. Beginning in 1893 with the seven one-act playlets featuring the adventures of Anatol, a young man very much like Schnitzler and his friends, he enjoyed a series of successes, notably with the novella *Sterben* (*Dying*, 1895), which diagnoses with psychiatric precision and detachment the emotions stirred in a love-couple by the man's lingering death; and the dramatic tragedy *Liebelei* (*Dalliance*, 1895), in which a young man, forsaking his affair with a married woman out of love for a simple young girl, is killed in a duel by the *mondaine's* husband, whereupon the beloved girl commits suicide.

In the winter of 1896–1897, Schnitzler was undergoing a period of doubt and depression: his current mistress was unexpectedly pregnant, and he was reluctant to forsake his happy bachelor-hood for marriage; he experienced the first onset of the hearing problems that gradually intensified and compromised his enjoyment of music; and he was beginning to be seriously torn between career choices—medicine or literature. In this spirit of doubt and skepticism he wrote the "ten dialogues" initially entitled *Liebesreigen* (*Dance of Love*) and later shortened simply to *Reigen* (*Round Dance*). Schnitzler realized from the start that these scenes, which deal frankly with the hypocrisy of the sexual rhythm that seemed to dominate the dance of the city's life, were "unperformable."[3] In the preface to the private printing (1896–1897) of 200 copies that Schnitzler presented "as a personal gift" to his friends, he noted explicitly: "Any appearance of the following scenes is for the time being out of the question."[4] But "dug up after a few hundred years," he believed, they would "uniquely illuminate an aspect of our culture."[5] Keenly aware of the differences between book and stage (discussed above in the Introduction), Schnitzler understood that his cynical exposé would be less explosive when read quietly by individuals than if performed in a theater.

Sex, as we have already seen in connection with *Salome*, was very much in the air at the century's turn, not just in practice but also in theory.[6]

Richard von Krafft-Ebing, a senior professor at the university whom Schnitzler knew well, had recently published his *Psychopathia sexualis* (1886), an explicit study of sexual perversions;[7] Sigmund Freud, who acknowledged an intellectual kinship with his contemporary Schnitzler and even superstitiously avoided him as his *Doppelgänger*, was contemplating the revolutionary ideas that resulted in his *Three Essays on the Theory of Sexuality* (1905); and in just a few years the young Otto Weininger would bring out the notorious treatise *Geschlecht und Charakter* (*Sex and Character*, 1903) in which he proclaimed the intellectual superiority of men over women, whom he viewed as utterly amoral in their sexuality. As an examination of the sense of despair and loss underlying the pervasive sexuality of the age, Schnitzler's work belongs very much in the context of those serious scientific expositions. But Schnitzler, who had studied Greek at the Gymnasium, chose for his presentation a literary form with which he was familiar from the satirical dialogues of the second-century Greek satirist Lucian (notably his *Dialogues of the Dead*).[8]

It was clear from the start that the dialogues would be linked in the ingenious cyclical form that Schnitzler on the title page of the original manuscript termed a "Hemicyclus."[9] Each scene or dialogue displays essentially the same structure—one familiar from William Hogarth's engravings *Before and After* (1730–1731):[10] a man and woman come together and engage in verbal foreplay; then a series of dashes (represented later on the stage by a brief curtain-fall) signifies the completed sexual act; and afterwards, following post-coital conversations, they go their separate ways. The originality of Schnitzler's literary kaleidoscope stems from the fact that a single figure, characterized only by profession or social class, always constitutes the transition from one scene to the next:

1. the prostitute and the soldier;
2. the soldier and the chambermaid;
3. the chambermaid and the young man;
4. the young man and the married woman;
5. the married woman and her husband;
6. the husband and the *süsses Mädel;*
7. the *süsses Mädel* and the writer;
8. the writer and the actress;
9. the actress and the count;
10. the count and the prostitute (from the first scene).

Schnitzler indicates in several scenes that one of the speakers is about to go off in a different direction with another partner: for instance, the soldier, who at the end of Scene 2 sends the chambermaid off to get a beer while he approaches a different woman. In several scenes, the speakers recall past affairs with other partners. There is also no suggestion that the prostitute and the count in the last scene will next couple with any of the partners to whom we have already been introduced; indeed, it is highly unlikely. Obviously, then, the circle is not closed, as is sometimes assumed, because the prostitute does not come together again with the soldier. Instead, it is a "hemicycle," a semicircle whose serpentine windings could go on endlessly.

It has often been noted that the structure resembles that of another dance without end, the Dance of Death (*Totentanz*) frequently depicted in medieval paintings and woodcuts: in this case, however, the common denominator that brings all men and women down to the same level is raw sex, not death—a parallel that inevitably brings to mind the pervasive theme of *eros* and *thanatos* found in so many works of the period, from Wilde's *Salome* and Hugo von Hofmannthal's *Der Tor und der Tod* (*Death and the Fool*, 1894) to Thomas Mann's *Tod in Venedig* (*Death in Venice*, 1912)[11]—not to mention Schnitzler's own recent story *Dying* and his play *Dalliance*. Moreover, specific references to death occur in the opening and concluding scenes of the play.

A structure that in less talented hands could have resulted in interminable and tedious repetitions undergoes almost endless variation in Schnitzler's presentation, which displays a virtuosity akin to that of Beethoven's *Diabelli Variations* or Brahms's *Variations on a Theme of Haydn*. The ten scenes introduce us to the strata of Viennese society from the lower classes (prostitute, soldier) through the working class (chambermaid) and prosperous middle class (young man, young women, husband) to the bohème (writer, actress) and the aristocracy (count). Each class is precisely characterized by typical linguistic features of dialect and jargon (to which no translation can do justice). The settings constitute a topography of Vienna and its environs: from the initial couplings under bushes on the bank of the Danube canal (1) and the Prater amusement park (2) by way of bourgeois households (3, 4, 5) to the chambre separée of a suburban restaurant (6), the writer's apartment (7), a country inn (8), the actress's luxurious city bedroom (9), and the prostitute's cheap quarters (10).

The relationships also differ markedly from case to case: the soldier in the first scene is quick and brutal in his conquest, while the count in the final scene is so drunk when he wakes up in the same prostitute's room that he no longer remembers whether they had sex or not. Yet sex with the same prostitute is the common denominator that links the lowest and the highest social classes. The young man, who matter-of-factly seduces the submissive chambermaid while his parents are out of the house, is initially impotent when confronted with the self-assurance of the bourgeois matron. The husband approaches his wife in a routine act of domestic coupling and lectures her (who has just returned from her ultimately satisfactory liaison) on womanly virtue while thinking ahead to his upcoming encounter with the *süsses Mädel*. Unlike the other women, the actress is a fierce and wholly self-centered dominatrix as portrayed in many of Klimt's paintings (for instance, his *Judith and Holofernes* [1901]) or as known from such real-life *femmes fatales* as Lou Andreas-Salomé, who in a famous photograph from the year 1882 is shown flourishing a whip in a cart drawn by Nietzsche and his friend Paul Rée; or Alma Mahler, who had an affair with Oskar Kokoschka and later married Franz Werfel. (Kokoschka was so smitten that he made a life-size doll of her, which accompanied him everywhere and which he depicted in his *Self-Portrait with Life-Size Doll Made in the Likeness of Alma Mahler* [1922].) Literary scholars have uncovered further motifs that Schnitzler used and varied in most of the scenes: for instance, suggestions of haste; comments on light/dark and on the heat; the fear of interruption; eating, drinking, and smoking; and so forth.[12]

The play, which begins and ends with prostitution, is constructed so that the scene in the married couple's bedroom constitutes its satirical center—no uncertain hint that the author regarded conventional *mariages de convenance* as a kind of prostitution. While in every scene both figures clearly have one goal in mind, they engage in the most varied subterfuges, deceits, and pretenses in order to conceal their true motives from their partners and, above all, from themselves. What Schnitzler regarded as the basic mendacity of society is cynically exposed by the juxtaposition of scenes in which one party or the other protests his or her loyalty and then immediately goes on to yet another rendezvous.

In sum, then, the play is anything but pornographic. On the contrary, the potentially "pornographic" moment is suppressed in every scene. Rather than depicting the joy of sex, Schnitzler was diagnosing the lack of intimacy in those mindless promiscuities and the essential loneliness of the individual amid the gay whirl of the Viennese social waltz—the hollowness of life. Their namelessness, rather than anticipating the symbolic figures of Expressionist drama, suggests the depersonalization of the individual, who is reduced to mere animal function. In a few cases, to be sure, a name slips out; it is no accident that the married woman's name, Emma, is reminiscent of the heroine of Flaubert's famous novel of adultery. But in other cases when the woman demands her partner's name as a sign of intimacy, it is refused or a false name is given. The sex is thereby reduced from an act of love to sheer animal lust—and, not incidentally, to a struggle for power and mastery between man and woman. The "hemicycle" of the dance, in turn, suggests a society constantly in motion without progress—what has often been called the "joyous apocalypse"[13] of turn-of-the-century Vienna, whose atmosphere Schnitzler so brilliantly captures.

More generally, the play attacks the widespread hypocrisy of the period with its double standards: the husband and wife who discuss morality while contemplating their respective extramarital affairs; the actress who brings a small statue of the Madonna to place on the bedside table during her trysts; the soldier's coarseness and the count's drunkenness, which belie the loudly touted military code of honor. Yet, as the continued fascination with the play for more than a century attests, as well as the ease with which it can be updated, the social and existential paradigms that Schnitzler outlines are no less valid for Western society in the twenty-first century than for fin-de-siècle Vienna.

All these considerations regarding Schnitzler's intentions, which he clearly expressed in his letters and diaries, and regarding its artistic merits, which have been widely recognized by scholars and critics of the past century, became irrelevant in the face of the scandals that erupted around the work even before its premiere in 1920. Schnitzler, who wrote *Reigen* early in his literary career, went on to become one of Europe's most highly regarded *hommes de lettres*, with an influence extending into the present: for instance, his early experiment with stream-of-consciousness narrative in *Leutnant Gustl* (*Lieutenant Gustl*, 1900); his portrayals of the failures of Jewish integration in the face of anti-Semitism in *Professor Bernhardi* (1912) and other works; or the subtle analysis of marital infidelities, *Traumnovelle* (*Dream Novel*, 1927), that inspired the 1999 American film *Eyes Wide Shut*. Meanwhile, *Reigen* continued to live a life of its own, quite distinct from that of the author, his intentions, and his achievements.[14]

Schnitzler had good grounds for believing that his work was unsuitable for public distribution. During that same decade, Frank Wedekind's "childhood tragedy" of youthful sexual awakening, *Frühlings Erwachen* (*The Awakening of Spring*, 1891, 1891), was pursued by the censor and not released for performance until 1912—and then only in a toned-down form. Wedekind's "Lulu tragedy," *Die Büchse der Pandora* (*Pandora's Box*, 1902), was also prosecuted three times from 1903 to 1906, with the result that, while the author was exonerated, his work was prohibited. In 1900, accordingly, Schnitzler had the manuscript published at his own expense and "not for sale," sharing it only privately with his friends. But as the private printing became more widely known and was even reviewed—the prominent critic Alfred Kerr called it "a little Decameron of our time" and alluded to the Hogarth etchings[15]—Schnitzler began to revise his opinion. He approached his friends Hugo von Hofmannsthal and Richard Beer-Hofmann for advice, which they offered in a jointly written ironic letter addressed jokingly to "Dear Pornographer" and warning him to find a respectable publisher and to insist on a sizeable advance since the book would surely be confiscated.[16] The respectable Fischer Verlag, on the advice of its legal counsel, declined to take on the work. So Schnitzler turned to the Wiener Verlag, a flashy firm concerned more with profits than propriety and counting on the notoriety that the work had already acquired to help its heavily advertised sales. The calculation paid off: following its publication in April 1903 sales soared, reaching 4,000 copies within the first two weeks and 11,000 by year's end. And the "unprecedented" success claimed by the firm in its advertisements continued for years to come: by 1927, 100,000 copies of the work had been sold in various editions.

While several of Schnitzler's friends from the intellectual community heralded the courageous work and praised its linguistic prowess,[17] the success was not unqualified, and critical voices were soon heard. Only five days after its publication, Schnitzler noted in his diary the "general indignation about *Reigen:* insincerity, cowardice, aggravation."[18] A few days later his publisher reported an "enraged attack" in the *Deutsche Zeitung*.[19] Apart from criticisms of its frivolities and warnings about its dangers for young readers, the Workers Party complained that Schnitzler's *süsses Mädel* was a literary figure that had little to do with reality in the outlying districts and that he showed little insight into the lives of the homeless or the lower-class figures who lived crowded five or more into filthy rooms with illness and venereal disease.[20]

While the Social Democrats felt that Schnitzler had not gone far enough with his social commentary and while the general Viennese press largely ignored it, the rightwing notably in Germany found other reasons to attack the work, both moral and political. The reviewer for Munich's *Neue Bahnen* called *Reigen* "nothing but a *Schweinerei* or, if that's too German, a *cochonnerie*" by an author without the moral ability to elevate his topic from pornography to art.[21] Two weeks later another reviewer wrote in the *Ostdeutsche Rundschau* that Schnitzler was obsessed with sex in its crudest form and, adding an anti-Semitic twist, that "the familiar *foetor judaicus*" ("Jewish stench") could be sensed everywhere in this work "written with such a doglike sex-lust that it disgusts us."[22] The anti-Semitic chorus swelled rapidly. The reviewer in one Viennese newspaper complained that it was difficult to escape the smut streaming in from Paris and Berlin, Vienna and Budapest. For Catholic and Protestant alike, for Christian and atheist, at stake are "purity of family life, chastity of the woman, loyalty of the man, purity of youth, health of the races."[23] The attacks soon became more explicit with complaints about "writers alien by country or race to the German people. Schnitzler's *Reigen* was too dirty even for our realistic stages. It is rampant only in book-form, within the German people."[24]

As a result of such reactions the work was soon banned in Germany. That same year students from the University of Munich who staged the three middle scenes of the play (4–6) were expelled by the Bavarian Minister of Culture. Nevertheless, despite various prohibitions and confiscations the work continued to be published by the Wiener Verlag, then (after 1908) by the Harz Verlag, and after 1919, when the old censorship regulations in Germany—the notorious *Lex Heinze:* §§183–184 of the penal code—had been relaxed, by the more cautious Fischer Verlag. Over Schnitzler's objections it was occasionally given public readings, although in 1903 a public reading by the prominent critic Hermann Bahr was prohibited by the police in Vienna. In 1912 the play was performed in its entirety for the first time in Budapest (in Hungarian translation)—only once, however, before being prohibited—and, immediately after the 1917 revolution, in Moscow and St. Petersburg.[25]

The growing success of the printed editions, the general interest in these unauthorized performances, and Fischer's encouragement led Schnitzler finally—more than twenty years after the work's conception and composition—to consider a performance in German.[26] In April 1919 he approached the famed director Max Reinhardt at the Berliner Theater, who responded enthusiastically, saying that a performance would be "not only artistically opportune but also unquestionably desirable."[27] Yet for all his interest Reinhardt delayed any action for more than a year. Then in the summer of 1920 his successor at the Berliner Theater, Felix Hollaender, passed the project along to Josef Hubert Reusch, General Manager of Berlin's Kleines Schauspielhaus, a theater attached to Berlin's Hochschule für Musik. It was here that the first authorized performance of *Reigen* took place on December 23, 1920, under the direction of Maximilian Sladek and Gertrud Eysoldt.

On the day of the premiere—at the instigation of the Hochschule für Musik, which regarded the play as a violation of its rule against performances that would arouse moral objections—the 6th Civil Chamber of the State Court III issued, with no prior verbal negotiation, a temporary injunction ("Einstweilige Verfügung") against the performance,[28] but the directors refused to comply. On opening night, Frau Eysoldt and her co-director Sladek stepped before the curtain, informed the audience of the injunction, and expressed their intention not to be intimidated. Gertrud Eysoldt, a distinguished actress who had earlier been Reinhardt's Salome and Lulu in the plays by Oscar Wilde and Frank Wedekind, declared that she would rather go to jail than concede the freedom of art in the face of philistine persecution.[29] As it happened, the performance took place with no immediate repercussions, and several of Berlin's leading critics followed with generally favorable reviews as well.[30] Many praised the wit, elegance, and irony of the piece, and it was applauded by the socialists for its social commentary. Others found it old-fashioned and questioned the relevance of fin-de-siècle imperial Vienna for a postwar democratic Berlin. Inevitably a wave of parodies followed.[31] In light of the many protests against the injunction the court requested affidavits from various critics and theater professionals, while the theater provided a supporting statement from the president of the German Theater Association. On January 3, 1921, the injunction was suspended so that two members of the court could attend performances of the play. Since they found it to be "an ethical act" ("*eine sittliche Tat*") in its exposure of the consequences of mindless abuse of mankind's most sacred experience,[32] on January 6 the injunction was cancelled.

The honeymoon following the love dance was brief, however. In view of the long-standing prohibitions in the 1920s against such "immoral" and "indecent" works as James Joyce's *Ulysses* (1922) and D. H. Lawrence's *Lady Chatterley's Lover* (1928), it is hardly surprising that voices continued to criticize the sexual content of the play. In addition, Schnitzler became engaged in literary feuds with two leading figures of Berlin's cultural elite: the actress Tilla Durieux and Maximilian Harden, editor of the cultural-political journal *Die Zukunft*.[33] But the protests soon shifted to another level altogether, and sexual morality became simply a pretext.

On January 7, the day following the cancellation of the injunction, certain officials within Berlin's Central Office for Combatting Immoral Writings sought to circumvent the court's action by bringing a suit against the theater for selling copies of the text—an act that allegedly violated the 1906 prohibition against the book itself. Meanwhile, other activists were stirring up public indignation. Erich Schlaikjer, a journalist and literary critic for the once liberal but increasingly nationalist *Tägliche Rundschau* and himself close to the proto-Nazi German National People's Party (Deutsch-nationale Volkspartei), published on January 11 the first in a series of articles claiming that "the esthetic cult of the sex act has in this case not only been victorious over the quiet majesty of the Nazarene, but has also shoved aside the majesty of the law with a derisive kick"[34]—thereby simultaneously raising the issue of anti-Semitism and attacking an all-too-liberal justice system. His main ally was the one-time history teacher Karl Brunner, who regarded it as his life mission to protect Germany from trashy literature. To that end, in 1910 he founded the journal *Die Hochwacht* and became in 1911 the literary expert for Berlin's Imperial Police Headquarters and in 1914 an official movie censor, proudly appropriating the intendedly offensive appellative "Schmutz-Brunner" ("Filth-Brunner").[35] In the new government after World War I he continued in his capacity as chief consultant for the Berlin Police on issues of morality as well as counselor in the Prussian Welfare Ministry. As such he was invited to address the female members of the Reichstag, who on February 14 issued their "Proclamation of German Women" declaring that the continued daily performances of *Reigen* represented "a prostitution of women in outrageous brazenness in violation of the simplest commandments of decency and good morals."[36] Together they motivated protests by such groups as the German Officers League, the League of Nation-Minded Soldiers, the German National Social Organization, and other nationalistic groups.

All this activity resulted in the notorious riot at the theater on February 22. The co-director Sladek was warned ahead of time by two members of the German National League for Protection and Resistance (Deutschvölkischer Schutz und Trutzbund) who were concerned about the plan. The police, alerted by Sladek, stationed 40 detectives inside the theater while another 100 policemen were stationed out of sight in other rooms of the building. Outside the theater, a group of boys in shorts were chanting "Jews to Palestine!"[37] In the middle of Scene 4 (young man and married woman), one of the rioters shouted the cue-word "*Schweinerei*," whereupon his companions hurled stink bombs from the galleries down onto the stage and into the parterre. The police moved into action and arrested a number of the disturbers. Although the riot was quelled, the incident brought hostilities out into the open, and it became increasingly clear that the occasion was being preempted as an occasion to vent anti-Semitic hatred.[38] Sladek, who was himself Catholic, reported that he received letters addressing him as "fat Jew" and "fat pig" and warning him "Take care, Judaea!"[39] The state prosecutor also received threats, accusing the police who suppressed the demonstration as having been reduced to "defenders of a whore house" and signing with a seal showing a death's head and the same inscription "Take care, Judaea!"[40]

When the riot and the legal maneuvers to prohibit the play and the book failed, the opponents settled on a second procedure. Since the play itself had been deemed legally decent and moral, in September 1921 Brunner and Schlaikjer persuaded the state prosecutor to lodge a complaint against the directors and the actors on the grounds (a) that the stage action was indecent according to §183 of the German Penal Code, in that it openly depicted the circumstances leading to the completion of the sexual act; and (b) that the objectionable music that filled the pauses suggested copulation in no uncertain terms. The trial that took place from November 5 to 11 constituted one of the most spectacular events of the Weimar Republic.[41] Witnesses for the prosecution maintained repeatedly that they had been offended and found the whole performance "indecent" ("*unzüchtig*"), that the play was calculated to denigrate the German people, and that the morally decadent atmosphere of the age could only be further poisoned by the piece.[42] One witness, a house-mother in a boy's school who had left the performance early in disgust, asserted that "as a German citizen and a woman and human being I have the right to demand that such a thing never be performed." An officer's wife observed that the defamation of family life, of marriage, of religious life, of the Christian religion, and of officers must have been intended to demoralize the German people and specifically its youth following the revolution.[43] Other more openly proto-Nazi witnesses were more specific. "This is what we owe to the Jewish rabble!" "We've got to put an end to these Jews! After all, we are Germans. These Jewish pigs [...] must be smoked out. This riff-raff ought to go to Palestine."[44] Immediately after the trial, on November 16, the National Democratic Party, a Nazi organization, announced a meeting of citizens, workers, and women to discuss the implications for true Germans of (a) the pacifists as champions for the enslavement of Germany; and (b) Schnitzlers *Reigen* and free love.[45] Clearly the performance was happily instrumentalized by the Nazis for their own purposes.

The defending attorney was Wolfgang Heine, a former Minister of the Interior and a leading defender of freedom of speech. Over and over again in his brilliant defense he was able to demonstrate that some "witnesses" had never actually seen the play, that others had received free tickets for the performances from Brunner's office, and that the objections were often based on faulty memories of the occasion and otherwise on utterly trivial grounds: that an actress had straightened her blouse suggestively, that beds appeared in many of the scenes, that an actor had wrapped his legs around his partner (while in fact he stood at a respectful distance), that the actress prayed and had an image of the Madonna, and so forth. The co-counsel for the defense, Justizrat Dr. Arthur Rosenberger, concluded "that we are not dealing with a battle against *Reigen* but a fight against the Jews, that *Reigen* was used only in order to instigate in this form an anti-Semitic action"[46]—and forced Brunner to reject any suggestion that the indictment had been made for anti-Semitic and nationalistic reasons. In view of the weak case presented by the prosecution and the compelling statements by witnesses for the defense—the directors, the actors, the composer of the music—as well as Heine's impassioned summarizing argument, the judges concluded that "in the court's view no indecent action occurred in any objective connection."[47] *Reigen* continued in Berlin with a run of some 300 performances.

The scandal accompanying the premiere in Vienna, which took place a few weeks later, was if anything rowdier and more blatantly political and racist than in Berlin.[48] Schnitzler himself had been concerned for several years about the growing anti-Semitism in Austria, noting in his diaries as early as June 16, 1918, that pogroms were no longer unimaginable.[49] As the postwar years brought hard times—inflation, unemployment, homelessness, strikes, hunger—to a country that was depressed at finding itself reduced from a great empire to a small nation, it was easy to blame the Jews. "The Jew is to blame!" (*"Der Jud ist schuld!"*) for the lost war, the unfavorable peace treaty, the housing problem, the social displacement of the middle class, the Russian Revolution—in short, for everything wrong with modern European society.[50] In 1920, the coalition of Christian Socialists and Social Democrats collapsed. The Christian Socialists, allying themselves with such parties as the Greater German Peoples Party (Grossdeutsche Volkspartei) and the Austrian National Socialists, won the fall elections and took over the government, promising a "spiritual cleansing," which would place moral imperatives above the law. This unleashed a cultural war with the Social Democrats and other liberal groups, which believed in the rule of law and the freedom of art. It was in this climate that *Reigen* premiered on February 1, 1921.

The occasion was unexpectedly peaceful, receiving respectful applause and favorable reviews from critics in the more liberal newspapers.[51] But the rightwing press began its campaign immediately. The reviewer for the *Reichspost*, the official organ of the Christian Socialists and Austrian Catholicism, reported on the day of the premiere that "it is difficult to keep one's blood cool in the face of this truly shameful deed that the Wiener Theater has accomplished."[52] Schnitzler's play "has turned the theater, which ought to be a house of noble joy, into a house of prostitution, a showplace for shameless actions and conversations that would not be out of place in any whore's lair." Further attacks followed, labeling the work "bordello prologues of the Jew Schnitzler" and "the most lecherous pornography."[53] An initial disturbance occurred on February 8, when a group of twenty young members of an anti-Semitic Peoples Party sneaked into the theater and tried to interrupt the performance with cries of "Cultural Disgrace!" (*"Kulturschande"*) and "Stop!" and insulted the audience as blackmarketeers and pushers (*"Schieber"*); but they were immediately arrested by the police.[54]

This disturbance catalyzed speculation about the possible prohibition of the play. On February 11 a loud debate took place in the parliament, pitting conservatives against the liberal Social Democrats, who were lampooned in the reactionary press as "shameless advocates of pornography."[55] Two days later, the Catholic People's League (Katholischer Volksbund für Österreich) organized a demonstration attended by 800 people and addressed by Ignaz Seipel, the leader of the Christian Democrats, who told the audience among other things that "the moral sensibility of our indigenous Christian people continues to be most sorely offended by the performance of a filthy work from the pen of a Jewish author" and that the Social Democrats were prepared to mount tumultuous scenes in parliament "whenever it involves protecting some Jewish machinations."[56] That same evening several hundred demonstrators lined up outside the theater, reviling Schnitzler as he entered and protesting the shaming of women and the protection of the Social Democrats.

Then on February 18, at the same point in the performance that triggered the scandal in Berlin, someone (later identified as a high government official) released a powerful stink bomb of hydrogen sulfide. To allow the audience to escape the stench the doors were opened. At that point several hundred protestors assembled outside invaded the theater and overpowered the small security force. They hurled seats from the boxes into the parterre, tossed tar-filled eggshells at the audience, tore clothes from women's bodies, and attacked individuals with clubs, fists, and brass knuckles. Members of the audience as well as protesters rushed onto the stage, where the stagehands drenched them with powerful streams of water and drove them out of the building, where several were arrested.[57] (The incident provided material for several newspaper cartoons in the following days.)[58] Alarmed by these developments, the police prohibited further performances "for reasons of public peace and order," an action hailed by the anti-Semitic *Volkssturm* as "Victorious Christian Wrath"[59] and as "A Success of Vienna's Christian Youth" in *Wiener Stimmen*.[60] The anti-Semitic *Reichspost* even blamed the turmoil on "several Jewish youths, who were embittered at being disturbed in their entertainment" and the "foreign profiteers" who constituted the audience.[61] When the Social Democratic *Arbeiter-Zeitung* criticized the demonstrators, its journalists were labeled "A. Z. Jews" and "the agitators of the A.-Z."[62] The triumphant account in the *Volkssturm* on February 20, under the heading "The Cultural Disgrace of *Reigen*," reported that "the Jewish writer Arthur Schnitzler" wrote his series of pornographic dialogues in the 1890s but did not dare for years to publish the work.[63] But now, in the age of the glorious Jewish, black-marketeering demagogue-republic, when all order has been dissolved in a boundless dictatorship of common nastiness, a theater with a Jewish managing director has put this *Schweinerei* on public display. But the "protest of Christian people" succeeded in stopping "Juda and its servants of filth." The article goes on to attack the "Jewish-red proletarian leaders" who take the part of the "Jewish swine-literati" ("*Schweineliteraten*") and defend the disgusting work on the grounds that it is art. True art of truth, goodness, and beauty can be recognized, however, in its perfect ur-type: in the eternal order and in God—not in the lies and evil of such Jewish *Schweinerei*. Other rightwing newspapers carried similar jubilant messages and gloated because the theater suffered a financial disaster.[64]

A year later, when the public furor had died down, the play was staged again from March 7 to June 30, 1922. At that point, a discouraged Schnitzler withdrew his permission for all further performances, and *Reigen* was not seen on stage again in German-speaking lands until 1982.

As far as the successive scandals surrounding the work are concerned, for the first twenty years opponents objected to the published book largely on grounds of its presumed immorality and, thanks to the severe censorship laws, often succeeded in having the work prohibited and confiscated in German-speaking countries—and contributed thereby to its publicity and continuing strong sales. But by the time it was first performed after World War I the nature of the opposition had changed. Because the censorship laws had been relaxed it was more difficult for the opponents to prevent its performance on legal grounds. Indeed, the response of the premiere audience in Berlin and the representatives of the Civil Court suggests that the play enjoyed a triumph in Schiller's sense as well. Schnitzler originally wrote his work as an indictment of the emptiness and hypocrisy dominating Viennese society of the fin-de-siècle. The fact that the Civil Court deemed his work "an ethical act" confirms his success in achieving and communicating that intention. And the fact that the victory occurred more than twenty years after the publication of the play, in the wholly different atmosphere pervading Europe after World War I, is a tribute to the supratemporal power of Schnitzler's vision, which characterizes all true art.

However, the rampant nationalism and anti-Semitism managed to harness the conservative sense of morality and decency, already upset by the 1918 revolution, the dissolution of the former imperial order in Austria and Germany, and the alleged moral laxness of the new republics, to support their own political and racist agenda. As Defense Attorney Heine observed in his publication of the court proceedings, the volume amounted to "a document of the intellectual battles that had to be fought out in Germany three years after the revolution."[65] Schnitzler's ten subtle scenes, intended to unmask with irony the moral hypocrisy of prewar Viennese society and to reflect on the fallibility of the human condition generally—in short, to serve as a moral institution in Schiller's generous understanding of the term[66]— were co-opted politically to support the crudest Nazi view of a sinister Jewish conspiracy determined to undermine the moral standards of decent citizens and to corrupt the national identity of the indigeneous German with their radically liberal thinking—in sum, to add fuel to the fires that within two decades enflamed the Holocaust. As the drama critic Ludwig Marcuse put it, the scandal of 1921 was "a first rehearsal for the great premiere of 1933."[67]

TROUBLE IN MAHAGONNY (BRECHT/WEILL'S AUFSTIEG UND FALL DER STADT MAHAGONNY)

On March 9, 1930, the actress-singer Lotte Lenya attended the premiere of *Aufstieg und Fall der Stadt Mahagonny* (*Rise and Fall of the City Mahagonny*) by her husband Kurt Weill and Bertolt Brecht in Leipzig's Neues Theater in a production directed by Walther Brügmann, conducted by Gustav Brecher, and designed by Caspar Neher. The area around the opera house was filled with brown-shirted Nazis carrying placards protesting the performance, and inside there were "black-white-red rabble-rousers who had been paid to come as a kind of claque by instigators with plenty of capital."[68] She soon became aware of "an electrical tension" in the atmosphere, "something strange and ugly."[69] Toward the end of the opera, she continues, "the whistling and booing began, and during the last scene fights broke out in the corridors, and the whole theater was filled with a screaming mob of people. The racket rapidly expanded because panicked members of the audience tried to escape across the stage." The disturbance was quelled only by the arrival of the police. The drama critic Alfred Polgar, who had come down from Berlin for the occasion, noticed in the "electrically charged hall" "a tension, an anticipatory disquiet, a readjustment of the passions [...] It also smelled strongly of an accompanying indignation that was simply waiting to be aroused."[70] Polgar describes various scenes: a woman on his left attacked by heart spasms and struggling to get out; a graying Saxon on his right gripping his wife's knee in agitation; warlike cries, fights, hissing, clapping, "enthusiastic bitterness, embittered enthusiasm." Polgar was impressed by a dignified gentleman who took out his keyring and blew a piercing sound through his cashbox key. Meanwhile, his Valkyrielike wife stuck two fat fingers into her mouth, shut her eyes, puffed up her cheeks, and outblew her husband. The critic for *Weltbühne* observed that "Saxon women, young and old, shouted 'Pfui!' 'Stop it!' and *'Pfui Teufel!'*"—that people were "terribly agitated, furious with rage, passionately angry."[71] The notorious evening has been described in similar terms by many others who were in attendance.

Disturbed by these outbursts, the theater committee of the city council met the next day to decide whether or not further performances should be allowed.[72] With a vote of five to three, and two abstentions, it was resolved that the show might continue. But a rightwing member of the committee (from the German National Peoples Party) demanded a hearing by the full city council, which by a vote of thirty-four to ten supported the committee's decision. The next performance, on March 16, monitored by policemen and conducted under full house lights, took place without incident, but after only three more performances the work was removed from the repertoire.

Three days following the premiere in Leipzig the opera with various mitigating changes was performed without incident in Kassel, but in Braunschweig on that same evening a Nazi student group from the Technical University caused disturbances during the performance and then rioted with shouts and shrill whistling, with the result that the opera was removed from the schedule. Other companies were reluctant to take the risk. Performances scheduled for that fall in Essen and Dortmund were cancelled, as was that in Oldenburg at the behest of a Nazi-led faction in the city council, which introduced a bill calling it "a shoddy patchwork of low-quality and immoral content."[73] A shortened version of the opera enjoyed a public success in Frankfurt during the festival for the fiftieth anniversary of its opera house on October 16, 1930.[74] But at the second performance three days later, a gala occasion attended by the Japanese prince and his wife along with their entourage, a mob of 100–150 Nazi demonstrators tried to break into the hall during the first intermission and had to be repulsed by the police. Then at the beginning of the second act demonstrators posted in the upper tiers hurled down stink bombs and firecrackers, causing panic in the audience. (Despite the turmoil the production had ten further performances.)

At Berlin's Kroll Opera, where the premiere had originally been scheduled to take place, Otto Klemperer was so dismayed by the text that he lost his nerve and rejected the work. On April 12, a radio station in Berlin aired an hour-long program called *"Mahagonny* Pro and Con," featuring seven numbers from the opera, which in turn stirred up new controversy.[75] By December 1931, however, when the opera in a drastically abbreviated version had its first performance in Berlin at the Theater am Kurfürstendamm, public resistance—for reasons discussed below—had calmed to the extent that the work could be repeated fifty times. Earlier works by Brecht and Weill had unsettled audiences and aroused controversy, but none had previously produced such an enormous theatrical uproar. Why this one?

The productive collaboration between Brecht and Weill began and ended with *Mahagonny*. In March 1927, Kurt Weill (1900–1950), regarded along with Paul Hindemith as one of the most promising young composers in Germany, was invited to create a short opera for performance at the prestigious German Chamber Music Festival in Baden-Baden that summer. As he cast about for a suitable libretto, he read the recently published poem-cycle *Hauspostille* (*Domestic Breviary*, 1927) by his bold young contemporary and approached Brecht (1898–1956) with the idea of setting five of the poems, the so-called "Mahagonny Songs," as a *Songspiel* (operatic cantata) for the occasion.[76] The performance, which launched Lotte Lenya's career for her famous rendition of the "Alabama Song," was the sensation of a program that also featured short operas by Hindemith, Darius Milhaud, and Ernst Toch.[77] The festival audience was prepared for avantgarde music but not the jazzy and politically tendentious *Gebrauchsmusik* ("functional music") offered by the adventuresome young collaborators who were intent on overturning all traditional conceptions of the arts. The audience's indignation was restrained by the need to remain in their places for Hindemith's concluding piece. The ambivalent but vociferous response encouraged the two young radicals to expand their thirty-minute *Songspiel* into a full-fledged opera that would exemplify their conception of the new "epic opera."[78]

As they worked on *Mahagonny*, the fruitful collaboration yielded various other works: the cantata *Das Berliner Requiem* (1928), the *Lehrstück* ("didactic play") *Der Lindberghflug* (*The Lindbergh Flight*, 1929), two choral pieces based on poems by Brecht (1929), songs and choruses for the play *Happy End* (1929), the pedagogical "school opera" *Der Jasager* (*The Yes-Man*,

1930), and notably the enormously successful *Dreigroschenoper* (*Threepenny Opera*, 1928). However, the most representative and, in many senses, greatest team effort was *Mahagonny*, which was completed in March 1929. The *Threepenny Opera* was in fact not an opera but a play that rose from time to time to musical expression in songs that Weill composed. But *Mahagonny* was conceived from the start as an opera—albeit an opera to end all operas, or at least the traditional opera as it had been known for three centuries in Europe. As such, it represented the fulfillment of theoretical ideas held by the two collaborators.

Brecht had been profoundly affected by his recent (albeit inadequate) study of Marx and in particular by the view that traditional art supports the existing society while concealing its evils. He stated his ideas most clearly in his "Notes on the Opera *Rise and Fall of the City Mahagonny*" (1930), which announces the principles elaborated more fully in his later *Kleines Organon für das Theater* ("*Little Organon for the Theater*," 1948).[79] It was Brecht's ambition to replace the traditional "culinary" opera with a new "epic" opera. At present, he argues, musicians and writers believe that they are in control of the "apparatus" or institution of the theater, but in reality the institution controls them and simply exploits their material for the benefit of a society that takes from it whatever it needs to reproduce itself. "Art is a ware—not to be produced without the means of production (apparatus)."[80]

Mahagonny proclaims itself an opera because it uses the traditional "culinary" genre of entertainment and amusement, but it exploits that genre for its own purposes. Brecht lists the contrasting (and by now familiar) characteristics of "dramatic" versus "epic" theater: notably, the one imitates an action while the other narrates it so as to produce not feelings—the Aristotelean fear and pity—but rational decisions. The application of these principles to opera leads first of all to a "radical separation of the elements" of word, music, and representation. Rather than enhancing the text, the music should explicate it; instead of illustrating the words, it should state its own position vis-à-vis the text. By making the content into an independent element to which both music and image take a position—by prioritizing the didactic over the culinary—the "illusion" is destroyed in favor of "discussability" and the viewer is forced to think and make decisions, thereby fulfilling the social function of theater—and, not incidentally, Schiller's conception of the theater as a moral institution. No matter how "culinary" *Mahagonny* may be, it attacks the society that still needs and enjoys such operas. In short, it uses traditional means to undermine that tradition. (Although Brecht does not put it in these terms, he is making a radical distinction between Horace's *dulce* and *utile*, emphasizing the "useful" over the merely entertaining.)

To this end, and on the basis of the earlier "Mahagonny Songs," Brecht created an explicitly ideological storyline that, like *Ubu Roi*, makes no demands upon the audience's psychological subtlety and that uses stage devices remarkably reminiscent of Jarry: notably a loose succession of scenes announced by placards.[81] Three swindlers in flight from the police—the widow Leokadja Begbick, Trinity Moses (Dreieinigkeitsmoses), and Willy the Accountant (Willy der Prokurist)—have a breakdown of their truck on a coast in an imaginary America somewhere vaguely between Florida and Alaska.[82] (People can reach it by sailing down the coast from Alaska, but the area is threatened by a hurricane that devastates Pensacola.) They decide to found a city named Mahagonny on the spot—a city full of "gin and whiskey, girls and boys" where the gold prospectors will be caught as though in a net and will spend their hard-earned money.[83] As Begbick tells the two men, "You can get gold more easily from men than from rivers." The city is intended to be a paradise for the rich, dedicated to "peace and harmony" insured by a table of rigid laws determining proper behavior. (Various suggestions have been advanced for the name Mahagonny: a record featuring the "American shimmy" *Komm nach Mahoganne!* (1922) that enjoyed a wild popularity in Germany; the brown or mahogany-colored shirts worn by the Nazis; the sinful city of Magog from the Bible.)[84]

In the next few months and years, as stated by the placards and projections announcing each scene, the city grows quickly around the Widow Begbick's Hotel Rich Man with its bar-room and brothel; and the first "sharks" make their way there—notably the prostitute Jenny and six other girls, who sing the now popular "Alabama Song." Soon, too, four lumberjacks who have made their fortunes during seven years in Alaska show up: Jimmy Mahoney, Jack, Pinchpenny Billy, and Alaska Wolf Joe.[85] As they announce in their first song, they are looking for a place without the evils of civilization, including venereal diseases: "Die Zi-zi-zi-zi-zivilis / Die wird uns dort geheilt" ("Our ci-ci-ci-ci-civilis—there it's cured").[86] In a purely commercial transaction Jimmy buys Jenny from Widow Begbick for thirty dollars.

After the astonishing "rise" of Mahagonny, however, it becomes rapidly clear to all that this city of peace and harmony with its well-regulated sin and its signs forbidding loud singing, soiling the chairs, and so forth, is in fact deadly boring. Its residents have little to do but fish and smoke and swim. As people begin to depart in hordes, prices fall and business wanes.

When Jimmy threatens to leave, the men lead him back to the hotel, where they listen to a pianist playing the popular *"Gebet einer Jungfrau"* (*"Maiden's Prayer"*) in a corny salon style, which Jack in a pointed reference to the kitschy taste of the bourgeoisie, proclaims "timeless art." Suddenly a hurricane, which has already devastated Pensacola, approaches the city, and Jimmy urges his fellows, in view of the coming disaster, to feel free to do whatever is forbidden. Despite a sign prohibiting singing he sings a lusty song announcing that nothing is forbidden.

At the last minute, the hurricane makes a detour around the city, but from that night on, order is replaced in Mahagonny by anarchy. Everything is allowed according to the principle that happiness is tantamount to unrestrained freedom, and business booms again—but the city's "fall" begins. Four scenes—"Sittenbilder des 20 Jahrhunderts" ("Moral Images of the Twentieth Century")[87]—illustrate the vices of this new society: "Eating" (*Essen*) in which Pigout Jack eats himself to death; "Loving" (*Lieben*) in which the men of Mahagonny are serviced in the whorehouse, while in another room Jimmy and Jenny sing a lovely love duet, the "Crane Song"; "Fighting" (*Kämpfen*) in which Alaska Wolf Joe, upon whom Jimmy has bet all his money, is killed in a boxing match with Trinity Moses; and "Boozing" (*Saufen*), in which Jimmy, to commemorate Joe's death, treats everyone to drinks and, standing on a billiard table, reminisces in song about the good old days in Alaska. Because he is unable to pay Widow Begbick, and none of his "friends," including Pinchpenny Billy and Jenny, will lend him money, he is put on trial and tickets are sold for the occasion: "only $5 to hear justice speak."[88]

In the first case, with Trinity Moses as prosecutor, Willy the Accountant for the defense, and the Widow Begbick as judge, a murderer is freed when he is able to bribe the judge (in front of a projection claiming that this is "no worse than other courts"). But Jimmy has no such luck: for indirectly contributing to the murder of his friend Joe he is sentenced to two days in jail; for disturbing the peace, to two months' loss of civil rights; for seduction of a girl named Jenny, to four years' prison; for singing during the hurricane, to ten years' imprisonment; and because he cannot pay for three bottles of whisky and a broken curtain-rod, he is condemned to death—"For lack of money, which is the greatest crime that occurs on this earth."[89] After his execution by electric chair, a projection depicts the now failing Mahagonny in flames while groups circle the stage carrying placards with various messages. Widow Begbick, Trinity Moses, and Willy proclaim "For Rising Prices," "For the Battle of All against All," "For the Chaotic Condition of our Cities," "For the

Continued Existence of the Golden Age."[90] The next group displays signs with conflicting messages, such as "For Private Property" and "For the Expropiation of the Others." The third group argues "For the Freedom of the Rich" and "For Bravery against the Defenseless." In the fourth group the girls, singing the "Alabama Song," carry Jimmy's watch, revolver, checkbook, and shirt. Other groups bear single signs "For Justice," "For Stupidity," and "For the Continuation of the Golden Age." As the opera ends the whole chorus joins in with the cynical refrain: "We can't help ourselves or you or any one."[91]

Brecht's angry libretto amounts to a modern morality tale depicting the fate of an innocent Everyman in the capitalistic and, in his eyes, Americanized world of the twentieth century. By implication it insults the theater audience, which has come professing belief in the same culinary delights offered by the boring city of pleasures portrayed in the first half, but in reality enjoying the evils of capitalistic overindulgence and corruption depicted in the second half.[92] An early reviewer, understanding these intentions clearly, pointed out that the aesthetic aspects of the work had become unimportant.[93] "People were furious and became ever more furious in the course of the three acts because—they themselves didn't know why. Their honest outrage broke out as redemptively as a delayed sneeze when finally the impudent Bolshevik showed his true face."[94] But Brecht doesn't offer the usual Communist theater, he continued. "Brecht seeks out the ladies and gentlemen where they believe themselves safest from him and his kind"—that is, in the bourgeois opera houses.[95] But he is not making Communist propaganda. "In this inconsistent opera, which is constructed with an almost intentional casualness, he tears down with every word a piece of bourgeois heaven, at every step kicks at the façades of bourgeois society, beginning with its traditional representational theater, to which he offers his most profound disrespect."[96] This opera, "which only pretends to be one, is an advance not to the renewal but to the abolition of the aesthetic genre: opera."[97] Another critic realized that "*Mahagonny* challenges us to take a position—not by its aesthetic form but by its content."[98] Unlike the *Threepenny Opera*, he goes on, which could be taken from its cheerful side, "*Mahagonny* wants the audience to take it seriously" and introduces politics into opera.

In the German press, where the issue was widely debated, most reviewers were less tolerant and understanding. (In 1930, thanks to the staggering unemployment statistics, the Nazis won 107 of 583 in the national Reichstag—up from only twelve seats two years earlier—and now constituted a significant public voice.) Alfred Heuss, editor of the respected

Zeitschrift für Musik and a vigorous opponent of modern music, addressed Brecht and Weill with the ominous threat that "your days may well be just as numbered as those of your scum-city Mahagonny."[99] He called the work "the nastiest imaginable, shabby, and above all artistically impotent." The entire evening, he concluded, went well beyond a theatrical scandal and amounted to a people's court (*Volksgericht*). What was still permissible in 1928 is no longer acceptable, he gloated. "The golden age for poets of pimping is over." Heuss, a Nazi sympathizer, detested the work so heartily that he returned to it in a lengthier article the following month, where he justified his use of the term "*Volksgericht*."[100] The scandal, he argued, was much more than the "opposition of nationalistic rowdies" to a work designed for "a parquet of pimps and similarly disposed individuals"—a work that relied on "the tacit acknowledgment of present-day cloacal circumstances."[101] Brecht, a "driveling fool who often doesn't remember what he wrote a few lines earlier," presents a "Marxist view of the world," which levels down all differences between high and low, noble and common, while Weill's score implies that "it doesn't matter whether a composer concerns himself with pimp-verse or with religious poetry."[102] The government has closed down the brothels in Germany, only to open them again in the theaters, justifying their actions with the freedom of art.[103] But the public outrage in Leipzig, he believed, constituted "a breach in the wall" of unwholesome cultural values espoused by the theater managers and the metropolitan press and marked a healthy sign of the public's faith in "a new, great and strong, soberly realistic age"—in other words, National Socialism.[104] In Braunschweig the rightwing press had a field day, saying that the public for all too long had shown "an angelic patience vis-à-vis the goat-leaps of the radicals."[105] The director "has granted admission to the worst kind of cultural bolshevism (*Kulturbolschewismus*) and now must suffer the financial consequences."[106] The cloacal image was popular among rightwing critics. In Frankfurt, the reviewer wrote that "the opera house jubilee ended in the cloaca, with a coffin at the end, which was the symbol for the good taste, here borne to the grave, of those who see anything applaudable in such miserable incapacity in the artistic shaping of nihilistic feelings."[107]

By the time the opera reached Berlin in December 1931 it had been toned down so greatly—morally, religiously, and politically—that it caused little offense and, in the process, lost its bite. One critic could not understand what all the hue and cry in Leipzig two years earlier had been about. "Have chaos and catastrophes dulled us so greatly that what excited people yesterday seems tame today? Or is the Berlin production simply less energetic?"[108] Brecht's text, he suggests, is "on the whole ineffective and wearisome." Another critic advanced much the same opinion, saying that not only was there no scandal; the team had to work hard even to get applause. Following the Leipzig premiere, the opera was thoroughly revised and the crudest passages deleted. "Not much remained that could wound sensitive spirits. What does remain, to be sure, is the banality of the subject, which is all the more off-putting because it marches in rather pretentiously with the claim of being especially clever."[109] A third summarized that "the opera today has a far less aggressive effect than [in Leipzig]. Its theses, for all their daring and brutality, are in the last analysis literary theses."[110] A critic with Nazi sympathies described the opera under the heading "For the Grandeur of Filth."

A procuress and a couple of pimps establish the fun-city Mahagonny for a public of scoundrels, and the author is surprised that it doesn't turn into a nice town. The contents: pigging out, whoring, boxing, boozing, purchasable excess. A Parsifal from the Alaskan forests is condemned to death for avoiding his bar bill by a court in which the procuress and her·pimps pass judgment, and over his corpse Mahagonny demonstrates for its ideals [...] In a word: Irony of the contemporary theater.[111]

But this "revolutionary joke" doesn't work, he concludes. "The whole thing is impudent and cold," displaying a juvenile temperament and sentimentality.[112]

While the rightwing press attacked the work for its immorality, there were also objections from the other wing. After the Leipzig premiere, the leftist pacifist Kurt Tucholsky, writing under the pseudonym "Peter Panter," pointed out that the audiences, including the Nazis, had protested because the opera represented everything they despised: "socialism, Jews, Russia, pacifism, the revocation of paragraph 218,[113] disturbance of their morality and disturbance of business, common people, everything common ... Pfui! Outrageous! Stop it!"[114] But how much energy is being wasted, he continues. "This threepenny philosophy: 'Wie man sich bettet, so liegt man' [actually a refrain from *Mahagonny:* "If you make your bed, you have to lie in it."], this carefully glazed roughness, these sharply calculated gold-digger curses [...] that's not life! Not even in yesterday's Klondike, and certainly not in today's America [...] even the connection to Germany in 1930 remains slack. It is stylized Bavaria." (A later Marxist critic confirmed these typical objections, pointing out that Brecht had only an incomplete understanding of Marxism and materialistic dialectics.[115] In fact, Brecht was only fulfilling the pessimism that characterized all bourgeois literature. "Mahagonny is a depiction of that atomized, anarchic capitalistic society about which the young Marx was writing [...] But Brecht presented only the superficialities of this anarchy without exposing the basis, the anarchic means of production."[116] What is false about Brecht's presentation, he continues, is that "the maxim of capitalistic society—everything is permitted for money—is discovered under the impression of a natural catastrophe.")[117]

These examples suggest the tone of the immediate reaction to the opera from left and right and the reasons governing the "scandal" of its premiere, the protests of the Nazis and other rightwing groups, and the German bourgeoisie generally.[118] From Brecht's point of view, indeed, the Leipzig premiere may be regarded as an effective realization of Schiller's theory. The author had a clear "moral" intent—to lampoon the values of capitalist society—and the frenzied reponse of the audience in Leipzig suggests that he achieved his result, even though of course there was no immediate acknowledgment of the validity of his critique.

Weill had an equally clear theoretical agenda. But, as in the case of the Wilde/Strauss's *Salome*, the aesthetic goal of the composer was initially overlooked in the scandal surrounding the more explicitly political-ethical intent of the author. What got lost in the furor was any appreciation of Weill's contribution and of the work as an opera rather than a piece of Marxist agit-prop. As the musicologist Alfred Einstein noted at the time, "the people of Leipzig who hissed and left the theater certainly felt Bert Brecht's and Kurt Weill's aggressiveness but not their seriousness."[119] And even that perceptive critic believed that "musically *Mahagonny* is no opera. It's a sequence of songs or songs expanded to scenes, not dramatic music." Those who deigned to notice the music condemned it as did the anonymous Viennese reviewer who observed that "the dramatic content [is] not worth mentioning." As for the music, "the nihilism of the text-author is matched by that of the composer Kurt Weill. This music, which prefers jazz rhythms, doesn't recoil from the harshest cacaphonies and professes melody only rarely and even then only for a few bars in a couple of songs."[120] Even the leftwing press found the music as unconvincing as the story. The anonymous reviewer for the Leipzig socialist workers' newspaper objected that the music did not attain the level of the *Threepenny Opera*. The various musical parodies prove simply that the composer has no original ideas.

Even the music makes only modest revolutionary starts. Often it "jazzes" along comfortably and without irony, in a genuinely American manner. Those are the passages that will no doubt find a receptive ear in our theater public. Otherwise the general mood of the evening is that of Spengler's *Decline of the West*, which was also at home on every bourgeois Christmas gift-table.[121]

The critic for the "theoretical organ" of the Nazi Party offered a few "fundamental words" on the musical aspect of Weill's score, tying his remarks explicitly to Nazi anti-Semitism.

The most prominent characteristic of Weill's music is jazz rhythm. If Weill here consciously introduces Negro rhythms into German art-music, and with a serious intention, then he is only carrying out in practice what the Jew Bernhard Sekles as director of the Hoch Conservatory in Frankfurt am Main more or less stated at the introduction of the class for jazz music: that a transfusion with Negro blood wouldn't hurt us. So the people that brought forth a Bach, Mozart, Beethoven, Wagner, needs to be reinvigorated by Negro blood. Negro blood, which is no doubt related to Sekles and his Semitic racial compatriots.[122]

Only a few critics were perceptive enough to recognize the true originality of Weill's score. H. H. Stuckenschmidt, writing in a prominent journal for the theater arts, acknowledged that "for a long time no dramatic work of art has been exposed to more impassioned resistance than Brecht-Weill's *Mahagonny*."[123] His balanced discussion, unlike many earlier reviews, does justice to both collaborators. "The primitive and rough magnificence of these incidents tied together by ballad-like transitional titles, demanded a wholly elemental music."[124] Holding to the principle that made the success of the *Threepenny Opera*, Weill "dissolves the action into songlike episodes and thus creates operatic numbers of great melodic penetration."[125] The work, he concludes, "stands historically at the developmental peak of the musical-dramatic production of the present."

However, it was the young leftist philosopher and musicologist Theodor W. Adorno whose extensive appreciation of the opera in 1930 essentially set the tone for all future serious musicological considerations. "The city Mahagonny is a depiction of the social world in which we live," he begins, "cast from the bird's-eye view of a truly liberated society."[126] Adorno devotes the first half of his essay to the plot, which he approves as far as it goes, but with a keen awareness of Marxist critiques of the work: "the bourgeois world is exposed as absurd, measured by a socialistic world that keeps itself hidden."[127] Brecht uses Marxist dialectics to expose the inevitable fall of capitalism by the "dialectics of the anarchy inherent in it" while presenting no positive countermodel.[128] In the second half of his essay, Adorno analyzes the form of the work and justifies its loose succession of scenes.[129] "It serves its purpose of replacing the closed bourgeois totality with the fragmentary succession of its ruins."[130] Above all, "the intentions of *Mahagonny* are borne by the music, which from the first note to the last is devoted to the shock produced by the abrupt confrontation with the utterly dilapidated bourgeois world."[131] Accordingly, Adorno speaks approvingly of the music,

which except for a few polyphonic moments like the introduction and a few ensemble passages makes do with the most primitive means; or rather he drags the worn-out, shabby household goods of the Sunday parlor onto a children's playground, where the old wares seen from the rear spread horror as totemlike figures—this music, patched together with triads and false notes, with old music-hall songs that are not really known but recalled as genetic material, hammered firm, glued with the stinking glue of softened opera potpourris, the music made from ruins of past music is wholly present.[132]

Following further careful analysis, Adorno summarizes that "*Mahagonny* goes far beyond the stage music of *The Threepenny Opera*; the music no longer serves, but dominates in the through-composed opera and unfolds according to its infernal measure".[133] Adorno hears echoes of *Carmen*, of cantus firmus, of archaic power of memory, of the satanic kitsch of the nineteenth century, and of Mahler's marches.

Adorno's perceptive analysis accurately summarized Weill's intentions, which the composer stated in a number of articles written during the composition and staging.[134] In his suggestions for the director and actors he explained that, unlike the *Threepenny Opera*, which was a "dialogue opera," *Mahagonny* was shaped according to pure musical principles. "The chronicle form used here is nothing but a 'linking of episodes.'"[135] The behavior of the singers, the movement of the chorus, as well as the entire representational style of this opera is determined by the style of the music. "This music is at no moment illustrative. It seeks to realize the attitude of human beings in the various situations that the rise and fall of the city precipitates."[136] Elsewhere he explained that he and Brecht envisioned

the ur-type of an opera in which the music begins only when the action has reached a static moment that permits a standstill of incidents, lasting as long as necessary, in favor of an unrestrained unfolding of the music. In order to apply this principle to opera, that is, to a genre in which the musical phenomena move more strongly into the foreground, it is important to move these static moments when music is possible closer together and to give to the connections between the musical numbers a form that interferes as little as possible with the musical structure of the whole.[137]

For this reason, the dialogues are replaced by projections that provide the transition from scene to scene.

.

The "epic opera" resulting from these innovations shares many features of conventional opera: a fugue-like orchestral prelude, interludes, and a grand finale recapitulating the principal motifs; recitatives, ensembles, chorales, and arias—many of which betray their origin in songs with memorable melodies. One hears sophisticated parodies of many works familiar to the bourgeois audience: Weber's *Freischütz*, the Temple Guards in Mozart's *The Magic Flute*, waltzes, Mahler's symphonies, and various popular songs—Weill's musical counterpart to Brecht's *Verfremdung*-techniques.[138] But in an effort to make his music more accessible and less expensive, Weill scored for a much smaller orchestra—some forty instruments—than the massive ones introduced immediately before the war by Strauss and Stravinsky, as well as an instrumentation clearly influenced by the jazz bands of the 1920s. The result, with its syncopated rhythms, fox trots, and blues that color the whole, is a music never before heard on the opera stage. In its reworking of these various fragments of the contemporary cultural memory into a consistent whole, Weill's score to *Mahagonny* constitutes a surprising yet close analogy to T. S. Eliot's *The Waste Land*.[139]

While the *Songspiel Mahagonny* had initially brought Brecht and Weill together in 1927, their work on the 1931 Berlin production drove the temperamentally different artists apart again. The poet and the composer initially shared a similar view of an epic opera that would put an end to traditional opera and make the form socially and musically more relevant, but their conceptions gradually grew further apart.[140] Brecht's text stressed through its names the American nature of the action and the capitalism that he detested. Weill, a pacifist but no Marxist, had a less political and more generally ethical view: he saw Mahagonny as a parable of human greed. "The content of this opera is the story of a city, its origin, its first crises, then the decisive turning point in its development, its glorious time and its decline. It offers 'moral images of our time,' projected onto an enlarged plane."[141] Accordingly he urged Brecht to change the names in order to play down the specifically American aspect and to alter the projections and placards so that their message would be more generally ethical and less specifically Marxist-ideological. Above all, the two men differed on the relative significance of their roles: Brecht did not want to be reduced to a mere librettist while Weill, the proud student of such composers as Humperdinck and Busoni, wanted to be regarded as more than a simple songwriter. In response to public pressure and the demands of the various theater directors, the libretto was gradually toned down so appreciably that Brecht eventually rejected the work, believing that it had been reduced to nothing more than a "culinary" entertainment without significant social relevance.[142] (It is characteristic of this breach that recordings of the opera—for instance, the 1956 Nordeutscher Rundfunk or the 1958 CBS Masterworks versions—bear only Weill's name on the cover.) In the course of the rehearsals for the Berlin performance their increasingly personal disagreements erupted into a major quarrel that put an end to their friendship. As a result, the opera has come gradually to be treated almost exclusively as an innovative musical achievement by Weill and not as the Schillerian "moral" achievement of the young radical Brecht to shock the bourgeoisie out of their capitalist satisfactions.[143]

The opera was produced a few more times in the early 1930s, notably in Vienna, Prague, and Copenhagen. But Nazi condemnations of the Marxist poet and the Jewish composer prohibited their works during the Hitler years. In the notorious 1937 Nazi exhibition of "Degenerate Art" in Munich and Berlin, recordings of songs from *Mahagonny* were played to illustrate "cultural bolshevism" and the degeneracy of Jewish music. The 1933 performance in Copenhagen was the last production of *Mahagonny* during the lifetimes of Brecht and Weill. But in the postwar era, and notably since 1962, the opera has again enjoyed successful revivals on opera stages around the world, including no fewer than three (Boston, Los Angeles, and the Spoleto Festival) in 2007 in the USA alone.[144] In the process, Weill's aesthetic achievement has been more appreciatively emphasized while Brecht's political-social attack on capitalism has most often been reduced to an ironic commentary appropriate to contemporary society. Audiences, while enjoying the music, can nod knowingly at the action without being scandalized. Anthony Tommasini, in his review of a 2008 performance at the Tanglewood Music Center observed: "Weill's music, though mostly stern and rigorous, has stretches of plaintive lyricism and searching harmony. Weill softens the anticapitalist screed in Brecht's text and humanizes the characters."[145]

Mahagonny mirrors in Brecht's text as well as Weill's score the cultural and political ambivalence of its own schizoid age. Yet with its social, political, and ethical critique expressed through brilliant musical effects it evidently still speaks to contemporary audiences, compelling them to engage in the kind of critical thinking about their societies demanded by the theater as a moral institution.

CHAPTER 6

Overcoming the past

DEFROCKING THE DEPUTY (HOCHHUTH'S
DER STELLVERTRETER)

The controversy aroused by Rolf Hochhuth's play *Der Stellvertreter* (*The Deputy*, 1963) has been called "one of the greatest publicity successes of the century"[1] and even "the largest storm ever raised by a play in the whole history of the drama."[2] Within six months of its premiere on February 20, 1963, more than 3,000 reactions—reviews, reports, letters—had been published in German newspapers and journals and documented in a collection commissioned by the publisher.[3] That same year, a Swiss publisher brought out an anthology of articles in response to the demonstrations that accompanied the play's performance in Basel.[4] A year later Eric Bentley released his *The Storm over the Deputy*, which was characterized on the cover as a collection of (mostly American) "essays and articles about Hochhuth's explosive drama." Meanwhile the play was being produced in London, Paris, Vienna, Athens, New York, Odense, Stockholm, the Netherlands (though it had to be shifted from The Hague to Rotterdam), and Tel Aviv (despite official statements supporting the Pope).[5] In Italy and Spain, Church pressure prevented performances; an attempt in Rome was stopped by the police.[6] In 1964, Jacques Nobécourt, an editor for German and Italian affairs at *Le Monde* in Paris, published a long and thoughtful account of the whole affair: the theme of the play and its repercussions around the world among Catholics, Protestants, and Jews; the historical reality of the various figures of the play and its background; and its critical reception.[7] His positive account was balanced that same year by the negative exposé of Rosario F. Esposito, who stoutly advanced the official Catholic position.[8] Since then the volumes of analysis and interpretation have continued to mount,[9] including voices such as those of Albert Schweitzer, Pope Paul VI, Pope Pius XII's personal secretary (Robert Leiber, S. J.), the historian Golo Mann, the philosopher Karl

113

Jaspers, the political theorist Hannah Arendt, members of the German Bundestag, and other prominent figures of church, State, and literature.[10]

Who was this hitherto-unknown playwright and why did his play arouse such an international scandal? Hochhuth might best be described not as a dramatist or even a writer but as a moralist in Schiller's sense who draws on recent history and contemporary events to explore the conscience and responsibility of the individual.[11] His second play, *Die Soldaten* (*The Soldiers*, 1967) dealt with Winston Churchill's decision to order the saturation bombing of German cities. The third, *Guerillas* (1970), imagined a wealthy, young US senator seeking to overthrow what he regards as the capitalistic government of the USA before he is forced into suicide by the CIA. This series was introduced by the first work of the young dramatist, *The Deputy*, which took the Holocaust and specifically the horrors of Auschwitz as an occasion to scrutinize the role of Pope Pius XII and the Catholic Church as well as the responsibility of German officers, scientists, and industrial leaders. As Hochhuth, an admirer of the great historian of Rome, Theodor Mommsen, put it in a 1964 interview: "man's bearing, his historic stance, can most readily be deciphered through the study of history. This, for me, is, and will surely remain the most interesting area for investigation."[12]

Rolf Hochhuth was born in 1931 in Eschwege, a town in central Germany near Kassel. Though his parents were opposed to Hitler and the war, he was himself, like most German boys of his age and that era, a member of Hitler youth groups and an enthusiastic supporter of the war who feared the Russians and disliked the Allies for their bombings of German cities. Soon after the war, however, his uncle, an anti-Nazi who was made mayor of the town by the American occupation authorities, appointed the young Hochhuth as a messenger to the occupiers, and his contacts with the Allies, as well as photographs from the death camps, forced him to rethink his assumptions. Disenchanted with what was being taught, he left school at age seventeen to undertake his own education through extensive reading: first, as a clerk in bookstores in Eschwege, Marburg, Heidelberg, and Munich; and then as an editor for Bertelsmann Publishing Company, sponsors of Europe's largest book club.

At the same time, Hochhuth had begun experimenting with his first writing efforts: both poetry and prose, including an unpublished novel, "Die Okkupation," concerning the end of the Nazi regime and the beginning of the Allied occupation. As a result of his first success at age thirty, the novella *The Berlin Antigone* (1961)—the story, based on an historical account, of a girl who in 1943 steals the corpse of her brother, who was executed by the Nazis for treason, and buries it illegally—and on the basis of his projected drama, he received the Gerhart Hauptmann Prize for the encouragement of young writers, with a citation praising him especially for "daring to seize the hot iron of recent European history."[13]

In the course of his readings in that recent history—including the protocols of the Nuremberg trials, Goebbel's diaries, the speeches of Pius XII, and notably the shocking documentary volume *The Third Reich and the Jews*—Hochhuth had encountered the cases of several figures who had individually resisted the Nazi tyranny.[14] Kurt Gerstein was a devout Christian and member of the Confessing Church (Bekennende Kirche) who, in order to undermine the Nazis from within, joined the SS. As a medically trained scientist he was responsible for disinfection in the Nazi Institute of Hygiene, where he was given the assignment of acquiring and transporting 100 kilograms of Zyklon-B to Belzec concentration camp for secret experiments. In this capacity he learned about the mass murders being carried out in the camps and at great personal peril reported them secretly to Protestant and Catholic leaders, including the Papal Nuncio in Berlin. (Despite these heroic efforts he disappeared after the war in a Paris prison, presumably a victim, because of his SS uniform, of partisan reprisals.) Hochhuth also learned of Father Maximilian Kolbe, a Polish Franciscan priest, who died at Auschwitz after taking the place of a Jewish prisoner sentenced to death by starvation in retaliation for the escape of a fellow prisoner. And he found accounts of Bernhard Lichtenberg, provost of St. Hedwig's Cathedral in Berlin, who offered public prayers for the Jews and asked to be allowed to accompany Jews to Auschwitz; instead he was sent to Dachau, where he died in 1943.

Powerfully moved by these tales, Hochhuth initially began to contemplate a story and then a play about Gerstein. In the process he imagined another (unhistorical) figure, the Jesuit Father Riccardo Fontana, whose life would be roughly based on Provost Lichtenberg's. (The completed work was dedicated to the memory of Father Kolbe and Provost Lichtenberg.) Eventually, after he had carried out extensive research in London, Paris, and Rome, studying archival documents and talking to survivors, he decided to include Pope Pius XII in order to personalize the question: "How, in this so-called Christian Europe, the murder of an entire people could take place without the highest moral authority of this earth having a word to say about it."[15]

It should be evident from the aforegoing that Hochhuth had developed a theory of history that differed conspicuously from the one currently fashionable among leftist thinkers, from Marx and Brecht to

Theodor W. Adorno and Herbert Marcuse: namely, that history is moved by anonymous powers over which the individual has little control.[16] In an important statement that he wrote in 1963 in response to a questionnaire from the journal *Theater heute*, Hochhuth argued, in contrast to this Hegelian detachment, that it is the essential task of drama "to insist that man is a responsible being."[17] While only a few prominent individuals have complete freedom of decision, every human subject enjoys a certain degree of freedom. The theater, he begins, "would be finished if it ever conceded that man even in masses is no longer an individual."[18] Drama should place human beings in situations where decisions must be made because "where he can no longer make decisions there is no drama."[19]

This view of the individual's responsibility and his view of theater as a vehicle for the dramatic presentation of history places Hochhuth much closer to his admired Schiller, the moralist and the dramatist, than, say, to Brecht or to such German-language contemporaries as Friedrich Dürrenmatt, who believed that in the totally bureaucratized states of postwar Europe the individual has no power and little responsibility and that "Creon's secretaries deal with the case of Antigone."[20] His work is not epic theater after the fashion of Brecht but rather traditional historical drama on a large scale, like Schiller's *Don Carlos* or *Wallenstein*.[21] It places individuals, carefully and elaborately characterized in the often extensive stage directions, in the foreground, rather than subordinating them to the masses or generalizing them into such Expressionistic abstractions as "man" or "the father." It is worth noting that this powerful tragedy of the individual appeared only two years after George Steiner, looking at the antidramas of Samuel Beckett, proclaimed "the death of tragedy."

While his work is based on extensive documentary materials, many of which are reproduced in the fifty-page appendix that follows the text of his play, in an effort to avoid the tone of documentary naturalism he fashioned a sort of free verse to concentrate the language, to suggest the ceremonious discourse used routinely by high church dignitaries—and, not incidentally, to enable the actors to memorize it more easily.[22] The resulting play has an elaborate structure, which because of the work's extraordinary length, can easily be overlooked. Acts I, III, and V have three scenes each, while the intervening Acts II and IV consist of a single long scene. The acts are punctuated temporally by three key events at roughly six-month intevals. The first act takes place in Berlin in August 1942, half a year after the notorious Wannsee Conference of January 20, 1942, where Nazi leaders determined to embark on the Final Solution to exterminate the Jews, and immediately following Gerstein's August visit to the death camps at Belzec and Treblinka, where he realized that the horrendous policy had already been put into effect. Act II takes place six months later on February 2, 1943, the day of the German surrender at Stalingrad, which marked a turning point in the war and gave new hope to the anti-Nazi opposition. The next three acts take place in October 1943: first in Rome, where the first deportation of Roman Jews to Auschwitz is carried out literally under the windows of the Vatican; and finally at Auschwitz, where clouds of smoke hover over the camp as the arriving prisoners are directed to their various fates. The action revolves around two opposed poles: the conversion of the young Father Riccardo Fontana from initial disbelief to action, when he learns of the killings in the concentration camps; and the inaction of various Church officials culminating in the Pope himself, who put political, diplomatic, and economic considerations ahead of moral action.

The tension begins in the first scene, when the SS officer Gerstein, at great personal risk, bursts into the papal legation in Berlin, where the (historical) Nuncio is meeting with the Jesuit Father Riccardo Fontana, to bring him proof of the horrendous murders in Poland. The Nuncio, unwilling to listen because of the existing concordat between Hitler and the Vatican, has Gerstein thrown out despite the pleas of Riccardo, whose order has received similar reports without giving them credence. The second scene, a raucous gathering of SS officers with Nazi scientists and industrialists hosted by Adolf Eichmann, exposes the cold-blooded calculation with which high officials in the Party condone the harsh treatment of Jewish workers in the Krupp factories and in the camps. Gerstein's report to Eichmann that he has been unable to carry out the ordered experiments with Zykon-B arouses suspicions of his loyalty; and we are introduced to the figure of the diabolical and seductively attractive "Doctor," based loosely on the historical figure of Joseph Mengele, the notorious camp physician, who emerges in the last act as an embodiment of evil. The third scene takes place in Gerstein's apartment, where he is giving refuge to a Jew named Jacobson. The Doctor, who seems to be suspicious of Gerstein, appears at the door and with cold logic destroys Gerstein's cautious arguments; when he leaves, Riccardo arrives to assure Gerstein that he will convey the message to the Vatican, which will surely act on the shocking information. Before Riccardo leaves, Gerstein tests his commitment by asking him to give his passport and clerical garb to Jacobson in exchange for the Jew's yellow star.

Act II takes place in the house of Riccardo's father, a papal counselor, on February 2, 1943, when it has just been learned that the German troops have surrendered at Stalingrad and that the momentum of the war has changed. Riccardo tries unsuccessfully to persuade first his father and then a visiting cardinal that they too are guilty if they simply stand by without taking action; it is the moment to persuade the Pope to make a statement about the fate of the Jews. The cardinal, with cynical *Realpolitik*, is dismayed by Riccardo's immoderate behavior and orders his reassignment from Berlin to Lisbon, where he can cause less trouble; but his father is reluctantly persuaded by his son's information and passion. The next act takes place half a year later, on October 16/17, when for the first time the Jews in Rome are rounded up for deportation to the camps. We first witness the specific case of a Jewish archaeologist and his family, who live in an apartment directly facing the Vatican. In Scene 2, Riccardo and Gerstein rush into the study of the Father General of the Salvatorian Order, who is chatting there with the cardinal, to announce that the Jews are being rounded up. The cardinal explains with his customary cynicism why the Church supports Hitler against the Bolsheviks. After his departure, the two young men try to persuade the Father General to allow Riccardo at least to make an announcement and appeal on Radio Vatican, but the abbot with growing impatience urges Riccardo to submit to the Church's authority. The last scene, in the Roman headquarters of the Gestapo, shows the arrest of the Jews (the family from the first scene) from the standpoint of indifferent Gestapo officers, even when Gerstein appears and questions the validity of their orders, which contravene earlier understandings between the Nazis and the Vatican.

In Act IV, finally, Pope Pius XII appears in person in the papal palace, and with clear, cool intelligence and subtle diplomatic reasoning counters the arguments brought forward by the impassioned Riccardo and the more restrained counsel of his father: Hitler is the bulwark of the West against Communism; the Pope hopes to negotiate a ceasefire between Germany and the Western Allies, not the unconditional surrender demanded by Roosevelt and Churchill; any statement from him at this point would simply worsen the fate of the Jews. To show his good faith he dictates a bland statement condemning the violence of war generally (with words borrowed from the Pope's actual Christmas message of 1943) and, with a Pilate-like gesture, washes his hands to cleanse them from ink dripped during his signature. Riccardo, in despair, pins to his soutane the yellow star that he received from Jacobson more than a year earlier and storms out of the audience, saying that "God should not destroy the church simply because one pope forsakes his calling."[23]

The last act begins with a dark scene in the train car transporting victims to Auschwitz, where we hear poetically generalized monologues of three typical figures: the old man, the woman, the girl. At the camp, the sinister Doctor recognizes Riccardo, whom he met in Berlin a year earlier and who has had himself taken to Auschwitz along with the Jews. In a great debate consciously reminiscent of a medieval morality play,[24] this "soul of Auschwitz" tells the priest that he too had once studied theology but, like Lucifer, fell away from God and now has sworn "to provoke the old gentleman so immoderately, so wholly without measure, that he must give me an answer" as to whether or not he exists.[25] Rather than allowing Riccardo to have the death he desires, the Doctor cynically condemns him to serve in the crematorium for nine hours a day and, there, to carry out his researches into God. In the last scene, Gerstein appears bearing false papers with which he hopes to rescue Riccardo; Riccardo refuses the offer but puts Jacobson, whose earlier escape attempt failed, in his place. They are foiled when the Doctor appears, recognizes everyone, and arrests Gerstein. Riccardo is shot dead when he tries to kill the Doctor, and Jacobson must carry his body off to the crematorium. At this moment, the camp loudspeaker announces that the Pope has not allowed himself to be persuaded to make any demonstrative statement against the removal of the Jews. As the curtain falls, we hear the words: "So the gas chambers functioned for another full year. Not until the summer of 1944 did the so-called daily quota of murders reach its apex. On November 26 Himmler had the crematoria blown up. Two months later the last inmates in Auschwitz were liberated by Russian soldiers."

If we now ask what provoked the scandal, it is necessary to discriminate. Great secrecy surrounded the premiere in Berlin:[26] by mutual agreement with the publisher, the first edition of the text, in paperback, was not released until the morning following the premiere, and the actors signed a pledge not to share their texts with outsiders. Consequently, no one apart from those directly involved had any official familiarity with the play. Yet many viewers that evening in Berlin's Theater am Kurfürstendamm had some suspicion of what they might expect. It was widely known that, out of concern for its explosive content, the first publisher, Rütten and Loening Verlag in Hamburg, had destroyed the type when the work was already in proofs and released the manuscript to the more courageous Rowohlt Verlag. A publicity campaign in Catholic newspapers and the Catholic news service, which admittedly had no firsthand knowledge of the work, had stirred up rumors and speculations.

On the day of the premiere, the Berlin diocese circulated a tract protesting the play. The anticipation of disturbances prompted the management
of the theater to post announcements asking the audience to refrain from
comments during the performance; and two policemen were in evidence,
strolling around the lobby. In addition, since the play at full length would
have required almost eight hours to perform, every director had to cut
it drastically, omitting entire scenes and many characters. (The production in Berlin reduced the play from eleven to six scenes and abbreviated
even those six, eliminating such secondary characters as Eichmann.) As
a result, viewers in different theaters saw what amounted to entirely different plays, depending on the emphasis the director wanted to give. (The
Paris performance, for instance, based on a translation by Jorge Semprun,
was given a pronounced Marxist slant.)

The audience at the premiere in Berlin was remarkably restrained—in
no small measure because Piscator, despite his long-standing reputation
for active political engagement, had cut such provocative scenes as the
one showing the jovial brutality of the Nazi bigwigs, much of the invec-
tive against the Pope, and—in the Western zone of the divided city of
Berlin—the final statement attributing the liberation of Auschwitz to the
Russians. Apart from a lone whistle and a few boos during the papal scene,
"a stormy ovation" greeted the author and the director when they took
their curtain calls,[27] and the play ran for five more months.

This was not the case at all the openings. In Basel, which followed
the Berlin premiere, some 10,000 youthful demonstrators both pro and
con from such groups as Action Catholique and the Action of Young
Christians for Denominational Tolerance took part in silent torch proces-
sions; the director received phone calls cursing him both as a Nazi and as a
"*Judenschwein*" (Jew-pig); anonymous threats were made against the theater, the synagogue, and even the Masonic lodge; the actors were exhorted
to strike; and the authorities in the Catholic canton of Zug cancelled the
residence permit that Hochhuth had requested. On opening night, the
theater was protected by 150 policemen while twenty others in plainclothes mingled with the audience inside.[28] The production was suspended
after seventeen performances. In Paris, the small Théâtre de l'Athénée was
besieged night after sold-out night by protestors, who stormed the stage,
screamed in rage, hurled stink bombs, tomatoes, and eggs, and handed
out broadsheets, until the management finally posted thirty policeman in
the auditorium.[29] The New York opening at the Brooks Atkinson Theater
was picketed by the American Legion, the American Nazi Party, and
Catholic groups inspired by a statement in *The New York Herald Tribune*

by Cardinal Spellman, attacking the "slanderous and divisive drama," which admittedly he had not seen or read.[30] But the performance itself was apparently anticlimactic, "a German doctoral dissertation in verse,"[31] thanks in no small measure to the poor translation and adaptation by Herman Shumlin.[32] (Within its first decade the play was produced in twenty-six different countries.)

The immediate protests in various cities can be easily explained as an instinctive and often ignorant reaction against a work regarded as generally anti-Catholic and specifically an attack on the character of Pope Pius XII. But to understand the larger debate, especially but not only in Germany, it is useful to recall as well the state of society in the early 1960s before the turmoils sparked in France by the general strike of May 1968, in Germany by the protests against the Shah of Iran, and in the USA by Vietnam. The *Wirtschaftswunder* of the Adenauer-era closely paralleled the prosperity of the Eisenhower years—a time of relative stability before the escalation of the Cold War, when few people were troubled by the events of the Nazi years and World War II, despite indisputable evidence presented by such scholars as Poliakov and Wulf in *The Third Reich and the Jews*.

Hochhuth's play burst upon a theatrical scene dominated in Germany by the theater of the absurd, lyrical dramas, conversation pieces, and text-faithful performances of classic works.[33] It was essentially a literature that avoided the large questions of guilt and repression, written for a society that had still not come to terms with its Nazi past. This public, comfortable in the German *Wirtschaftswunder*, had never before been confronted so directly with the question of collective guilt or individual responsibility.[34] Even dramas with a political message tended to avoid the immediate present, preferring historical analogies or parables.

A few writers in Germany sought to rouse literary awareness of the Holocaust. But the allusions in Günter Grass's *Die Blechtrommel* (*The Tin Drum*, 1959) were qualified almost humorously by the grotesqueries of the novel. Paul Celan's powerful poem "Todesfuge" ("Death Fugue," 1952) remained metaphorical, sublimating the smoke from the crematorium at Auschwitz into "the black milk of dawn." And Max Frisch's play *Andorra* (1961) dealt with the persecution of the Jews indirectly in the form of a parable. Then, in 1961, the consciousness of Auschwitz and the Holocaust was thrust upon the public in excruciating detail by the Eichmann trial in Israel, which was widely reported all over the world. Hochhuth's play, with its historical appendix, was the first literary work in any country to deal directly and specifically with the persecution of the Jews and the Final Solution.

Here, in contrast to some of the earlier works we have considered, the aesthetic element played no role in the scandal. Certainly the weaknesses of the young author's first play were generally acknowledged and criticized—not to mention the inadequacies of most of the translations and stage adaptations, which detracted from its cumulative effect. The language was routinely called colorless; the length was excessive even by Schillerian or Wagnerian standards; the characters showed no development; the depiction of the Pope was regarded as too much of a caricature to be true; the hero was too much of a Schillerian idealist, motivated by what one critic accurately called a "pathos of the absolute";[35] the Doctor became too much an embodiment of pure evil with no human qualities, unlike the "banality of evil" attributed to Eichmann; and the speeches, including those of many minor characters, were often set pieces, exemplifying a general type, and not individualized. But these criticisms are largely beside the point because almost all the critics, apart from those predisposed by their faith from any objective view, agree that the play's weaknesses are more than outweighed by its moral force. As Lionel Abel observed, "It is precisely the play which has made people realize its subject is great."[36]

In a sense, moreover, the Catholic defenders of the Pope also miss the point. Hochhuth does not assign sole responsibility to Pius XII; indeed, the Pope appears in only a single scene. No later than the second scene of Act I it is made clear that the German military leaders, scientists, and industrialists such as the Krupp management, who exploited slave labor, were heinously guilty. Moreover, through such figures as the Papal Nuncio, the Cardinal, and the Father General, the author shows that the reluctance to see or to act was widespread in the Vatican and the Church. At the same time, the references to Father Kolbe, to Provost Lichtenberg, and to King Christian of Denmark, who threatened to wear a yellow star if the Jewish citizens of Denmark were so required, along with allusions to others, including the Father General, who resisted actively or passively by giving shelter to Jews—all these examples show that Riccardo did not represent an exception in his heroism.

In this larger context, the Pope emerges as a symbolic figure for Christendom as a whole and all those who failed to take any action when confronted with indubitable evidence of the Holocaust. Hence the subtitle of the play: "A Christian Tragedy."[37] Hochhuth quotes Hannah Arendt's *Eichmann in Jerusalem* to the effect that

in the center of a trial can only be the accused […] a person of flesh and blood with an individual story. […] Everything that goes beyond that, like for instance the history of the Jewish people in the Diaspora and antisemitism or the behavior of the German people and other peoples [...] enters the trial only to the extent that it provides the background and the circumstances under which the accused committed his deeds.[38]

Just as Eichmann in the utter banality of his person became for Arendt a symbol for the evils of the Holocaust, by analogy Hochhuth's Pope exemplifies by his position as the Vicar of Christ the failure to accept moral responsibility. "To me," he said in an interview,

Pius is a symbol, not only for all leaders, but for all men—Christians, Atheists, Jews. For all men who are passive when their brother is deported to death. Pius was at the top of the hierarchy and therefore had the greatest duty to speak. But every man—the Protestants, the Jews, Churchill, Eden, Cordell Hull, all had the duty to speak.[39]

This message has been understood by most non-partisan critics. "Yes, Pope Pius is a symbol," writes a professor of theology. "He symbolizes the truth that 'the way for evil to triumph is for good men to keep silent.' To accuse him is to accuse ourselves. Pius XII was not only God's 'deputy': he is our 'representative'—the representative of our inhumanity."[40]

The play may be regarded in the last analysis as a moral parable illustrating Hochhuth's belief in the freedom and hence the responsibility of the individual. The scandal compels us as thinking viewers or readers to consider the facts and circumstances and to come to our own conclusions about the justification for the Pope's decision. We may come to conclusions different from Hochhuth's, but our conclusion in itself is less important than the fact that we have been forced to make a moral decision. Moreover, the process once begun does not allow us to remain complacently with historical-literary examples. We are driven to review our own past decisions: have we always passed the test to act in cases that require a moral decision or have we decided, for reasons that seem utterly plausible and diplomatic, to abstain? In his Poetics lectures, Hochhuth cites Schiller on "The Theater Considered as a Moral Institution," arguing that the essay is not simply a historical document and out of date because it is 200 years old.[41] Only in the theater are the mighty of the world forced to confront truths that they otherwise seldom or never hear and see. Has anyone, he asks, seen a German chancellor or president or minister at the premiere of a daring play? No, he maintains; they prefer to go safely to performances of *Everyman*. "For premieres might show them something surprisingly new, possibly objectionable, contemporary. And in that case one would prefer not to be said to have attended."

THE WRECK OF THE MEDUSA
(HENZE'S DAS FLOSS DER MEDUSA)

It was not the excesses of *Regietheater* but an original composition that provided the instigation for the most notorious scandal of German musical history from the second half of the twentieth century: the disrupted premiere in 1968 of the oratorio *Das Floss der Medusa* (*The Raft of the Medusa*), composed by Hans Werner Henze to a libretto by Ernst Schnabel. Henze (1926–), regarded by many as the most important composer of his generation,[42] often collaborated with poets and writers for his libretti and oratorios: with W. H. Auden and Chester Callman (*Elegie für junge Liebende*, 1961; *Die Bassariden*, 1966), Ingeborg Bachmann (*Der junge Lord*, 1965), and Edward Bond (*We Come to the River*, 1976; *Die englische Katze*, 1983). So it is no surprise that he had long contemplated a joint project with his friend, the novelist and radio-documentary writer Ernst Schnabel.

Schnabel (1913–1986) left school at age seventeen without graduating, spent twelve years sailing the world in the merchant marines, and then served as an officer in the German Navy during World War II. His early novels were adventurous sea stories after the fashion of Joseph Conrad (*Die Reise nach Savannah* [*Journey to Savannah*], 1939; *Nachtwind* [*Nightwind*], 1947); later he wrote several widely admired modernizations of ancient mythological themes: notably Odysseus (*Der sechste Gesang*, referring to the sixth book of the Odyssey, 1956) and Daedalus (*Ich und die Könige* [*The Kings and I*], 1958). It was as a natural outgrowth of both these tendencies that he proposed to his composer-friend a work based on a historic sea-adventure that could be presented in such a manner as to expose its relevance for contemporary society and politics. The result was their "Oratorio volgare e militare" *Das Floss der Medusa* (1968). (The form of oratorio for this work was the obvious choice because, historically, the oratorio has a propagandistic function: created initially by the Church for the performance of religious texts in the *oratorio*, or prayer hall, it was later appropriated by such Protestant composers as Bach and Handel and then adapted in the twentieth century by such secular composers as Prokofiev and Shostakovich for eulogies to socialism.[43])

The incident, made famous by Théodor Géricault's vast painting *Le Radeau de la Medusa* (1818), took place in the summer of 1816, when a convoy of four French vessels set sail on June 17 from La Rochelle with the mission of reoccupying the territories of Senegal, which Napoleon had lost to the English.[44] On July 2, after almost two weeks of smooth sailing and only thirty hours from its destination, the flagship *Medusa*—thanks to the negligence of its inexperienced captain, a politically appointed Bourbon émigré, and its incompetent navigator—became stranded on a clear day on a reef marked distinctly on the charts. Since the frigate, having sped ahead of the convoy, was alone, for three days the crew strove in vain to free it from the sands. On the evening of the third day most of the passengers, consisting primarily of the new governor of Senegal with his staff and their families, along with the ship's captain and other officers, boarded the six seaworthy lifecraft and sailed to safety. Seventeen sailors chose to remain on board and subsequently perished. The remaining 154—including a few sailors and passengers (among whom was one woman), but mainly the colonial African battalions of impressed (and now disarmed!) blacks and Muslims along with a small handful of their officers—constructed a large raft (8 meters by 15 meters) with neither oars nor rudder and supplied with twenty-five pounds of biscuits, six kegs of wine, and two of water, on which they drifted for two weeks. On the first night several men were swept overboard; on the second day a band of drunken mutineers attacked their officers clustered by the mast, and many were killed. When the food and drink were consumed, they resorted to blood and urine for drink and devoured the flesh from corpses of the dead. As a result of further mutinies and suicides only about thirty men remained alive after the first week, of whom the ill were killed until only fifteen remained. On July 17 the brig *Argus*, sent out to search for the stranded vessel, appeared on the horizon and rescued fourteen survivors. The incident, regarded by French historians as the beginning of the fall of the Bourbons in France,[45] was subtly politicized by Géricault's painting, in which the figure at the apex of the pyramidal group signaling to the ship on the distant horizon is a mulatto, named Jean-Charles in the sources, waving a tattered piece of red cloth: oppressed humanity signaling for liberation through socialism.[46]

Schnabel and Henze agreed in advance on a dramaturgical scheme that would involve two soloists—Henze specified Dietrich Fischer-Dieskau and Edda Moser—along with a large chorus and orchestra.[47] It was their idea to divide the chorus into two sections separated by the orchestra and representing the realms of the living and the dead. Each realm is exemplified by a soloist: the mulatto Jean-Charles (baritone) for the living and Madame La Mort (soprano; a figure suggested by Cocteau's film *Orphée*) for the dead. At the beginning the entire chorus is grouped on the side of the living, but as they die they are ferried from one side to the other by Charon, until only the few survivors are left. Charon, who serves as narrator, speaks words taken directly from the survivors' accounts of the incident and covering the period from June 17, when the convoy set sail, to the survivors' rescue on July 17. When the chorus passes from the side of the living to that of the dead, it speaks the language of the underworld—that is, lines in the Italian original borrowed directly from Dante's *Divine Comedy*. For the choral sections Henze devised a polyphonic style indebted to Bach's *Passions* in an effort to suggest "the voices of people thrown together, voices that rose to a scream or died away to a murmur and to silence."[48] The only explicitly political statements of the work are voiced by Charon. In his prologue he calls the work "a story of betrayal and steadfastness [which] aroused mistrust of a regime and its favorites, who later fell from power."[49] His concluding words—"The survivors returned to the world, having learned a lesson from reality and eager to overthrow it"—are accompanied by timpani pounding out in a driving, crescendoing ostinato the unmistakable rhythms of the familiar chant "Ho! Ho! Ho-Chi-Minh!"[50]

What was the appeal of this notorious incident to Henze, who was commissioned by North German Radio to set Schnabel's text to music for a performance scheduled for the late fall of 1968? Following the popular success of the comic opera *Der junge Lord* in 1965 and the acclaimed premiere at the 1966 Salzburg Festival of *Die Bassariden* (an opera based on Euripides' tragedy *Bacchae*), Henze was at the peak of his artistic career, yet he was slighted by many music critics and fellow composers, such as Luigi Nono and Pierre Boulez, as an eclectic aesthete favoring an irrepressible lyricism, resolved dissonances, and a refusal to adhere to the current vogue of aleatory and serial composition in his effort to combine dodecaphony with traditional harmony. *Der junge Lord*, in particular, with its brilliant text by Bachmann and metrically steady *belcanto*, and with its references to Mozart's *Entführung aus dem Serail* (*Abduction from the Seraglio*), struck adherents of the New Music as reactionary: an updated *Rosenkavalier*. In the words of one of the nastier articles by a leftwing critic, Henze's music "reproduces the bourgeois music-ideal" and provides "an opiate of melodiousness [...] His raft drifts, like all Henziads, in the wake of the musical counterrevolution."[51]

Henze, coming to maturity during the Nazi years as an apolitical and introspective youth despite his dedicated Nazi father—a familial situation almost precisely opposite that of Hochhuth—was made aware at an early age of the inherently subversive potential of art through the Nazis' repression of modernism and "degenerate" art, which included such early passions of his as Stravinsky and Mahler.[52] Even after he had won his first early prizes, Henze felt increasingly that the music he wanted to compose was irreconcilable with the trends represented in Germany by such composers as Karlheinz Stockhausen and propagated by the International Society for New Music and the country's dominant cultural arbiters and critics—a situation precisely analogous to the simultaneous rejection of figurative and socially oriented painting by the heralds of abstract expressionism. His compositions displayed an emotional dimension that was unfashionable and lacking discordant outbursts of angst and despair. (Reading his autobiography one senses an almost masochistic satisfaction in Henze's frequent mentions of premieres of his music at which Nono, Boulez, Stockhausen, and others got up after a few bars and stalked conspicuously out.[53]) The need to be alone with his compositions motivated his emigration in 1953 to Italy, which—first near Naples and then outside Rome—has been his permanent residence ever since.

What I was trying to escape from was not so much postwar Germany as the musical avant-garde in Germany and/or avant-garde music in general. I needed to be on my own in order to live like a hermit and discover what music meant to me as an individual, how it is bound up with our lives, what it must mean to us and what is the cultural role that the composer fulfils within human society.[54]

During his early years in Italy, Henze's fame, as well as his commissions, grew steadily as he enjoyed success after success with his operas and symphonies. After some ten or twelve years, however, this highly introspective composer began to feel that the private world of idealizing wishes and dreams that he had constructed, as well as the increasingly private nature of his music, had isolated him from the "real" world and enmeshed him in raw emotion and self-contemplation.[55] As one critic unkindly put it in a frequently quoted epithet: "It isn't the case that one is rooted in tradition simply because one roots around in it."[56]

Observing Germany from his remote and rather unworldly retreat, the hitherto politically indifferent Henze was dismayed by developments in the Bonn Germany of the 1960s and impressed by the demonstrations of the young protesters seeking to change the world. Taking a more active interest in politics, he participated along with Günter Grass, Ingeborg Bachmann, and other figures from the world of culture, in Willi Brandt's 1965 election campaign. He studied such fashionable texts as Herbert Marcuse's *Eros and Civilization*, Frantz Fanon's *The Wretched of the Earth*, and the Communist Manifesto. In the early summer of 1967 he followed with intense interest the reports on the mass demonstrations against the Shah of Iran in Berlin, which resulted in the killing of the student Benno Ohnesorg by a policeman. Later that summer, while serving as composer in residence at Dartmouth College in the USA, he was impressed by the nonviolent student protests against the war in Vietnam. That fall, in Berlin, at the home of the poet Hans Magnus Enzensberger, he met a number of the young leaders of the SDS (Socialist German Students), including their charismatic spokesman, Rudi Dutschke, and was excited by their heady, idealistic—and endless—debates, sit-ins, go-ins, marches, and demos. In February 1968, with members of the APO (Außerparlamentarische Opposition or non-parliamentary opposition), he helped to organize an international Vietnam Conference in Berlin, over-whelmed in a spirit of solidarity by the marches and songs and speeches. In April he learned that his new friend Rudi Dutschke had been shot and ser-iously wounded in the head by a young reactionary. Following Dutschke's operations, Henze brought him secretly to his home in Italy for a lengthy convalescence. (In 1979, Dutschke died from the effects of the injuries to his brain.)

It was in this time-out-of-joint and in this mood, which combined pol-itical idealism unconstrained by experience or education or realism with a genuine sense of identification with outsiders rejected by the domin-ant bourgeois society, that Henze in late 1967 and the first half of 1968 composed the music for *Das Floss der Medusa* in which he now saw "the dramatic death throes and struggle for survival of a group of Third-World people after they have been abandoned to their fate [...] by representa-tives of a heartless and thoughtless ruling class."[57] That October, as he was reading Che Guevara's diaries in this new spirit of humanitarian and social commitment, he learned of Guevara's execution in Bolivia and began to identify the Latin American revolutionary hero with the banner-waving mulatto in Géricault's painting and with Jean-Charles, the hero of the oratorio he was composing. He and Schnabel decided to turn their work into an allegorical requiem for Che Guevara, to whom it is dedicated.

Up to this point, Henze's political activity had been largely peripheral and understated. All that changed two months before the premiere of *Das Floss der Medusa*. Henze had been commissioned to write his Second Piano Concerto for the opening, on September 29, of a new center for the arts in the Westphalian town of Bielefeld, a work performed by Christoph Eschenbach. When Henze learned that the sponsors intended to name the museum for a family member who had been active in the Nazi SS, he was asked by his friends on the left to make a statement about the embar-rassing situation. Henze responded with an article that received enormous publicity across Germany and from which one statement, in particu-lar, was widely reprinted. "We don't need museums, opera houses, and premieres ... What we need is the creation of humanity's greatest work of art: the World Revolution."[58]

This statement guaranteed a controversial reception for the premiere of *Das Floss der Medusa*. When Henze arrived in Hamburg for rehearsals of the oratorio, which he was to conduct, he was greeted by an anonymously written article in the weekly magazine *Der Spiegel* (published in Hamburg), in which he was ridiculed for paying lip-service to radical political causes while remaining conservative in his music. "For the composer Henze his revolution takes place only in the dedication" (to Che Guevara).[59] Meanwhile, the article continued with *ad hominem* aspersions, he lives in the lap of luxury with huge commissions paid for his compositions by the bourgeois society he pretends to despise. "Two souls reside in his breast—here APO, there Lucullus." (Rudi Dutschke wrote a long response in defense of his friend, attacking the "lies and half-truths of the *Spiegel*-machinery and the 'neo-liberal' component of the preservation-strategy of late capitalism," which was printed on the day of the premiere.[60]) During the rehearsals Henze was invited by a group from the Socialist Music Students of Hamburg who wanted to discuss music and politics. "All I remember—and my memory is still as vivid as though it were yesterday—is the aggression and malice with which I found myself faced."[61] Henze, who up to this point had enjoyed good relations with members of the SDS, was perplexed by the hostile reception of the young musicians, who disparaged his politics as well as his music. A friendly member of the SDS warned Schnabel that the *Spiegel* piece had been taken by many students as a call to disrupt the premiere.[62] Asked by journalists how he intended to react to possible tumult at the coming performance, he invited friends from the Berlin SDS to the premiere to counteract the hostile Hamburg students and to persuade them not to interfere. Schnabel later heard that the aggressive critic from *Spiegel*, only two hours beforehand, had personally instigated the Hamburg SDS to sabotage the performance.[63]

It was against this background that the premiere of the oratorio was to take place on December 9, 1968. The venue was the vast multipurpose Hall B, the so-called Blue Hall, in the Hamburg park known in North German dialect as Planten un Blomen (Plants and Flowers), where a large concert platform had been erected (and where the final rehearsal was recorded).[64] The hall was packed with students, including members of the SDS from Berlin and Hamburg; such celebrities as Georg Solti, Peter Ustinov, Paul Dessau, Rolf Liebermann, and Ernst Schnabel; and plainclothed policemen, who had been forewarned of possible demonstrations.

Those entering the hall were handed copies of a manifesto by the Socialist Music Students declaring that any potential political content of the work would be nullified since the work was being performed as a "ritual concert" before a bourgeois audience; it demanded a musical life not controlled by the State—one in which the authoritarian structure of the traditional orchestra would be broken up.

As Henze waited backstage with Edda Moser, Dietrich Fischer-Dieskau, and the actor Charles Regnier as Charon, he could not see what was happening in the auditorium, where there was much activity.[65] Shortly before starting time, a student went up and hung a poster of Che Guevara from the rostrum, which an official immediately tore down. Other students—a "team of anarchists," according to the *Spiegel* report—went up with another portrait of Che, a red flag, North Korea's black flag, and banners reading "Revolutionary?" and "Expropriate the Culture-Industry." Then the conductor and soloists came out on stage although Henze was warned by a representative of North German Radio that he would be held responsible for the consequences if he did not remove the red flag. When Henze raised his baton, the famed RIAS Chamber Choir, brought from West Berlin for the occasion, began to chant: "Take down the flag, take down the flag." (Berlin was at that time still a divided city with fierce loyalties in both east and west, and RIAS was the US-sponsored Radio In the American Sector.) At that point Henze and the soloists left the stage again, followed by the chorus, who also led off the children from the Hamburg Boy's Choir of St. Nicolai. Backstage, Henze became engaged in a heated discussion with the men and women of the chorus, who said that they could not appear on stage with the same red flag that fluttered from the Brandenburg Gate in Communist East Berlin. Fischer-Dieskau reproached Henze for involving him in the controversy, but Edda Moser hugged him in solidarity.

In the hall outside, meanwhile, officials from North German Radio were scuffling with the students in an attempt to remove the offending objects, while Ernst Schnabel and Charles Regnier tried to calm the students. Suddenly some thirty riot police in white helmets, who had been stationed nearby, marched down the corridors and arrested the student demonstrators, along with Schnabel, who was injured in the fray. (They were driven off and jailed for a few hours in Hamburg's police headquarters.) When order had been restored, Henze came back on stage, which the orchestra had also deserted, protested the police intervention, which had made the performance or any discussion impossible, and joined some members of the audience in a chant of "Ho! Ho! Ho-Chi-Minh!"

As the audience filed out, students from the Berlin SDS's Project Group for "Culture and Revolution" handed out another manifesto, stating that "this concert should have taken place before an audience of workers [...] But in the future Henze will write revolutionary music and see to it that those for whom it is written can also hear and understand it."[66]

Henze had long ruminated intensively about the role of music in contemporary society. How was it possible, he now speculated, "to reconcile modern art—this product of the bourgeoisie—with the Socialist Revolution and whether, within the new context, such art might simply cease to be bourgeois of its own inevitable accord."[67] The immediate result was a more angular and less lyrical music incorporating radical political ideas, such as *El Cimarrón* (*The Runaway Slave*, 1970), his recital for baritone, and four instruments celebrating the Cuban national hero. In the later 1970s, however, he returned to more traditional forms in his string quartets and symphonies.

Henze had entertained the genuinely idealistic, if somewhat naive hope of transforming the bourgeois public through his socialist message, but he failed in his attempt to use the stage as a moral institution in Schiller's sense—and not only because the premiere failed to take place. The audience for *Das Floss der Medusa* was offended for a variety of reasons, but not for the reasons the composer had hoped. Some arrived with traditional expectations and were shocked by Henze's exploitation of music to advance political views. The more radical members of SDS were dismayed by the conservatism of his politics and by the bourgeois venue for the performance of what was supposed to be a revolutionary work. Others held advanced theories of the New Music and were affronted by Henze's more traditional aesthetics.

The scandal was widely reported in the German press; Schnabel mentions (and quotes from) 102 different accounts, including a predictably hostile review in *Der Spiegel*, which labeled the work—on the basis of the piano score and the recording of the dress rehearsal, which was broadcast instead of the interrupted live performance—a "tragicomic absurdity," in which the raft floated in "an ocean of sentimental, but all too expansive, lyrically colored monotony."[68] Andrew Porter more perceptively called it "a humanist tragedy, and classical in form."[69] Henze reacted with philosophical calm to the scandal, consoling himself with the thought that "it was now the height of fashion to boo our spiritual fathers" and citing from that same era Daniel Cohn-Bendit's public attack on Herbert Marcuse, Theodor W. Adorno's humiliations during lectures at the universities in Frankfurt and Berlin, and the interruption of a concert by Pierre Boulez in Berlin's Philharmonie, when a member of the Red Guard took the stage and recited from Mao's Red Book.[70]

Das Floss der Medusa finally had its radio premiere on January 29, 1971, in Vienna's ORF (the Austrian national radio station) and its stage premiere on April 15, 1972, in Nuremberg. Although it only gradually made its way into the international concert repertory, it has by now been accepted into the canon of twentieth-century classics, albeit hardly as a successful example of the theater as a moral institution.

CHAPTER 7

Conclusion

Readers who have followed my account to this point will surely recall other theatrical scandals that might have been included. Dublin's Abbey Theatre witnessed two of the most tumultuous happenings in Irish stage history: in 1907 the "Playboy Riots" aroused by the week-long stand of J. M. Synge's *The Playboy of the Western World;* and twenty years later the mobbing of the stage by spectators protesting against Sean O'Casey's *The Plough and the Stars* (1926).[1] At the 1923 Paris premiere of Tristan Tzara's Dadaist play *Le Coeur à gaz* (*The Gas Heart,* 1920), a brief hoax featuring six actors representing the mouth, the eye, the ear, and other parts of the human head, the author's friend Paul Eluard engaged in a fist fight on stage with André Breton, advocate of the new surrealist theater.[2] Following the 1926 premiere of Béla Bartók's musical pantomime *Der wunderbare Mandarin* (*The Miraculous Mandarin*) in Rhine-Catholic Cologne, the spectators who had not already stalked out in disapproval greeted the composer and conductor with such a chorus of hisses, whistles, and cries of "Pfui!" that then-mayor Konrad Adenauer summoned the General Manager of the opera company to his office and angrily demanded that the piece, dealing with three tramps and a prostitute, be removed from the schedule.[3] Dmitri Shostakovich's erotically suggestive opera *Lady Macbeth of Mzensk* (1930), based on Nikolai Leskov's novella, enjoyed remarkably successful premieres in Leningrad and Moscow in 1934 followed by two years of popularity. Then on January 26, 1936, Stalin accompanied by his chief officials attended a performance; two days later *Pravda* printed a damning review entitled "Chaos Instead of Music," whereupon all further performances were cancelled and the critics outdid themselves in revising their initially favorable opinions. As one of the less frequent postwar examples we might consider a late work of Thomas Bernhard, whose career had generated several earlier theater scandals. His last play *Heldenplatz* (1988), a depiction of lingering postwar Austrian anti-Semitism (written, not coincidentally, at the urging of Claus Peymann, the German director of Vienna's Burgtheater), was preceded by weeks of acrimonious public debate, seasoned at the last moment by a pile of horse manure dumped at the Burgtheater's entrance by rightwing activists. This publicity led to the posting of 200 policemen around the theater on the evening of the premiere, which in the event was interrupted by nothing more violent than a few catcalls.[4]

I have chosen not to consider that corpus of works, beginning around 1910 with Marinetti's Futurist *serate*, which were produced not so much as plays meant to provoke moral reflection as, rather, happenings intended to overthrow all conventional notions of theater. Marinetti organized claques to ensure that an uproar would accompany his spectacles, even when the audience was prepared goodnaturedly to accept them. Their nontheatrical nature is suggested by the fact that they were often moved out of theaters into such public locales as municipal buildings, galleries, clubs, and banquet halls.[5] Similarly, the various events presented in the years following 1916 at Zurich's renowned Café Voltaire and other venues of Dadaism in Berlin and Paris were not dramas but performance art, including poetry readings, musical entertainments, painting displays, and fashion shows. The 1935 production of Antonin Artaud's *Les Cenci*, a play teeming with rape, incest, and patricide and intended to illustrate Artaud's theory of "the theater of cruelty," derived from his admired Jarry, did not arouse the scandal the author had longed for but encountered instead an uncomprehending lack of interest. When Peter Handke's play *Publikumsbeschimpfung* (*Offending the Public*, 1966) amused audiences rather than enraging them, the chagrined author eventually prohibited further performances. The entire century of "director's theater" extending from Marinetti's *serate* to Hans Neuenfels's stagings in Berlin suggests that the directors, with their often conscious effort to shock and scandalize, often manage to irritate, dismay, disappoint, and anger their audiences but rarely succeed in stimulating them to the serious contemplation of moral, intellectual, or social issues.

Why is this the case? All too often and typically directors strive to achieve their effects by updating familiar material with modern sets, contemporary costumes or nude actors, and by imposing their own views, political, religious, or other, on well-known works and the audience, amusing those who have come in order to be titillated or to have their own views substantiated and annoying those with other expectations but hardly provoking anyone to serious reconsideration of their values. A current star of German stage, film, and television informed an interviewer that "in the theater the text is not at all primary. Theater is a *Gesamtkunstwerk* [total work of art] of all possible things."[6] She went on to defend a production in which Shakespeare's elves were portrayed by fat, hairy, naked men, arguing that "it was not Shakespeare, but Max Reinhardt who introduced romanticism into *A Midsummer Night's Dream* and made a fairy tale of it." By way of contrast, a young dramatist cited in 1908 by Thomas Mann told him that the rehearsals for his first play had been a painful experience. "In the hands of the director his work had become a textbook for something foreign, different, for something that had not yet been present."[7] More recently, the jury of the Mühlheimer Theatertage awarded a prize to a young writer's play but not to its production by the Bavarian State Theater, reasoning that it was "unsuitable for the text."[8] The indignant director spoke of "indirect censorship" and maintained loftily that "the director is an interpreter, hence an artist. It is his responsibility to give a new text a premiere performance according to his own ideas. This sovereignty ["Hoheit"] must be preserved."[9] In recent decades directors have often set out with the conscious and explicit will to be shocking: hence the decapitated heads that Neuenfels introduced into Mozart's opera. His device, though displaying appallingly bad taste, shocked no one. The scandal arose for a different reason: the controversy over the freedom of art when the performance was cancelled out of fear of anticipated (but unrealized) Muslim objections.

When the theater functions as a moral institution, it is the work of the creators, not of the directors. Directors are gratified when their productions shock the spectators; the creators, from Schiller by way of Hauptmann to Henze, have often been surprised and dismayed at the reaction, as was Stravinsky at the audience's hostile response to the music he had created with love and passion. Writers and composers have not customarily set out primarily to shock: the scandal is a secondary and often unanticipated side effect of a work whose primary purpose is to embody the creators' innovative conception of their art. As Thomas Mann's composer Adrian Leverkühn remarks: "In my opinion it suffices fully if a work is heard *one time*, namely, when the composer conceived it."[10] Romain Rolland's composer-hero Jean-Christophe shares this sentiment when he shuts himself in his room to write, not caring whether the people of Paris hear him or not. "He wrote for his own pleasure and not for success."[11] Schiller, realizing that the "public" for his works still lay in the future, wrote with his youthful friends in Stuttgart in mind. Hugo, Hauptmann, and Jarry were thinking primarily of their coteries of Jeunes-France, Gegenwart, and Décadence. Schnitzler was so certain that his work would not be accepted by the "public" that he refused for over twenty years to permit its performance and then, after the scandal and trial, denied permission for decades more. As we have seen, the premiere has not always produced in audiences scandalized by superficialities the moral effect advocated by Schiller and sought by many of his successors.

The artists' attitude is understandable if we look back at the two centuries and ten works that we have surveyed—no catalogue but a representative sampling—because the creators of works that evoke scandals on stage are usually young beginners, not experienced theater people. Schiller, Hugo, Hauptmann, and Jarry were all in their twenties when their plays—in each case their first performed work—premiered. Stravinsky, Brecht, Weill, and Hochhuth were all in their early thirties and not yet advanced in their careers. Schnitzler was thirty-four when he wrote *Reigen*, only his third play (which, however, was not produced until he was close to sixty). The forty-two-year-old Henze could be said to have been enjoying a second youth when he composed *Das Floss der Medusa*, closely associated as he was with the young men and women of the German student radicals. Strauss, at forty-five, is the old man of the group.

But if these youthful creators did not usually set out to scandalize their audiences, they did hope in Schiller's large understanding of the word to stimulate thoughtful questioning of existing "moral" conventions. Schiller belonged to the literary tradition inherited by most of the writers represented here. As Thomas Mann remarked in 1929, "the German has his conception of theater from [Schiller], a conception that is seriously distinguished from that of all other peoples."[12] The drama critic Otto Brahm explicitly compared the difficulty the young Schiller encountered in establishing himself, despite the popular success of *Die Räuber*, to the situation of Gerhart Hauptmann and his fellow Naturalists around 1890.[13] Schiller's plays as performed by the Meiningen ensemble belonged to Hauptmann's earliest and unforgettable dramatic experiences. Brecht's "epic theater" was explicitly designed to cause the audience to think and make decisions in a manner wholly at one with Schiller's model. Hochhuth referred specifically to Schiller's essay in his own theoretical remarks and, like Schiller's categorization of *Die Räuber*, called his plays "dramatic novels."[14] But Schiller's influence was not restricted to the German writers. Hugo, as we saw, paid frequent tribute to Schiller, who also belonged to the canon with which the voluminously read Jarry was familiar. The German-born composers Strauss and Henze were of course educated in that same tradition, and even artists unfamiliar with Schiller have often shared his goals. Stravinsky, who may not have read Schiller, created music and a scenario that challenged in a Schillerian manner the accepted views of his audiences, both aesthetic and ethical-religious.

Significant artistic success and advances depend extensively on what has been called a balance between recognition and irritation, between fulfillment and shattering of the horizon of expectations ("*Horizonterfüllung und Horizontdurchbrechung*").[15] This condition presupposes accepted aesthetic standards and a steady state of moral expectations in the theater, which, as we saw in Chapter 1, is by history and tradition a conservative institution. If the artist merely fulfills the expectations of the audience and critics, the result is entertainment after the fashion of boulevard theater—or today's Broadway productions—whereby drama, music, and ideas are not normally advanced. If, on the other hand, the expectations are too scandalously shattered, the initial result is often incomprehension; the progress achieved by the work is sometimes realized only years or decades later. As Otto Brahm put it in 1891, "the new literature is revolutionary; the theater is conservative—that is the decisive point for our problem."[16]

In every case our scandals on stage were generated by a conflict between the old and the new, between convention and the innovations of *Sturm und Drang*, *Jeune-France*, Naturalism, Décadence, non-Wagnerian opera, primitivism in music and theme, "epic" theater, documentary drama, and leftist radicalism in a lyrical form at odds with the reigning New Music. It was this conflict that in each case precipitated the scandal and forced audiences, sooner or later, to rethink and adjust their expectations to accommodate a new "horizon" that succeeding generations were able to take for granted. As Proust shrewdly remarks,

it was Beethoven's quartets themselves that devoted half a century to forming, fashioning, and enlarging the audience for Beethoven's quartets, thus marking, like every great work of art, an advance if not in the quality of artists at least in the community of minds, largely composed to-day of what was not to be found when the work first appeared, that is to say people capable of appreciating it.[17]

Because of these shifting horizons, Hugo was able to address a public of which Schiller had only dreamed. After World War II, Henze could be accused slightingly of composing after the fashion of Strauss, whose once-shocking harmonic innovations were now fashionable. Schiller, Hugo, Hauptmann, Jarry, Schnitzler, Brecht/Weill, Hochhuth, and Schnabel/Henze challenged the sociopolitical convictions of contemporary spectators and exposed their underlying flaws: the absolutism of eighteenth-century monarchy; the illiberal policies of royalism; the exploitation of workers in the *Gründerzeit* coupled with its rampant alcoholism; the underlying bestiality of fin-de-siècle bourgeois society; the sexual hypocrisy of that same era; the destructive capitalism of the West *entre deux guerres;* the denial of responsibility for the Holocaust in postwar Germany; and the lack of social conscience in the 1960s. Strauss, Stravinsky, and Hochhuth added religion to the already heady brew: a re-visioning of the New Testament in very human emotional terms; an exploration of primitive elements in the religious experience; and the hypocrisy of any religion that fails to speak up against the inhumanity of mankind. The differing reactions of different premiere audiences—for instance, to *Salome* or to *The Deputy*—highlighted in several cases the varying circumstances, whether political or social or religious, from city to city and from country to country.

In many cases, at the same time, the creators were also challenging the aesthetic standards of their time in a manner so radical that it often distracted the audience's attention from the moral message. Schiller, Hugo, and Jarry presumed to make brigands the heroes of their dramas and to permit them to speak in a language that offended contemporary standards of taste. Hauptmann introduced onto the stage a hitherto-unknown realism that took for granted, often in an earthy dialect, normal all-too-human impulses, including sexuality and childbirth. Strauss's lush orchestration created harmonies that pushed a Western musical tradition extending from Bach to the present into new dimensions; Stravinsky introduced the rhythms of a primitive culture into that same tradition; and Weill broadened it with the sounds and effects of jazz. With their "epic" devices, Jarry, Stravinsky, Brecht, and Hochhuth fashioned a theater that did not allow the spectators to enter into an Aristotelean complicity of pity and fear but forced them through a process of alienation to acknowledge within themselves unwelcome aspects of their common humanity and their societies.

Although our list of representative scandals extends from the late eighteenth to the late twentieth century, the incidents are conspicuously concentrated in France and Germany of the period from roughly 1890 until World War II.[18] Schiller and Hugo represent tentative overtures to the situation we have explored. Hochhuth and Henze/Schnabel are equally isolated postludes. Why should this be the case? As I argued in the Introduction, scandal on stage could take place only when a new public began to replace the authoritarian audiences of royalty and the elite who previously controlled the theater and its offerings. Both Schiller and Hugo, as we saw, came to grips with that issue in their respective critiques of absolutism and royalism. Schiller dreamed of a new public consciousness that might be helped into realization through the theater as a moral institution; Hugo spoke explicitly of the new public that was emerging in 1830. But it was only in the second half of the nineteenth century that this new public finally dominated the theater, replacing the former aristocratic demands with their bourgeois expectations. At that point, writers like Hauptmann and Jarry, and composers like Strauss and Stravinsky, emerged to challenge the assumptions and criteria of the new bourgeois establishment, just as Schiller and Hugo had questioned those of the earlier controlling elites. In the now more liberal, and commercialized, theatrical atmosphere preceding World War I they catalyzed with increasing frequency the "scandals" of their works.

During the decades between the two world wars the situation changed as the extreme nationalisms of the totalitarianism that had arisen in Italy, Germany, and Russia sought to dominate aesthetic standards as repressively as had the former monarchies. As a result we find new forms of resistance: not just the response of a bourgeoisie when its hypocrisy regarding alcoholism, sexuality, and brutality was exposed but now also the bitter anti-Semitism that greeted Schnitzler's play and Weill's opera, the hostility of the Nazis to Brecht's Marxism, and the hypocritical moralism with which Shostakovich's opera was rebuked by the spokesmen of Stalinism. In all these cases the dominant society was unified by its acceptance of the prevailing social mores, whether *Gründerzeit, Belle Époque*, Nazi, or Communist. These norms provided horizons of expectations challenged by the artists' visions. The predictable results of this friction were the scandals we observed.

The principle is borne out by the fact that the most conspicuous theatrical scandals in postwar Europe occurred in Germany, where for specific historical reasons the general public was unified to a degree unknown in most other countries. Germans of those years, enjoying the prosperity of their *Wirtschaftswunder*, were largely united by an unwillingness to confront their responsibility for the Holocaust, a past that Hochhuth for the first time forced them to acknowledge. The same problem of *Vergangenheitsbewältigung* did not exist, or at least not to the same degree, in other countries.[19] Similarly, the radicalism of the 1960s reached in the German RAF (Red Army Faction) extremes of violence rarely encountered elsewhere outside Italy. Henze's apparent complicity in that radicalism represented a threat to a society unified in its opposition to it, while his compositions stirred the contempt of a contemporary musical coterie enraptured with its own New Music.

At this point, the question thrusts itself upon us: is scandal on stage still possible in a Western society where Jarry's *mot de Cambronne* is one of the milder expletives worn on T-shirts and heard not just on the streets and in classrooms but on radio, television, internet blogs, and in film?

As I write these lines, a US federal appeals panel has just struck down a policy allowing the Federal Communications Commission to fine stations and networks for broadcasting shows that contain occasional expletives, on the grounds that the Government cannot punish broadcast stations for permitting words occasionally blurted out by various celebrities as well as the President and Vice President.[20] Can aesthetic scandal—that is, the outcry arising from the conflict between the old and the new, tradition and innovation—be aroused in a society that celebrates, according to the title of a well-known book by art critic Harold Rosenberg, *The Tradition of the New* (1959)? Where the walls of banks and boardrooms boast works of "corporate Modernism"?[21] Is scandal even theoretically conceivable in a society that has largely lost touch with the past? Where students graduate from high school and college having read less and less "literature" and often little or nothing written before their own birthdates? Where the youth of the twenty-first century relegates the Beatles and Bob Dylan to ancient history while the average age of concertgoers and operagoers steadily rises? How can there be "moral" scandal where artists and performers since the 1960s have outdone themselves to "provoke" and "offend" and "disturb" a public already inured to shock? Where audiences since the heyday of Mort Sahl flock each evening to clubs or tune in every morning to radio stations with the confidence that all accepted values—or at least those that they do not share—will be flouted and reviled in the filthiest possible terms? Indeed, it might well be argued that, in a multicultural age of competing value systems, the response to provocation is more often approbation than shock.

If scandal is no longer feasible or possible on our Western stages, can theater still function as a site for moral trial? In his 1986 talk on "The Theater as a Moral Institution Today," the Swiss dramatist Friedrich Dürrenmatt maintained that "the attempt to arouse protest with present-day art is becoming more and more difficult," arguing paradoxically that theater has become so free that it must "create its own non-freedom, if it still wishes to fight for its freedom."[22] This has come about, he believes, because in our increasingly interlinked world with its exploding populations the former smaller governments and personalized rulers have turned into "institutionally legitimated and functioning apparatuses, states, that are subject to no morality but only to laws" and that permit freedom only where it does no harm: in the cultural realm.[23] The social contract that Schiller envisaged—that the State maintain the theater financially in return for the theater's moral-ethical-political support for the State—is no longer valid because the State no longer pays any attention to the theater.

The public in Europe and the USA has become so diverse—politically, religiously, socially, and otherwise—that hardly any gathering outside denominational churches, synagogues, and mosques or political-party assemblies can claim any sort of coherent "moral" unity. Certainly not the theatergoing public! And if there are no longer any shared "moral" expectations, can the theater hope to challenge or change them? The logical if depressing conclusion arising from these ruminations is that Schiller's grand conception, which arose in response to a specific historical situation in the late eighteenth century and survived, explicitly or implicitly, through 200 years of Western culture, has itself been deflated into a quaint historical notion lacking validity and urgency. Should the idea of theater as a moral institution now be relegated to history along with the classical conception of theater as a communal celebration of shared beliefs? Theaters have become either museal repositories of the tried and tested canon or, like the *faux scandale* of *Idomeneo*, venues of frustrated directorial aggression. That is today's true scandal on stage.

Notes

PREFACE

1 Susan Bennett, *Theatre Audiences: A Theory of Production and Reception* (London: Routledge, 1990), p. vii.
2 Daphna Ben Chaim, *Distance in the Theatre: The Aesthetics of Audience Response* (Ann Arbor, Mich.: UMI Research Press, 1984).
3 James H. Johnson, *Listening in Paris: A Cultural History* (Berkeley, Calif.: University of California Press, 1995).
4 Neil Blackadder, *Performing Opposition: Modern Theater and the Scandalized Audience* (Westport, Conn.: Praeger, 2003).
5 Anya Peterson Royce, *Anthropology of the Performing Arts: Artistry, Virtuosity, and Interpretation in a Cross-Cultural Perspective* (Walnut Creek, Calif.: AltaMira, 2004).
6 Thomas Zabka and Adolf Dresen, *Dichter und Regisseure: Bemerkungen über das Regie-Theater* (Göttingen: Wallstein, 1995); Jürgen Schläder (ed.) *Oper-MachtTheaterBilder: Neue Wirklichkeiten des Regiethetaters* (Leipzig: Henschel, 2006); Johanna Dombois and Richard Klein, "Das lied der unreinen gattung: zum Regietheater in der oper," *Merkur*, 61 (2007), pp. 928–937.
7 Thomas Zabka, "Das wilde Leben der Werke," in Thomas Zabka and Adolf Dresen, *Dichter und Regisseure: Bemerkungen über das Regie-Theater* (Göttingen: Wallstein, 1995), pp. 9–57, here p. 10.

I INTRODUCTION

1 The incident was reported widely in the international press. See *The New York Times* front-page coverage on September 27 as well as follow-up pieces on September 28 (A10) and October 1 ("The Week in Review," p. 3).
2 For a lively account of the incident, reactions to it, and the often far-fetched appeasement moves in various European countries during the following months see Henryk Broder, *Hurra, wir kapitulieren! Von der Lust am Einknicken* (Berlin: WJS, 2006).
3 In the *Iliad* and *Odyssey* Idomeneus is mentioned several times in his capacity as a great warrior who brought his fleet of eighty ships safely home again. Virgil refers to Idomeneus at various points (*Aeneid* 3.121, 400; 11.264) but reports only

that he has left Crete and moved to the Sallentine Plains of Calabria, without giving any reasons. It was left to his commentator to fill in the blanks.

4 Georg Thilo and Hermann Hagen (eds), *Servii Grammatici qui feruntur in Vergilii carmina commentarii*, vol. I (Leipzig: Teubner, 1881), p. 365.

5 See the account of the performance in Maynard Solomon, *Mozart* (London: Hutchinson, 1995), pp. 229–237.

6 *The New York Times*, December 19, 2006, A5.

7 *The New York Times*, September 27, 2006, A8.

8 Quoted in *The New York Times*, October 1, 2006.

9 For summaries of world opinion see *Die Welt*, October 2, 2006; and *Die Zeit*, October 5, 2006, p. 49.

10 See the report in *The New York Times*, October 28, 2006, A10.

11 Der Spiegel Online, October 3, 2006.

12 Quoted in *Focus*, November 20, 2006, p. 70.

13 *Tagesspiegel*, November 14, 2006, p. 21; *Focus*, November 13, 2006, p. 13. That same year saw theatrical disturbances for religious reasons elsewhere in the world: in Saudi Arabia Islamic extremists stormed the stage during a performance, at a college in Riyadh, of a play critical of religious conservatives, and a brawl ensued as the police fired shots into the air (*The New York Times*, November 29, 2006, E1); and in the north Russian city of Syktyvkar a performance of Shostakovich's *Tale of the Priest and of His Workman Balda* (based on a story by Pushkin) by the State Theater of Opera and Ballet of the Republic of Komi was scaled back to a series of numbers from the opera, omitting all scenes portraying a greedy priest that offended the local clergy (*The New York Times*, October 5, 2006, E2).

14 See, for instance, the report in Faz.net, December 18, 2006.

15 Quoted in Der Spiegel Online, September 30, 2006.

16 The winning essays by Thomas Zabka and Adolf Dresen, representing positions respectively pro and con, were published under the title *Dichter und Regisseure: Bemerkungen über das Regie-Theater* (Göttingen: Wallstein, 1995).

17 Quoted in *Newsweek*, October 23, 2006, p. 27.

18 See Braque, *Illustrated Notebooks*, p. 10.

19 Quoted in Der Tagesspiegel Online, October 3, 2006.

20 Susan Sontag, *Against Interpretation and Other Essays* (New York: Noonday, 1966), pp. 8, 27.

21 I take the next four quotations in this paragraph from Michael G. Kammen, *Visual Shock: A History of Art Controversies in American Culture* (New York: Knopf, 2006), p. xxiii.

22 Quoted in Hans Haacke, "Museums, managers of consciousness," in *Hans Haacke: Unfinished Business*, ed. by Brian Wallis (Cambridge, Mass.: MIT Press, 1986), p. 8.

23 Quoted in Don Hawthorne, "Does the public want public sculpture?," *ARTNews*, 81 (May 1982), p. 61.

24 *Los Angeles Times*, October 21, 1990, Calendar sec., pp. 3–4.

25 Arthur C. Danto, *Encounters and Reflections: Art in the Historical Present* (New York: Farrar, 1990), p. 274.

26 See http://provocation.curtin.edu.au/11.html.

27 Theodore Ziolkowski, *German Romanticism and its Institutions* (Princeton, NJ: Princeton University Press, 1990), pp. 321–329.

28 The anthropologist Hans Peter Duerr, as quoted in Der Spiegel Online, September 30, 2006.

29 See René Wellek and Austin Warren, *Theory of Literature* (New York: Harcourt, 1956), pp. 17–26 ("The Function of Literature").

30 G. W. F. Hegel, *Werke*, ed. by Eva Moldenhauer and Karl Markus Michel, 21 vols. (Frankfurt: Suhrkamp, 1970), vol. XIII, pp. 20–21.

31 René Wellek, *A History of Modern Criticism 1750–1950*, 7 vols. (New Haven, Conn.: Yale University Press, 1955–1991), vol. III, p. xiv.

32 Edgar Allan Poe, *Complete Works* (New York: Putnam, 1900), 10 vols., vol. I, pp. 164–197, here p. 171.

33 See Wellek, *History of Modern Criticism*, vol. IV, p. 463.

34 Thomas Mann, *Gesammelte Werke in zwölf Bänden* (Frankfurt: Fischer, 1960), 12 vols., vol. VI, p. 384.

35 Kammen, *Visual Shock*, p. 181.

36 Siegfried Matthus, "Die Kunst ist nie frei gewesen," *Berliner Morgenpost*, October 1, 2006.

37 *The Poems of Samuel Johnson*, ed. David Nichol Smith and Edward L. McAdam, 2nd edn. (New York: Oxford University Press, 1974), p. 109. I am indebted for the quotation to Blackadder, *Performing Opposition*, p. 4.

38 Mann, "Rede über das Theater" (1929), in his *Gesammelte Werke*, vol. X, pp. 282–298, here p. 298.

39 Heinrich Detering, "Kunstreligion und Künstlerkult: Bemerkungen zu einem Konflikt von Schleiermacher bis zur Moderne," in *Schleiermacher-Tag 2005. Eine Vortragsreihe*, ed. by Günter Meckenstock, *Nachrichten der Akademie der Wissenschaften zu Göttingen, I. Philologisch-Historische Klasse 2006*, Nr. 4 (Göttingen: Vandenhoeck & Ruprecht, 2006), pp. 179–200, p. 180.

40 Ludwig Marcuse, *Obszön: Geschichte einer Entrüstung* (Munich: List, 1962), p. 210.

41 See Elizabeth Gilmore Holt (ed.), *The Triumph of Art for the Public: The Emerging Role of Exhibitions and Critics, 1785–1848* (Garden City, NY: Anchor Doubleday, 1979), p. 6.

42 Lawrence Kramer, *The New York Times*, June 3, 2007, sec. 2 (Arts & Leisure), p. 29.

43 Quoted in *Der Spiegel*, December 2, 1968, p. 182.

44 Walter Panofsky, *Protest in der Oper: Das provokative Musiktheater der zwanziger Jahre* (Munich: Laokoon, 1966), p. 8.

45 Kammen, *Visual Shock*, pp. 287–304.

46 See Jens Malte Fischer, "Oper wohin?," *Merkur*, 60 (2006), 1067–1072.

47 Der Tagesspiegel Online, October 5, 2006.

48 I refer to the controversies generated by the performance art of Karen Finley, by Chris Ofili's *The Holy Virgin* (1996), by André Serrano's *Piss Christ* (1989), and by the ninety cans of Piero Manzoni's *Artist's Shit* (1961).

49 Kammen, *Visual Shock*, p. 355.

50 David A. Lawton, *Blasphemy* (Hemel Hampstead: Harvester Wheatsheaf, 1993), p. 202.

51 Niklas Luhmann, *The Reality of the Mass Media*, trans. by Kathleen Cross (Cambridge: Polity, 2000), pp. 29–32.

52 Claudia Dürr and Tasos Zembylas, "Konfliktherde und Streithähne: Grenzzonen und Strategien im Literaturbetrieb," in Stefan Neuhaus and Johann Holzner (eds), *Literatur als Skandal: Fälle—Funktionen—Folgen* (Göttingen: Vandenhoeck & Ruprecht, 2007), pp. 75–88, here p. 76.

53 Blackadder, *Performing Opposition*, p. x, applies the term more narrowly "to the incident itself—to the clash between a performance … and a group of spectators protesting against that performance."

54 "The Futurist Cinema," in Filippo Tommaso Marinetti, *Selected Writings*, ed. R. W. Flint (London: Secker, 1972), p. 130. See Günter Berghaus, *Theatre, Performance, and the Historical Avant-garde* (New York: Palgrave Macmillan, 2005), p. 96.

55 Alan Sinfield, "The theater and its audience," in Alan Sinfield (ed.), *Society and Literature 1945–1970* (London: Holmes, 1983), pp. 173–197; p.181.

56 On the difference in reactions between the reading public and the theater audience in the light of reception theory see Marvin Carlson, "Theater audiences and the reading of performances," in Thomas Postlewait and Bruce A. McConadrie (eds), *Interpreting the Theatrical Past: Essays in the Historiography of Performance* (Iowa City, Iowa: University of Iowa Press, 1989), pp. 82–98.

57 Thomas Forrest Kelly, *First Nights: Five Musical Premieres* (New Haven, Conn.: Yale University Press, 2000), p. xii.

58 Blackadder, *Performing Opposition*, pp. x–xi.

59 Jürgen Habermas, *Strukturwandel der Öffentlichkeit: Untersuchungen zu einer Kategorie der bürgerlichen Gesellschaft* (Frankfurt: Suhrkamp, 1990), p. 116. Kierkegaard, to be sure, had a less charitable view of what he called that "monstrous abstraction," which can develop "only in a passionless but reflective age"—that is, his own post-revolutionary society—with the aid of the press. Kierkegaard disparages the very reason and "reflection" praised by Habermas, arguing that envy becomes the "negatively unifying principle in a passionless and very reflective age." "Only when there is no strong communal life [as in antiquity or ages unified by revolutionary passion] to give substance to the concretion will the press create this abstraction 'the public,' made up of unsubstantial individuals who are never united or never can be united in the simultaneity of any situation or organization and yet are claimed to be a whole." See Søren Kierkegaard, *Two Ages: The Age of Revolution and the Present Age, A Literary Review* (1846), ed. and trans. by Howard V. Hong and Edna H. Hong (Princeton, NJ: Princeton University Press, 1978), p. 81 and 90–91.

60 Editors' preface in Stefan Neuhaus and Johann Holzner (eds.), *Literatur als Skandal: Fälle—Funktionen—Folgen* (Göttingen: Vandenhoeck & Ruprecht, 2007), p. 12.

61 Habermas, *Strukturwandel*, p. 64.

62 Blackadder, *Performing Opposition*, p. 1–8.

63 Blackadder, *Performing Opposition*, p. 11–12. See also James H. Johnson, *Listening in Paris: A Cultural History* (Berkeley, Calif.: University of California Press, 1995) for the analogy in musical performances.

64 Philipp Ther, *In der Mitte der Gesellschaft: Operntheater in Zentraleuropa 1815–1914* (Vienna: Oldenbourg, 2006), pp. 55–60.

65 Hochhuth, "Räuber-Rede," in his *Räuber-Rede: Drei deutsche Vorwürfe—Schiller, Lessing, Geschwister Scholl* (Reinbek bei Hamburg: Rowohlt, 1982), pp. 7–103, here pp. 45 and 33. See Chapter 2 below.

66 Reinhart Koselleck, *Kritik und Krise: Ein Beitrag zur Pathogenese der bürgerlichen Welt* (Freiburg: Alber, 1954), pp. 81–87.

67 I cite the text from Friedrich Schiller's *Sämtliche Werke*, ed. by Gerhart Fricke and Herbert G. Göpfert, 5 vols. (Munich: Hanser, 1967), vol. V, pp. 818–831, here p. 819.

68 The lecture was originally called "Vom Wirken der Schaubühne auf das Volk" ("On the Effect of the Theater on the Public"). Schiller subsequently published it in 1785 under the title "Was kann eine gute stehende Schaubühne eigentlich wirken?" ("What Effect Can a Good Permanent Theater Actually Achieve?"). When he later included it in his shorter prose works he gave it the now familiar title. On the essay, its genesis, and its influence see Carsten Zelle's discussion in Matthias Luserke-Jacqui (ed.), *Schiller-Handbuch* (Stuttgart: Metzler, 2005), pp. 343–357.

69 Johann Christoph Adelung, *Grammatisch-kritisches Wörterbuch der Hochdeutschen Mundart*, 2nd edn., 4 vols. (Leipzig: Breitkopf, 1793–1801), vol. III, p. 280.

70 Friedrich Schiller, "Was kann eine gut stehende Schaubuehne eigentlich wirken?" *Samtliche Werke*, vol. V, pp. 818–31, here p. 823.

71 Schiller, "Was kann eine gut stehende Schaubuehne eigentlich wirken?" p. 823.

72 Schiller, "Was kann eine gut stehende Schaubuehne eigentlich wirken?" p. 826.

73 Schiller, "Was kann eine gut stehende Schaubuehne eigentlich wirken?" p. 827.

74 Schiller, "Was kann eine gut stehende Schaubuehne eigentlich wirken?" p. 828.

75 Schiller, "Was kann eine gut stehende Schaubuehne eigentlich wirken?" p. 830.

76 Schiller, "Was kann eine gut stehende Schaubuehne eigentlich wirken?" p. 830.

77 Schiller, "Was kann eine gut stehende Schaubuehne eigentlich wirken?" p. 831.

78 Schiller, "Was kann eine gut stehende Schaubuehne eigentlich wirken?" p. 831.

79 This point is often misunderstood. The literary historian Ludwig Marcuse (in *Obszön*, pp. 246–259), for instance, without mentioning Schiller's essay, objects at length to any "moral" function of art; but he identifies morality narrowly with the injunctions of religion.

80 Mann, "Versuch über das Theater" (1908), in his *Gesammelte Werke*, vol. X, pp. 23–62, here pp. 45–50. Mann cites the German Kaiser as remarking that, "as the university is the continuation of the gymnasium, so for us the theater is the continuation of the university"—a wholly Schillerian sentiment.

2 OVERTURES

1 On the background to Schiller's play see Gert Sautermeister, "Die Räuber: Ein Schauspiel," in Matthias Luserke-Jacqui (ed.), *Schiller-Handbuch* (Stuttgart: Metzler, 2005), pp. 1–45; and Lesley Sharpe, *Friedrich Schiller: Drama, Thought and Politics* (Cambridge: Cambridge University Press, 1991), pp. 6–30. The play has been discussed extensively in the vast secondary literature on Schiller.

2 See Schiller's self-review of *Die Räuber* in the *Wirtembergisches Repertorium 1* (1782); in Friedrich Schiller, *Sämtliche Werke*, ed. by Gerhart Fricke and Herbert G. Göpfert, 5 vols. (Munich: Hanser, 1967), vol. I, pp. 619–635, here p. 624.

3 See Sautermeister, "Die Räuber," pp. 6–8.

4 In his preface to the first edition, in *Sämtliche Werke*, vol. I, p. 487.

5 Schiller, *Sämtliche Werke*, vol. I, p. 488.

6 This phenomenon has been widely studied since Wolfgang Riedel, *Die Anthropologie des jungen Schiller: Zur Ideengeschichte der medizinischen Schriften und der "Philosophischen Briefe"* (Würzburg: Königshausen & Neumann, 1985).

7 In the suppressed preface to the first edition; *Sämtliche Werke*, vol. I, p. 482.

8 In his preface to the first edition; *Sämtliche Werke*, vol. I, p. 484.

9 Christian Friedrich Timme in the *Erfurtische Gelehrte Zeitung*, July 24, 1781; rpt. in Friedrich Schiller, *Die Räuber: Texte und Zeugnisse zur Entstehungs und Wirkungsgeschichte*, ed. by Herbert Kraft and Harald Steinhagen (Frankfurt: Insel, 1967), pp. 67–77, here p. 68.

10 On the repertoire of the court theater in Stuttgart and Ludwigsburg see Jean-Jacques Alcandre, *Écriture dramatique et pratique scénique: Le "Brigands" sur la scène allemande des XVIIIe et XIXe siècles*, 2 vols. (Berne: Lang, 1986), vol. I, pp. 110–123.

11 Alcandre, *Écriture dramatique et pratique scénique*, vol. I, pp. 150–160.

12 Herbert Stubenrauch and Günter Schulz (eds.), *Schillers Räuber: Urtext des Mannheimer Soufflierbuches* (Mannheim: Bibliographisches Institut, 1959). The changes from scene to scene are conveniently itemized in Alcandre, *Écriture dramatique*, vol. I, pp. 161–166. Essentially the same text, albeit with the restoration of a few scenes (e.g., Karl once again kills Amalia), was published by Schiller in 1782 under the title *Die Räuber: Ein Trauerspiel* in order to distinguish it from the earlier *Schauspiel*. Today most interpretations are based on the original *Schauspiel* of 1781.

13 Otto Schmidt, "Die Uraufführung der 'Räuber'—ein theatergeschichtliches Ereignis," in *Mannheimer Soufflierbuch* (as in note 12), pp. 151–180, here p. 151.

14 As reported by Schiller's friend Jakob Friedrich Abel; in Bodo Lecke, *Dichter über ihre Dichtungen: Friedrich Schiller von den Anfängen bis 1795* (Munich: Heimeran, 1969), p. 137. The volume reprints (pp. 84–160) most of the relevant contemporary documents.

15 "Avertissement zur ersten Aufführung der Räuber," in Lecke, *Dichter über ihre Dichtungen: Friedrich Schiller*, pp. 104–105; also in Schiller, *Sämtliche Werke*, I, p. 489.

16 "Avertissement zur ersten Aufführung der Räuber," pp. 104–105.

17 See the account in Streicher's later book on Schiller's flight from Württemberg to Mannheim (1836); rpt. in its entirely in Max Hecker (ed.), *Schillers Persönlichkeit: Urtheile der Zeitgenossen und Documente*, 3 vols. (Weimar: Gesellschaft der Bibliophilen, 1904), vol. I, pp. 191–192. Streicher, who did not in fact attend the performance, based his account on Schiller's own report of the event.

18 Reported in Anton Pichler, *Chronik des Großherzoglichen Hof und National-theaters in Mannheim* (Mannheim, 1879), pp. 67–68; reproduced in Schiller, *Die Räuber: Texte und Zeugnisse*, pp. 77–78, and in most books on Schiller.

19 Quoted in Gertrud Rudloff-Hille, *Schiller auf der Bühne seiner Zeit* (Berlin: Aufbau, 1969), pp. 20–21.

20 The anonymous review is now attributed to Adolf Freiherr von Knigge, *Allgemeine Deutsche Bibliothek* 49/1 (1782), p. 127; rpt. in Norbert Oellers (ed.), *Schiller: Zeitgenosse aller Epochen: Dokumente zur Wirkungsgeschichte*, 3 vols. (Frankfurt: Athenäum, 1970), vol. I, p. 57.

21 On the "Mannheim style" in general and Iffland's acting in particular see Schmidt, "Die Uraufführung"; and Alcandre, *Écriture dramatique*, pp. 183–232.

22 Schiller, *Die Räuber: Texte und Zeugnisse*, p. 77.

23 See the full documentation in Jean-Marc Civardi (ed.), *La Querelle du Cid (1637–1638)* (Paris: Champion, 2004).

24 Augustin Simon Irailh, *Querelles littéraires, ou Mémoires pour servir à l' Histoire des Révolutions de la République des Lettres, depuis Homere jusqu' à nos jours* (Paris: Durand, 1761), pp. 334–348, here p. 335.

25 Irailh, *Querelles littéraires*, p. 347, as in the case of Racine's Athalie.

26 See the detailed account by Robert Jouanny in his edition of *Oeuvres com-plètes de Molière*, 2 vols. (Paris: Garnier, 1962), vol. I, pp. 621–628, as well as Molière's own account in his preface to the 1669 edition (vol. I, pp. 628–632).

27 For a list of performances from 1782 to 1785 see Alcandre, *Écriture dramatique*, pp. 242–245.

28 Bertolt Brecht, "Schillers Räuber im Stadttheater," in his *Gesammelte Werke in 20 Bänden* (Frankfurt: Suhrkamp, 1970), vol. XV, pp. 21–23.

29 Brecht, "Zur Gewerkschaftsvorstellung am Mittwoch," November 16, 1920; in *Gesammelte Werke*, vol. XV, pp. 27–28.

30 On performances of the play since 1959 see Sautermeister, "Die Räuber," in *Schiller-Handbuch*, pp. 17–20.

31 Rolf Hochhuth, "Räuber-Rede," in *Räuber-Rede*, pp. 7–103, here p. 96. Hochhuth is no doubt referring to the wave of books and articles that accom-panied the 200th anniversary of Schiller's birth in 1959.

32 Hochhuth, "Räuber-Rede," p. 102.

33 Hochhuth, "Räuber-Rede," p. 102.

34 Hochhuth, "Räuber-Rede," p. 102.

35 Théophile Gautier, *Victor Hugo* (Paris: Charpentier, 1902), pp. 13, 33.

36 Jean-Marc Hovasse, *Victor Hugo, vol. I: Avant l'exil (1802–1851)* (Paris: Fayard, 2001), p. 795.

37 *Cromwell* (1827), though its famous preface became a manifesto of French Romanticism, was much too long and ungainly to be performed; *Amy Robsart* (written in 1822), was so weak that Hugo refused to acknowledge his authorship when it was staged in 1828 in a glaring failure; *Marion de Lorme* (1829), was prohibited for lèse-majesté by the censor.

38 Victor Hugo, "Sur M. Dovalle," in his *Oeuvres complètes*, XII, pp. 173–176, here p. 173.

39 I take the phrase from Pierre Halbwachs, "A propos de la 'Bataille d'Hernani,'" in *Romantisme et politique*, pp. 99–109, here 100.

40 Victor Hugo, "Préface de Cromwell," in *Oeuvres complètes*, ed. by Jean-Pierre Reyaud, 14 vols. (Paris: Laffont, 1985), vol. XII, pp. 1–44, esp. pp. 16–30.

41 Adèle Hugo, *Victor Hugo raconté par Adèle Hugo: texte intégral*, ed. by Evelyne Blewer (Paris: Plon, 1985), pp. 456–477, here p. 459.

42 The quotations in this paragraph and below are taken from Gautier's *Victor Hugo*, pp. 4, 8, 27, 5, 10. Essentially the same text appears in Gautier's *Histoire du romantisme*, pp. 77–98.

43 Gautier, *Victor Hugo*, p. 36.

44 Gautier, *Victor Hugo*, p. 43.

45 Danielle Molinari, *Voir des étoiles: Le Théâtre de Victor Hugo mis en scène*, Catalogue of an exhibition at the Maison de Victor Hugo, April 12–July 28, 2002 (Paris: Paris-Musées, 2002), pp. 144–145.

46 Hugo, *Victor Hugo*, p. 461.

47 Hugo, *Victor Hugo*, p. 464.

48 Gautier, *Victor Hugo*, p. 49.

49 Gautier, *Victor Hugo*, p. 49.

50 Here, unless otherwise indicated, I follow Adèle Hugo's description, pp. 464–467.

51 Gautier, *Victor Hugo*, pp. 43–44.

52 Hugo, *Victor Hugo*, p. 465.

53 Hugo, *Victor Hugo*, p. 465.

54 Hugo, *Victor Hugo*, p. 467.

55 Here I follow Hugo, *Victor Hugo*, pp. 467–477.

56 Hugo, *Victor Hugo*, p. 470.

57 On March 2, 1830, 221 liberal deputies sent an appeal to the King demanding the resignation of the ultraroyalist ministers.

58 Polignac had become the symbol for the unpopularity of the regime.

59 Victor Hugo, *Victor Hugo: Hernani*, ed. by Anne Ubersfeld (Paris: Librairie Générale Française, 1987), pp. 9–14; here p. 10. The first half of the preface actually amounts to an extended quotation from his review "Sur M. Dovalle," written only a few weeks earlier.

60 Hugo, "Preface," p. 10.

61 Hugo, "Preface," p. 10.

62 Hugo, "Preface," p. 10.

63 Hugo, "Preface," p. 11.

64 Hugo, "Preface," p. 11.

65 Hugo, "Preface," p. 12.

66 Hugo, "Preface," p. 12.

67 Letter of November 18, 1830, in Carl Carl and Margaretha Carl, *"Kann man also Honoriger seyn als ich es bin?" Briefe des Theaterdirektors Carl Carl und seiner Frau Margaretha Carl an Charlotte Birch-Pfeiffer*, ed. by Birgit Pargner and W. Edgar Yates, Quodlibet, 6 (Vienna: Lehner, 2004), pp. 54–55. I am indebted for this reference to one of the anonymous readers of my manuscript.

68 Halbwachs, "A propos," p. 108.

69 Gautier, *Victor Hugo*, pp. 44–48. For an analysis of the purely poetic/lyrical aspects of the work as "a part of a poet's consciousness" see Charles Affron, *A Stage for Poets: Studies in the Theatre of Hugo and Musset* (Princeton, NJ: Princeton University Press, 1971), pp. 21–61, here p. 22.

70 Quoted in Ubersfeld's edition of Hernani, pp. 202–203.

3 SCANNING THE SURFACE

1 Richard Hamann and Jost Hermand, *Gründerzeit* (Berlin: Akademie, 1965).

2 Hamann and Hermand, *Gründerzeit*. See also Marvin Carlson, *The German Stage in the Nineteenth Century* (Metuchen, NJ: Scarecrow, 1972), esp. pp. 203–226.

3 On the Freie Bühne, see Roy C. Cowen, *Naturalismus: Kommentar zu einer Epoche* (Munich: Winkler, 1973), pp. 68–97; and Peter Sprengel, *Gerhart Hauptmann: Epoche—Werk—Wirkung* (Munich: Beck, 1984), pp. 48–54.

4 Otto Brahm, "Zum Beginn," in his *Theater—Dramatiker—Schauspieler*, ed. by Hugo Fetting (Berlin: Henschel, 1961), p. 30.

5 Otto Brahm, "Freie Bühne," in his *Theater—Dramatiker—Schauspieler*, ed. by Hugo Fetting (Berlin: Henschel, 1961), p. 32.

6 Otto Brahm, "Zur Eröffnung der Freien Bühne," in his *Theater—Dramatiker—Schauspieler*, ed. by Hugo Fetting (Berlin: Henschel, 1961), p. 27.

7 See Wolfgang Leppmann, *Gerhart Hauptmann: Leben, Werk und Zeit* (Berne: Scherz, 1986); also Bernhard Zeller (ed.), *Gerhart Hauptmann: Leben und Werk*, Catalogue for the Memorial Exhibition at the Deutsches Literatur-Archiv of the Schiller-Nationalmuseum Marbach, May–October 1962 (Stuttgart 1962) and especially Hauptmann's own autobiography, *Das Abenteuer meiner Jugend*, in *Die großen Beichten* (Berlin: Propyläen, 1966), pp. 7–638.

8 Diary notice of December 18, 1897; in his *Die Kunst des Dramas: Über Schauspiel und Theater*, ed. by Martin Machatzke (Frankfurt Ullstein, 1963), pp. 196–197; here p. 196.

9 Diary notice of December 18, 1897, p. 196.

10 In Hauptmann, *Notiz-Kalender 1889 bis 1891*, ed. by Martin Machatzke (Vienna: Propyläen, 1982), p. 291 (November 1890).

11 See Peter Sprengel, *Gerhart Hauptmann: Epoche—Werk—Wirkung* (Munich: Beck, 1984), pp. 36–37, 54–56.

12 Theodore Ziolkowski, *Fictional Transfigurations of Jesus* (Princeton, NJ: Princeton University Press, 1972), pp. 99–110.

13 W. A. Coupe, "An ambiguous hero: in defense of Alfred Loth," *German Life and Letters*, 31 (1977/78): pp. 13–22.

14 For analyses and bibliographies of the play, which has been extensively discussed in the secondary literature, see Sprengel, *Gerhart Hauptmann*, pp. 65–74; Cowen, *Naturalismus*, pp. 156–163; and Cowen, *Hauptmann-Kommentar zum dramatischen Werk* (Munich: Winkler, 1980), pp. 35–44.

15 To be sure, a stylized Viennese dialect was featured in Ludwig Anzengruber's *The Fourth Commandment* (Das Vierte Gebot, 1877), which had earlier been performed on Austrian stages and arrived at the Freie Bühne only two weeks after *Vor Sonnenaufgang*. I am indebted for this reminder to one of the readers of my manuscript.

16 Letter of June 7, 1889; in *Notiz-Kalender*, p. 90.

17 Letter of August 19, 1889; in *Notiz-Kalender*, pp. 153–156, here p. 154.

18 Letter of September 3, 1889; in *Notiz-Kalender*, pp. 164–167, here p. 165. The *Notiz-Kalender* contains other letters of praise from Hauptmann's friends and colleagues. See Felix Voigt, "Die Aufnahme von 'Vor Sonnenaufgang' in Hauptmanns Freundes und Bekanntenkreis," in his *Hauptmann-Studien: Untersuchungen über Leben und Schaffen Gerhart Hauptmanns*, vol. I: 1880 bis 1900 (Breslau: Maruschke, 1936), pp. 63–80.

19 Gerhart Hauptmann, "Vor Sonnenaufgang: Fragment" (1889), in his *Die Kunst des Dramas: Über Schauspiel und Theater*, ed. by Martin Machatzke (Frankfurt: Ullstein, 1963), pp. 93–95. The criticism of both has continued down to the recent past, when some postwar German scholars have even called Loth a forerunner of Nazi eugenic policies.

20 Letter of September 8, 1889, to Paul Ackermann; in *Notiz-Kalender*, pp. 169–170.

21 Letter of September 10, 1889; in *Notiz-Kalender*, p. 171.

22 Letter of October 19, 1889; in *Notiz-Kalender*, pp. 183–184.

23 Letter of October 19, 1889; in *Notiz-Kalender*, pp. 183–184.

24 From Paul Lindau's autobiography *Nur Erinnerungen* (Stuttgart, 1917), vol. II, p. 33; quoted in the editor's postscript to *Notiz-Kalender*, p. 473.

25 Paul Schlenther, *Wozu der Lärm? Genesis der Freien Bühne* (Berlin: Fischer, 1889), p. 23.

26 Gerhart Hauptmann, *Das zweite Vierteljahrhundert* (ch. 1); in his *Die großen Beichten* (Berlin: Propyläen, 1966), pp. 642–643.

27 Otto Brahm, "Theater-Kalender auf das Jahr 1911," in his *Theater—Dramatiker—Schauspieler*, ed. by Hugo Fetting (Berlin: Henschel, 1961), p. 35.

28 I follow the firsthand account by Paul Schlenther, one of the founding members of Freie Bühne, in his Gerhart Hauptmann: *Sein Lebensgang und seine Dichtung* (Berlin: Fischer, 1898), pp. 81, 100–101.

29 On Kastan, who was taken to court by the Freie Bühne when he refused to accept expulsion from his subscription membership for his behavior, see Blackadder, *Performing Opposition*, pp. 27–32.

30 Blackadder, *Performing Opposition*, p. 101.

31 *Berliner Tageblatt*, October 21, 1889; in Zeller, *Gerhart Hauptmann*, p. 56.

32 *Vossische Zeitung*, October 20, 1889; in Theodor Fontane, *Aufsätze, Kritiken, Erinnerungen*, part 3, vol. 2 of *Sämtliche Werke*, ed. by Walter Keitel (Munich: Hanser, 1962), pp. 817–822, here p. 821.

33 Hermann Bahr, "In Erwartung Hauptmanns," in his *Mit Gerhart Hauptmann: Erinnerungen und Bekenntnisse aus seinem Freundeskreis*, ed. by Walter Heynen (Berlin: Stilke, 1922), pp. 34–68; here p. 67.

34 Fontane, *Aufsätze*, p. 824.

35 Walter Requardt, *Gerhart Hauptmann Bibliographie: Eine Zusammenstellung der von und über Gerhart Hauptmann im In und Auslande erschienenen Werke*, 3 vols. (Berlin: Selbstverlag, 1931), vol. III, pp. 445–448, lists many reviews with a generous selection of quotations. See also Zeller, *Gerhart Hauptmann*, pp. 52–61.

36 Brahm, *Theater—Dramatiker—Schauspieler*, p. 35.

37 "Die 'Freie Bühne.' Ein Nekrolog von Conrad Alberti," *Die Gesellschaft*, 6 (August 1890): pp. 1104–1112, here pp. 1110–1111.

38 "Die 'Freie Bühne,'" p. 1111.

39 "Die 'Freie Bühne,'" p. 1111.

40 Walter Requardt, *Gerhart Hauptmann Bibliographie: Eine Zusammenstellung der von und über Gerhart Hauptmann im In und Auslande erschienenen Werke*, 3 vols. (Berlin: Selbstverlag, 1931), vol. III, p. 445.

41 Requardt, *Bibliographie*, vol. III, p. 445.

42 Requardt, *Bibliographie*, vol. III, p. 446.

43 Requardt, *Bibliographie*, vol. III, p. 446.

44 Requardt, *Bibliographie*, vol. III, p. 447.

45 Requardt, *Bibliographie*, vol. III, p. 448.

46 According to Hauptmann's account in his 1912 talk "Kunst und Jugend"; in Zeller, *Gerhart Hauptmann*, p. 68.

47 *Notiz-Kalender*, pp. 405–406.

48 *Notiz-Kalender*, p. 198.

49 *Notiz-Kalender*, pp. 409–410.

50 Alfred Kerr, "Der Ahnherr" (1896), in his *Gesammelte Schriften*, 7 vols. (Berlin: Fischer, 1917–1920), vol. I, pp. 46–68, here p. 67. Kerr goes on to distinguish between Ibsen's plays and those written by his younger German contemporaries: namely, a looser, more narrative technique; and bodies rather than thoughts.

51 See Roy C. Cowen, *Naturalismus: Kommentar zu einer Epoche* (Munich: Winkler, 1973), p. 8 and passim.

52 Arthur Symons, "A Symbolist Farce," in his *Studies in Seven Arts* (London: Constable, 1906), pp. 371–377, here p. 373.

53 I take the details from Paul Chauveau, *Alfred Jarry, ou la naissance, la vie et la mort du Père Ubu* (Paris: Mercure de France, 1932), p. 77.

54 Alfred Jarry, "Discours de Alfred Jarry," in his *Tout Ubu*, ed. Maurice Saillet (Paris: Le Livre de Poche, 1962), pp. 19–21. This edition contains the text of all

the "Ubu" plays as well as the various accompanying comments. Essentially the same material is available in the more recent *Ubu: Publiés sur les textes définitifs*, ed. by Noël Arnaud and Henri Bordillon (Paris: Gallimard, 1978).

55 Jarry, *Tout Ubu*, pp. 22–24.

56 Letter of August 1, 1896, to Lugné-Poe; in Jarry, *Tout Ubu*, p. 135.

57 For biographical information I have relied on a variety of sources: the early biographies by "Rachilde" (pseud. of Marguérite Vallette) and Chauveau; Roger Shattuck, "Alfred Jarry, 1873–1907," in his *The Banquet Years: The Arts in France 1885–1918* (New York: Harcourt, 1958); Keith Beaumont, *Alfred Jarry: A Critical and Biographical Study* (New York: St. Martin's, 1984); and Noël Arnaud, *Alfred Jarry d'Ubu Roi au Docteur Faustroll* (Paris: La Table Ronde, 1974), who provides an almost day-by-day account of the year 1896.

58 Shattuck, *The Banquet Years*, p. 154.

59 For the present purposes the question of Jarry's originality or even plagiarism ("l'Affaire Ubu"), which was heatedly debated following Jarry's rediscovery in the 1920s is irrelevant. See Charles Chassé, *Sous le masque d'Alfred Jarry (?): Les Sources d'Ubu Roi* (Paris: Floury, 1921) and Beaumont, *Ubu Roi*, pp. 12–14.

60 Jarry wrote three more Ubu plays: *Ubu Cocu, Ubu enchaîné*, and *Ubu sur la Butte;* but Ubu Roi marked the apogee of Jarry's literary career.

61 Rachilde, *Alfred Jarry*, p. 80.

62 Letter of January 8, 1896, to Lugné-Poe; in Jarry, *Tout Ubu*, p. 133.

63 Detailed analyses of the play are provided, among others, by Judith Cooper, *Ubu Roi: An Analytical Study*, Tulane Studies in Romance Languages and Literatures, 6 (New Orleans, 1974), and Beaumont, *Ubu Roi*.

64 Rachilde, *Alfred Jarry*, p. 70. I refer in the following description to the premiere. The dress rehearsal before an invited audience on the preceding evening appears to have taken place fairly peacefully with only minor disturbances during the third act. See Blackadder, *Performing Opposition*, pp. 41–68, for a detailed analysis of the audience and its reaction.

65 "The Guermantes Way"; in Marcel Proust, *Remembrance of Things Past*, trans. by C. K. Scott Moncrieff and Terence Kilmartin, 2 vols. (New York: Random House, 1981), vol. II, p. 496.

66 Rachilde, *Alfred Jarry*, p. 78.

67 Günter Berghaus, *Theatre, Performance, and the Historical Avant-garde* (New York: Palgrave Macmillan, 2005), pp. 1–45. See also Chauveau, *Alfred Jarry*, p. 76; and Beaumont, *Alfred Jarry*, pp. 85–88.

68 Chauveau, *Alfred Jarry*, p. 82. For a thorough analysis of the play's names, neologisms, and slang along with its vulgarisms, see Cooper, *Ubu Roi*, pp. 75–104; and Beaumont, *Ubu Roi*, pp. 46–54. Blackadder, *Performing Opposition*, pp. 46–50, 58–62, 66–67, also includes perceptive comments on "merdre."

69 Romain Coolus in *Revue Blanche* (January 1, 1897); in Henri Robillot, "La Presse d'Ubu Roi," *Cahiers du Collège de 'Pataphysique*, 3–4 (1950): pp. 73–88; here p. 74. Robillot's collection reprints many contemporary reviews of the premiere.

70 These phrases occur in the text as cited in Jarry, *Tout Ubu*, pp. 39, 82, 94, 115, 86, 92, 96, respectively.
71 Here I follow Rachilde, *Alfred Jarry*, pp. 80–81; here p. 80.
72 Rachilde, *Alfred Jarry*, p. 81.
73 Chauveau, *Alfred Jarry*, pp. 82–83.
74 Rachilde, *Alfred Jarry*, p. 81.
75 Sarcisque Francey, *Temps*, December 14, 1896; in Robillot, "La Presse," p. 75.
76 I base the following generalizations on the reviews reproduced in Robillot, "La Presse."
77 Camille Mauclair, *Revue Encyclopédique*, p. 172; Robillot, "La Presse," p. 80.
78 A respected (but unnamed) critic cited by Henry Fouquier in *Le Figaro*, December 11, 1896; Robillot, "La Presse," p. 80.
79 Louis Claveau, *Le Soleil*, December 11, 1896; Robillot, "La Presse," p. 75.
80 Robillot, "La Presse," p. 76.
81 Robillot, "La Presse," pp. 76–77.
82 Robillot, "La Presse," p. 78.
83 Robillot, "La Presse," pp. 78–79.
84 Robillot, "La Presse," p. 81.
85 W. B. Yeats, *Autobiographies* (New York: Macmillan, 1938), p. 297.
86 I assume that Cyril Connolly had tongue in cheek when he called Ubu "an epitome of the common man struggling for decency in the world we live in" and "the Santa Claus of the Atomic Age." See his *Ideas and Places* (London: Weidenfeld & Nicolson, 1953), pp. 38–39.
87 Symons, *Studies in Seven Arts*, pp. 371, 375.
88 Cooper, *Ubu Roi*, p. 105.
89 Beaumont, *Ubu Roi*, pp. 46, 57.
90 Catulle Mendès, "Ubu Roi: Comédie guignolesque," *Journal*, December 11, 1896; in his *L'Art au théâtre*, 3 vols. (Paris: Fasquelle, 1897–1900), vol. II, pp. 438–440.
91 Mendès, "Ubu Roi," p. 440.
92 Mendès, "Ubu Roi," p. 439.
93 Letter of October 27, 1896; in Stephane Mallarmé, *Correspondance*, ed. by Henri Modor and Lloyd James Austin, 11 vols. (Paris: Gallimard, 1959–1985), vol. VIII, pp. 255–256.
94 *Revue Blanche*, January 1, 1897; in Robillot, "La Presse," 74.
95 Louis Dumur, "Théâtre," *Mercure de France*, September 1896, pp. 544–545.
96 *Mercure de France*, January 1897, p. 219.
97 Pulcinella and Polichinelle, Punch and Karageuz are, respectively, Italian, French, English, and Turkish figures from guignol theater, Punch and Judy shows, and shadow plays; Mayeux is the caricatured personification of the bourgeois created after the Revolution of 1830 and Joseph Prudhomme the type of complacent petty-bourgeois banality; Robert Macaire was a popular literary figure used by Daumier as the typical swindler and Adolphe Thiers the president of the Republic after 1871; Torquemada was the notorious Inquisitor General; and Edouard Vaillant the renowned socialist and revolutionary of 1871.

98 Quoted in François Caradec, *À la recherche de Alfred Jarry* (Paris: Seghers, 1974), p. 68. Nicolas Chauvin was a soldier of the Republic and Empire, whose name became the term for a fanatical patriotism (chauvinism).

99 Quoted by Beaumont, *Alfred Jarry*, p. 102.

100 Alfred Jarry, "Les Paralipomènes d'Ubu," in his *Tout Ubu*, pp. 165–175, here p. 165.

101 I am indebted for this insight to Beaumont, *Alfred Jarry*, p. 107.

102 Alfred Jarry, "Questions de Théâtre," in his *Tout Ubu*, pp. 152–155, here p. 153. Marie Leprince de Beaumont (1711–1780) was renowned for her edifying fairy tales, the best known of which is "Beauty and the Beast." The critic who has best understood that Jarry's play is "the projection of a moral vision" is Beaumont, *Ubu Roi*, pp. 45, 87.

103 Rachilde, *Alfred Jarry*, p. 79.

104 George Wellwarth, *The Theater of Protest and Paradox: Developments in the Avant-Garde Drama* (New York: University Press, 1964), pp. 1–14.

105 Rachilde, *Alfred Jarry*, p. 88.

106 Martin Esslin, *Theatre of the Absurd*, rev. edn. (Garden City, NY: Doubleday, 1969), pp. 308–314. This often loosely applied association is rightly criticized by Beaumont, *Ubu Roi*, p. 87.

107 Beaumont, *Ubu Roi*, p. 41.

108 Beaumont, *Ubu Roi*, pp. 59–85. Beaumont provides a detailed account of performances in France and Great Britain.

4 SOUNDING THE DEPTHS

1 *Dresdner Nachrichten*, December 10, 1905; quoted in Friedrich von Schuch, *Richard Strauss, Ernst von Schuch und Dresdens Oper*, 2nd edn. (Leipzig: Breitkopf, 1953), p. 72.

2 Telegraphed report in Vienna's *Neue Freie Presse*, December 10, 1905.

3 Schuch, *Richard Strauss*, p. 73. On the effect of *Salome* within the specific tradition and history of the Dresden court theater see Philipp Ther, *In der Mitte der Gesellschaft: Operntheater in Zentraleuropa 1815–1914* (Vienna: Oldenbourg, 2006), pp. 167–170.

4 Letter of December 15, 1905, to Ernst von Schuch; quoted in Schuch, *Richard Strauss*, p. 74.

5 Walter Panofsky, *Richard Strauss: Partitur eines Lebens* (Berlin: Deutsche Buch-Gemeinschaft, 1967), p. 119.

6 Alma Mahler, *Gustav Mahler: Memories and Letters*, ed. Donald Mitchell and trans. Basil Creighton, 3rd edn. (Seattle, Wash.: University of Washington Press, 1975), p. 88.

7 Thomas Beecham, *A Mingled Chime: An Autobiography* (New York: Putnam, 1943), pp. 169–171.

8 Beecham, *A Mingled Chime*, p. 171.

9 Arnold Bax, *Farewell, My Youth, and Other Writings*, ed. Lewis Foreman (Aldershot: Scolar, 1992), p. 28.

10 "How the audience took it," *The New York Times*, January 23, 1907, p. 9.

11 Helen G. Zagona, *The Legend of Salome and the Principle of Art for Art's Sake* (Geneva: Droz, 1960), p. 132.

12 Michael T. R. B. Turnbull, *Mary Garden* (Portland, Oreg.: Amadeus, 1997), pp. 66–67.

13 Quoted in Panofsky, *Richard Strauss*, p. 117.

14 Richard Strauss, "Erinnerungen an die ersten Aufführungen meiner Opern" (1942), in his *Betrachtungen und Erinnerungen*, ed. Willi Schuh (Zurich: Atlantis, 1981), p. 227.

15 Panofsky, *Richard Strauss*, p. 116.

16 *Bibliothek der Kirchenväter* (Munich: Kösel, 1916), vol. XXVI, pp. 68–72, here p. 72. Quoted from Thomas Rohde (ed.), *Mythos Salome: Vom Markusevangelium bis Djuna Barnes* (Leipzig: Reclam, 2000), pp. 68–72. On the history of the legend see Rohde's afterword (pp. 265–290), but especially the three volumes of *Reimarus Secundus, Geschichte der Salome*.

17 On early painting see especially Karstin Merkel, *Salome: Ikonographie im Wandel* (Frankfurt: Lang, 1990); and more generally Hugo Daffner, *Salome: Ihre Gestalt in Geschichte und Kunst, Dichtung, bildende Kunst, Musik* (Munich: Schmidt, 1912).

18 See the list in Rohde, *Mythos Salome*, pp. 316–317; the rubric "Johannes der Täufer" in Elisabeth Frenzel, *Stoffe der Weltliteratur: Ein Lexikon dichtungsgeschichtlicher Längsschnitte*, 9th edn. (Stuttgart: Kröner, 1998), pp. 382–387; and Mario Praz, *The Romantic Agony*, trans. by Angus Davidson (New York: Meridian, 1956), pp. 291–303 and passim.

19 See especially Daffner, *Salome*, pp. 298–388; and Mireille Dottin (ed.), *Salomé dans les collections françaises* (Saint-Denis: Musée d'Art et d'Histoire, 1988).

20 Elaine Showalter (*Sexual Anarchy: Gender and Culture at the Fin de Siècle*, New York: Viking, 1990) adds to this the element of homoeroticism, which can be illustrated by the notorious photograph of Wilde himself dressed for the role of Salome.

21 Ludwig Marcuse, *Obszön: Geschichte einer Entrüstung* (Munich: List, 1962), pp. 226–227. See also Sander Gilman, "Salome, syphilis, Sarah Bernhardt, and the 'modern Jewess,'" *The German Quarterly*, 66 (1993): pp. 195–211, for the association of the iconic figure with disease.

22 Praz, *Romantic Agony*, p. 302.

23 Richard Ellmann, *Oscar Wilde* (New York: Knopf, 1988), pp. 339–342.

24 Derrick Puffett (ed.), *Richard Strauss: Salome* (Cambridge: Cambridge University Press, 1989), p. 2.

25 On Wilde's use of Flaubert, see Helen G. Zagona, *The Legend of Salome and the Principle of Art for Art's Sake* (Geneva: Droz, 1960), pp. 121–132; and Rainer Kohlmayer, "Oscar Wildes Einakter Salome und die deutsche Rezeption," in Winfried Herget and Brigitte Schultze (eds), *Kurzformen des Dramas* (Tübingen: Francke, 1990), pp. 159–186.

26 In this connection see especially Richard Ellmann, "Overtures to Wilde's *Salomé*," *Tri-Quarterly*, 5 (1969): pp. 45–64.

27 See Marni Reva Kessler, *Sheer Presence: The Veil in Manet's Paris* (Minneapolis, Minn.: University of Minnesota Press, 2006). Kessler, who restricts herself to the period 1852–1889, does not discuss or mention Wilde or Salome.

28 Ernest Renan, *The Life of Jesus*, Garden City, NY: Dolphin Books, 1863.

29 Here I differ with Rohde, who in his afterword to *Mythos Salome* (p. 287) argues that both veils conceals emptiness and intangibility ("ihre Leere, ihre Ungreifbarkeit"). In Lamentations 1:8–10, for instance, the fallen Jerusalem, destroyed by the Babylonians and her sanctuaries invaded, is compared to a woman whose nakedness is revealed when her unclean skirts are torn away. And at Genesis 38:15–16 the widowed Tamar puts on a veil to seduce her father-in-law Judah, who therefore mistakes her for a harlot.

30 Ellmann, *Oscar Wilde*, pp. 372–373.

31 Ellmann, *Oscar Wilde*, pp. 374–375.

32 Lachmann was the wife of the radical anarchist Gustav Landauer, who later translated Wilde's *The Soul of Man under Socialism*, *Portrait of Dorian Grey*, and (with his wife) Wilde's essays on life and art.

33 On Lachmann's translation see Kohlmayer, "Wildes Einakter," pp. 169–173.

34 Kohlmayer, "Wildes Einakter," pp. 174–176. For a description of Eysoldt's performance see Marie Luise Becker, "Gertrud Eysoldt," *Bühne und Welt*, 5 (1903), pp. 635–641, especially p. 640.

35 Strauss, "Erinnerungen," pp. 224–229. See also the accounts in Panofsky, *Richard Strauss;* and Norman Del Mar, *Richard Strauss: A Critical Commentary on His Life and Works*, 2 vols. (London: Barrie & Rockliff, 1962), vol. I, pp. 239–246.

36 Strauss, "Erinnerungen," p. 224.

37 For a detailed comparison of Strauss's treatment of Lachmann's text see Roland Tenschert, "Richard Strauss' Opernfassung der deutschen Übersetzung von Oscar Wildes *Salome*," in Willi Schuh (ed.), *Richard Strauss Jahrbuch 1959–60* (Bonn: Bossey, 1960), pp. 99–106; English translation in Puffett, *Salome*, pp. 36–50.

38 Bax, *Farewell, My Youth*, p. 28.

39 Strauss, "Erinnerungen," p. 225.

40 John Williamson, "Critical Reception," in Puffett, *Salome*, p. 138, 172 n.37. Puffett cites a letter of August 8, 1929, from Strauss to his nephew Rudolf Moralt, in which the composer reports that Hitler told his son "that Salome was one of his first operatic experiences and that he had cadged the money from his relations in order to travel to the first performance in Graz." On the Graz premiere see also Alex Ross, *The Rest is Noise: Listening to the Twentieth Century* (New York: Farrar, Straus & Giroux, 2007), pp. 3–4; and on Strauss and Mahler, pp. 4–6.

41 Mann, *Doktor Faustus*, in his *Gesammelte Werke in zwölf Bänden* (Frankfurt: Fischer, 1960), vol. VI, p. 205.

42 Mann, *Doktor Faustus*, vol. VI, p. 208.

43 Romain Rolland, *Jean-Christophe*, trans. by Gilbert Cannen, 3 vols. (New York: Modern Library, 1938), vol. II, pp. 407–408.

44 Julius Korngold, "Salome (Ein Gespräch)," *Neues Wiener Tagblatt*, May 28, 1907; reprinted in his *Deutsches Opernschaffen der Gegenwart: Kritische Aufsätze* (Leipzig: Leonhardt, 1921), pp. 136–146.

45 Korngold, "Salome (Ein Gespräch)," p. 136.

46 Korngold, "Salome (Ein Gespräch)," p. 141.

47 Korngold, "Salome (Ein Gespräch)," p. 143.

48 Korngold, "Salome (Ein Gespräch)," p. 143.

49 Ten years later, reviewing "Salome im Hofoperntheater" (*Deutsches Opernschaffen*, pp. 179–184), Korngold revised his opinion somewhat; he still objected to the story, but he had come to better appreciate the musical language of the opera. "Salome is a brilliant work, but often painfully brilliant. It arouses the imagination, titillates, overstimulates the nerves; the nobler powers of the music recede too greatly."

50 See "Richard Strauss and the Viennese Critics (1896–1924)," ed. Leon Botstein, trans. Susan Gillespie, in Bryan Gilliam (ed.), *Richard Strauss and His World* (Princeton, NJ: Princeton University Press, 1992), pp. 311–371, esp. pp. 324–335.

51 Hans Warbeck, "Salome," *Die Schaubühne* 2 (December 13, 1906), pp. 579–584.

52 Warbeck, "Salome," p. 582.

53 Hans von Dettelbach, *Breviarum Musicae: Probleme, Werke, Gestalten* (Darmstadt: Wissenschaftliche Buchgesellschaft, 1958), p. 252.

54 Warbeck, "Salome," p. 583.

55 Warbeck, "Salome," p. 584.

56 Warbeck, "Salome," p. 584.

57 Rudolf Louis, "Die erlöste Salome," *Süddeutsche Monatshefte* 4 (1907), pp. 246–249.

58 Louis, "Die erlöste Salome," p. 247.

59 Louis, "Die erlöste Salome," p. 246.

60 Bax, *Farewell, My Youth*, p. 28.

61 Bax, *Farewell, My Youth*, p. 131.

62 J. C. Lusztig, "Richard Strauss' Musikdrama Salome," *Bühne und Welt* 8 (1906), pp. 298–300.

63 Lusztig, "Richard Strauss' Musikdrama Salome," p. 299.

64 Lusztig, "Richard Strauss' Musikdrama Salome," p. 300.

65 Henry T. Finck, *Richard Strauss: The Man and His Works* (Boston, Mass.: Little, Brown, 1917), pp. 234–243.

66 Finck, *Richard Strauss*, p. 235.

67 Finck, *Richard Strauss*, p. 234.

68 Finck, *Richard Strauss*, p. 234.

69 Finck, *Richard Strauss*, p. 239.

70 Finck, *Richard Strauss*, p. 240.

71 Finck, *Richard Strauss*, p. 240.

72 Finck, *Richard Strauss*, p. 243.

73 Panofsky, *Richard Strauss*, p. 120.

74 Quoted in Panofsky, *Richard Strauss*, p. 120.

75 Panofsky, *Richard Strauss*, p. 121.

76 Adam Röder, *Salome* (Wiesbaden: Berend, 1907).

77 Röder, *Salome*, p. 7.

78 Röder, *Salome*, p. 13.

79 Röder, *Salome*, p. 14.

80 Röder, *Salome*, p. 23.

81 Röder, *Salome*, pp. 29–30.

82 Röder, *Salome*, p. 31.

83 Reimarus Secundus, *Geschichte der Salome von Cato bis Oscar Wilde, gemeinverständlich dargestellt* (Leipzig: Wigand, 1907–1908); Röder, *Salome*; and Lawrence Gilman, *Strauss' "Salome": A Guide to the Opera* (London: Lane, 1907), p. 55.

84 Williamson, "Critical Reception," p. 131.

85 Puffett's introduction to his volume, *Salome*, p. 7. See also Williamson's chapter on "Critical Reception," pp. 131–144.

86 Del Mar, *Richard Strauss*, vol. I, p. 281.

87 Del Mar, *Richard Strauss*, vol. I, p. 8.

88 In Puffett, *Salome*, pp. 145–160; here p. 160.

89 Dettelbach, *Breviarum*, pp. 247–248. See also Williamson, "Critical Reception," 139–140.

90 Both passages are quoted in this context by Günter Berghaus, *Theatre, Performance, and the Historical Avant-garde* (New York: Palgrave Macmillan, 2005), pp. 31, 51.

91 Stephen Walsh, *Stravinsky: A Creative Spring: Russia and France, 1882–1934* (London: Cape, 2000), p. 209.

92 Thomas Forrest Kelly, *First Nights: Five Musical Premieres* (New Haven, Conn.: Yale University Press, 2000), p. 258. (Kelly's splendid chapter on this work was printed in a much briefer form as *The Disastrous Premiere of the Rite of Spring*, The John R. Adams Lecture in the Humanities, San Diego, Calif.: Department of Classics and Humanities, San Diego State University, 2006.) Kelly's view is widely shared. See, for instance, Helmut Kirchmeyer, *Strawinskys russische Ballette* (Stuttgart: Reclam, 1974), p. 102, who compares it as a "Jahrhundertwerk" to Beethoven's Eroica and Wagner's Tannhäuser—works that "forced the history of music onto a new course."

93 Modris Eksteins, *Rites of Spring: The Great War and the Birth of the Modern Age* (Boston, Mass.: Houghton Mifflin, 2000), p. xiv.

94 Roger Shattuck, *The Banquet Years: The Arts in France 1885–1918* (New York: Harcourt, 1958), p. 3.

95 Gustave de Pawlowski's review in *Comoedia*, May 31, 1913; quoted in Kelly, *First Nights*, p. 308.

96 Quoted in Kelly, *First Nights*, p. 263.

97 See Margaret Ziolkowski, *Hagiography and Modern Russian Literature* (Princeton, NJ: Princeton University Press, 1988), pp. 3–19; and her (trans. and ed.) *Tale of Boiarynia Morozova: A Seventeeth-Century Religious Life* (Lanham, Md.: Lexington, 2000), esp. pp. 32–41.

98 Igor Stravinsky, *Autobiography* (1936) (London: Calder, 1975), p. 31. It should be noted that the set and costume designer Nicholas Roerich later claimed that the original idea was his. See Walsh, *Stravinsky*, p. 138.

99 The information in this paragraph is based on the composer's account in Igor Stravinsky and Robert Craft, *Memories and Commentaries* (London: Faber & Faber, 2002), pp. 88–89.

100 Quoted by Kirchmeyer, *Russische Ballette*, pp. 103–104.

101 Stravinsky, *Autobiography*, pp. 26–27. See also his letter of July 21, 1911, to Rimsky-Korsakov, as he was composing Petrushka: "I am interested in ballet and love it more than anything else." Quoted in Wolfgang Burda, *Stravinsky: Leben, Werk, Dokumente* (Munich: Piper, 1993), p. 60.

102 Jacques Rivière, "Le Sacre du Printemps," *La Nouvelle Revue Française* 5 (November 1, 1913), pp. 706–730, here p. 706.

103 Stravinsky, *Autobiography*, p. 71.

104 Rivière, "Le Sacre du Printemps," p. 728. See also Kirchmeyer, *Russische Ballette*, pp. 104–105.

105 On the musical effects see Ross, *The Rest is Noise*, pp. 90–92.

106 Burda, *Strawinsky*, p. 79.

107 Giacomo Puccini, *Letters*, ed. by Giuseppe Adami and trans. by Ena Makin, rev. edn. (London: Harrap, 1974), p. 251. For the most complete and entertaining description of the circumstances surrounding the premiere— including the still-new theater, the advertisements in the programs, and translations of contemporary reviews—see Kelly, *First Nights*, pp. 256–334, from which I cite several of the reviews (here p. 327). See also Ross, *The Rest is Noise*, pp. 74–76. For the originals of many contemporary reviews see François Lesure (ed.), *Igor Stravinsky, Le sacre du printemps: dossier de presse/ press-book* (Geneva: Minkoff, 1980).

108 Doris Monteux, *It's All in the Music: The Life and Work of Pierre Monteux* (London: Kimber, 1965), p. 90; quoted in Kelly, *First Nights*, p. 318.

109 Kelly, *First Nights*, p. 318.

110 Kelly, *First Nights*, p. 274.

111 Léon Vallas, in *La Revue Française de Musique*, June–July 1913, pp. 601–603; quoted in Kelly, *First Nights*, p. 317.

112 Quoted in Kelly, *First Nights*, p. 312.

113 Kelly, *First Nights*, pp. 313–314.

114 Stravinsky, *Autobiography*, p. 52.

115 Ernest Newman, in *The Sunday Times*, July 3, 1921.

116 Gustave de Pawlowski, in *Comoedia*, May 31, 1913; quoted in Kelly, *First Nights*, p. 309.

117 From *Le Coq et l'Arlequin* (Paris, 1918); reprinted in Margaret Crosland (ed.), *Cocteau's World: An Anthology of Writings by Jean Cocteau* (London: Owen, 1972), pp. 322–336, here p. 325. Also in Kelly, *First Nights*, pp. 324–326.

118 Stravinsky, *Autobiography*, p. 97. For Stravinsky's complete view of Nijinsky see pp. 40–42, pp. 95–99.

119 Stravinsky, *Autobiography*, p. 97.

120 Stravinsky, *Autobiography*, p. 97.
121 Stravinsky, *Autobiography*, p. 97.
122 Stravinsky and Craft, *Memories and Commentaries*, pp. 37–38. Also in Kelly, *First Nights*, p. 333.
123 Adolphe Boschot, *Echo de Paris*, May 30, 1913; quoted in Kelly, *First Nights*, pp. 305–306.
124 Kelly, *First Nights*, p. 307.
125 Kelly, *First Nights*, p. 314.
126 Kelly, *First Nights*, p. 316.
127 Kelly, *First Nights*, p. 316.
128 Carl Van Vechten, *Music after the Great War* (New York: Schirmer, 1915), pp. 87–88. Also in Kelly, *First Nights*, p. 323.
129 [H. Colles], "The Fusion of Music and Dancing," *The Times*, July 12, 1913.
130 Here I disagree with Modris Eksteins (*Rites of Spring: The Great War and the Birth of the Modern Age*, Boston, Mass.: Houghton Mifflin, 2000, p. 50), who believes that "the theme was devoid of readily identifiable moral purpose."

5 DIAGNOSING THE PRESENT

1 Editors' preface to Schnitzlers "Reigen," ed. Alfred Pfoser, Kristina Pfoser-Schewig, and Gerhard Renner, 2 vols. (Frankfurt: Fischer, 1993), vol. I, p. 9.
2 See, for instance, Carl E. Schorske, *Fin-de-Siècle Vienna: Politics and Culture* (New York: Knopf, 1980), pp. 10–15; and Peter Gay, *Schnitzler's Century* (New York: Norton, 2002). Both works mention *Reigen* only in passing.
3 Letter of January 7, 1897, to Otto Brahm; Arthur Schnitzler, *Briefe 1875–1931*, ed. Therese Nickl, Heinrich Schnitzler, Peter Michael Braunwart *et al.*, 2 vols. (Frankfurt: Suhrkamp, 1981–1984), vol. I, p. 309.
4 Reproduced in Schnitzler, *Schnitzlers "Reigen,"* p. 45.
5 Letter of February 26, 1987, to Olga Waissnix; Schnitzler, *Briefe*, vol. I, p. 314.
6 Gay, *Schnitzler's Century*, pp. 63–94.
7 On Schnitzler and Krafft-Ebing, see Horst Thomé, "Arthur Schnitzlers 'Reigen' und die Sexualanthropologie der Jahrhundertwende," *Text + Kritik*, 138/39 (1998), pp. 102–113.
8 On Schnitzler and Lucian see the editor's introduction to Arthur Schnitzler, *Ein Liebesreigen: Die Urfassung der "Reigen,"* ed. by Gabriella Rovagnati (Frankfurt: Fischer, 2004), pp. 30–31.
9 Reproduced in Schnitzler, *Liebesreigen*, pp. 25–28.
10 On this frequently noted parallel, see Alfred Pfoser, "Rund um den Reigen: Eine interpretatorische Einführung" in *Schnitzlers "Reigen,"* pp. 13–42; here p. 15.
11 Carl E. Schorske, *Fin-de-Siècle Vienna: Politics and Culture* (New York: Knopf, 1980), p. 11; Pfoser, "Rund um den Reigen," p. 19; Schnitzler, *Liebesreigen*, pp. 38–42.
12 Erna Neuse, "Die Funktion von Motiven und stereotypen Wendungen in Schnitzlers Reigen," *Monatshefte für deutschen Unterricht*, 64 (1972), pp. 359–367.
13 Pfoser, "Rund um den Reigen," p. 31.

14 The story of the work's publication has often been recounted: I follow mainly the documented account in *Schnitzlers "Reigen,"* pp. 43–71; but see also Thomas Koebner, *Arthur Schnitzler: Reigen. Erläuterungen und Dokumente* (Stuttgart: Reclam, 1997), pp. 10–14; Gerd K. Schneider, "The social and political context of Arthur Schnitzler's Reigen in Berlin, Vienna, and New York: 1900–1933," in Dagmar Lorenz (ed.), *A Companion to the Works of Arthur Schnitzler* (Rochester, NY: Camden House, 2003), pp. 27–57; and Gerd K. Schneider, *Die Rezeption von Arthur Schnitzlers "Reigen," 1897–1994: Text, Aufführungen, Verfilmungen, Pressespiegel und andere zeitgenössische Kommentare* (Riverside, Calif.: Ariadne, 1995).

15 In *Neue Deutsche Rundschau*, November 1900; reproduced in Thomas Koebner, *Arthur Schnitzler: Reigen. Erläuterungen und Dokumente* (Stuttgart: Reclam, 1997), pp. 11–12.

16 The letter of February 15, 1903, is reproduced in Schnitzler, *Schnitzlers "Reigen,"* vol. I, pp. 213–214.

17 See the reviews in Schneider, *Rezeption*, pp. 44–47.

18 Arthur Schnitzler, *Tagebuch*, ed. by Kommission für Literarische Gebrauchsformen (Werner Welzig, Peter Michael Braunwarth *et al.*), 10 vols. (Vienna: Österreichische Akademie der Wissenschaften, 1981–2000), vol. VI, p. 24 (April 7, 1903).

19 Schnitzler, *Tagebuch*, vol. VI, p. 24 (April 10, 1903).

20 Schneider, *Rezeption*, pp. 66–67.

21 Friedrich Törnsee, "Bücherschau: Arthur Schnitzlers Reigen," *Neue Bahnen*, May 1, 1903, p. 245; quoted in Schneider, *Rezeption*, p. 50.

22 Ottokar Stauf von der March, "Reigen," *Ostdeutsche Rundschau*, May 17, 1903, p. 15; quoted in Schneider, *Rezeption*, p. 51.

23 "Schnitzlers Reigen," *Neues Wiener Journal*, July 2, 1903; quoted in Schneider, *Rezeption*, p. 51.

24 *Allgemeine Rundschau*, May 15, 1905; quoted in Schneider, *Rezeption*, p. 75.

25 Kristina Pfoser-Schewig, "Erste Aufführungsversuche," in *Schnitzlers "Reigen,"* pp. 73–79.

26 In addition to the information in the second volume of *Schnitzlers "Reigen"* and the full documentation of the court proceedings reproduced in Wolfgang Heine (ed.), *Der Kampf um den Reigen: Vollständiger Bericht über die sechstägige Verhandlung gegen Direktion und Darsteller des Kleinen Schauspielhauses Berlin* (Berlin: Rowohlt, 1922); see Heinz Ludwig Arnold, "Der falsch gewonnene Prozess," *Text + Kritik*, 138/39 (1998), pp. 114–122.

27 See his letters in *Schnitzlers "Reigen,"* vol. II, pp. 99–102, here p. 99.

28 Schneider, *Rezeption*, pp. 94–95.

29 See the account in Wolfgang Heine (ed.), *Kampf um den Reigen: Vollständiger Bericht über die Sechstägige Verhandlung gegen Direktion und Darsteller des Kleinen Schauspielhauses Berlin* (Berlin: Rowohlt, 1922), p. 6; and Eysoldt's own statement at the trial, p. 427.

30 See the selection in *Schnitzlers "Reigen,"* vol. II, pp. 105–141; and in Schneider, *Rezeption*, pp. 96–99.

31 See the contemporary examples reprinted in *Ringel-Ringel-Reigen. Parodien von Arthur Schnitzlers "Reigen,"* ed. by Gerd Klaus Schneider and Peter Michael Braunwarth (Wien: Sonderzahl, 2005). On subsequent parodies and adaptations down to the recent past, see Gerd K. Schneider, *"Ich will jeden Tag einen Haufen Sternschnuppen auf mich niederregnen sehen:" Zur künstlerischen Rezeption von Arthur Schnitzlers "Reigen" in Österreich, Deutschland und den USA* (Vienna: Praesens Verlag, 2008).

32 *Schnitzlers "Reigen,"* vol. II, pp. 137–140, here p. 139.

33 Schneider, *Rezeption*, pp. 104–110.

34 Reproduced in *Schnitzlers "Reigen,"* vol. II, pp. 141–142.

35 On Brunner see Ludwig Marcuse, *Obszön: Geschichte einer Entrüstung* (Munich: List, 1962), pp. 232–241, as well as Brunner's own extensive statement in *Kampf um den Reigen*, pp. 296–340.

36 Reproduced in *Schnitzlers "Reigen,"* vol. II, p. 145.

37 Marcuse, *Obszön*, p. 214.

38 Marcuse, *Obszön*, pp. 226–227.

39 See his testimony in Heine, *Kampf um den Reigen*, pp. 24–36, here p. 29.

40 Arnold, "Der falsch gewonnene Prozess," p. 18.

41 Extensive excerpts from the trial proceedings are readily available in the article "Literatur vor Gericht: Von 'Les Fleurs du Mal' bis 'Notre-Dame-des-Fleurs,'" *Akzente*, 12 (1965): pp. 210–251, here pp. 211–230. For a narrative account and analysis of the trial see Marcuse, *Obszön*, pp. 207–263.

42 Heine, *Kampf um den Reigen*, pp. 124, 44. In his summation (pp. 379–380) the defense attorney questioned whether or not any of these witnesses—representing groups dedicated to social service, protection of youth, the salvation of fallen sinners, and other "duties of love"—could be regarded as "ordinary citizens."

43 Heine, *Kampf um den Reigen*, pp. 58, 93.

44 Heine, *Kampf um den Reigen*, pp. 95, 161–165.

45 See the poster reproduced in Schneider, *Rezeption*, p. 598.

46 Heine, *Kampf um den Reigen*, p. 164.

47 Heine, *Kampf um den Reigen*, p. 432.

48 Here I follow mainly Alfred Pfoser, "Die Wiener Aufführung," in *Schnitzlers "Reigen,"* vol. I, pp. 81–175.

49 Schnitzler, *Tagebuch*, vol. III, p. 152.

50 Pfoser, "Die Wiener Aufführung," vol. I, p. 96.

51 Schneider, *Rezeption*, pp. 97–99.

52 The lengthy attack is reproduced in *Schnitzlers "Reigen,"* vol. I, pp. 293–296.

53 *Neues Montagsblatt*, February 7, 1921; quoted in Schneider, *Rezeption*, p. 130.

54 Pfoser, "Die Wiener Aufführung," vol. I, pp. 121–122.

55 *Reichspost*, February 14, 1921; in *Schnitzlers "Reigen,"* vol. I, p. 343.

56 Pfoser, "Die Wiener Aufführung," vol. I, p. 135.

57 See the police report of the incident in *Schnitzlers "Reigen,"* vol. I, p. 143; Schnitzler's diary entry for February 16, 1921, in *Tagebuch*, vol. VII, pp. 144–145; and several newspaper accounts in Schneider, *Rezeption*, pp. 163–171.

58 Reproduced in *Schnitzlers "Reigen,"* vol. I, pp. 142–143; and Schneider, *Rezeption*, pp. 592–595.

59 "Der siegreiche Christenzorn," *Volkssturm*, March 1, 1921; in *Schnitzlers "Reigen,"* vol. I, pp. 363–374.

60 "Ein Erfolg der Wiener christlichen Jugend," *Wiener Stimmen*, February 17, 1921; *Schnitzlers "Reigen,"* vol. I, pp. 374–376.

61 Schneider, *Rezeption*, pp. 169–170.

62 Schneider, *Rezeption*, p. 174.

63 *Schnitzlers "Reigen,"* vol. I, pp. 346–353.

64 Schneider, *Rezeption*, p. 176.

65 Heine, *Kampf um den Reigen*, p. 5. The concluding pages of Heine's summation (pp. 401–404) constitute a thoughtful analysis of the current sociopolitical situation in Germany.

66 Heine insisted on the "morality" of Schnitzler's play; Heine, *Kampf um den Reigen*, pp. 397–399.

67 Marcuse, *Obszön*, p. 214.

68 *Sächsische Arbeiterzeitung*, March 11, 1930; quoted in Fritz Hennenberg and Jan Knopf (eds.), *Brecht/Weill "Mahagonny"* (Frankfurt: Suhrkamp, 2006), pp. 265–266.

69 Lotte Lenya, "Erinnerungen an Mahagonny" (1957), from the program notes for the performance at the Deutsche Staatsoper Berlin, 1964; rpt. in Hennenberg and Knopf, *Brecht/Weill "Mahagonny,"* pp. 187–191, here pp. 189–190.

70 Review in *Das Tagebuch* (Berlin), March 22, 1930; rpt. in *Polgar Kleine Schriften*, ed. by Marcel Reich-Ranicki and Ulrich Weinzierl, 6 vols. (Reinbek bei Hamburg: Rowohlt, 1982–1986), vol. VI, pp. 272–276.

71 Klaus Pringsheim, "Mahagonny," *Weltbühne* 26 (March 18, 1930), pp. 432–434.

72 See "Aus dem Protokoll der Sitzung des gemischten Theaterausschusses der Stadt Leipzig Nr. 4/1930," in Hennenberg and Knopf (eds.), *Brecht/Weill "Mahagonny,"* pp. 258–262; and in the same volume: Jürgen Schebera, "Zur Wirkungsgeschichte bis 1933," pp. 219–246, here p. 223; and Ronald Sanders, *The Days Grow Short: The Life and Music of Kurt Weill* (New York: Holt, 1980), pp. 150–151.

73 Ernst Schumacher, *Die dramatischen Versuche Bertolt Brechts 1918–1933* (Berlin: Rütten, 1955), p. 275.

74 According to the report in the *Frankfurter Nachrichten*, October 20, 1930; rpt. in Hennenberg and Knopf, *Brecht/Weill "Mahagonny,"* pp. 236–237.

75 Jürgen Schebera, *Kurt Weill: An Illustrated Life*, trans. by Caroline Murphy (New Haven, Conn.: Yale University Press, 1995), p. 160.

76 On the disturbances, which came to less than full-fledged scandals, surrounding the performances of two earlier plays by Brecht: *Im Dickicht der Städte* (1923; *In the Jungle of the City*) and *Baal* (1923)—see Blackadder, *Performing Opposition*, pp. 131–148.

77 Blackadder, *Performing Opposition*, pp. 89–99.

78 On the unusually complicated genesis of the opera, including its various
adaptations and name changes to meet local specifications, see Jan Knopf,
"Aufstieg und Fall der Stadt Mahagonny," in Jan Knopf (ed.), *Brecht
Handbuch*, 5 vols. (Stuttgart: Metzler, 2001), vol. I, pp. 178–197; here
pp. 178–182.

79 Brecht, "Anmerkungen zur Oper 'Aufstieg und Fall der Stadt Mahagonny,'" in
his *Gesammelte Werke in 20 Bänden* (Frankfurt: Suhrkamp, 1970), vol. XVII,
pp. 1004–1016.

80 Brecht, "Anmerkungen zur Oper 'Aufstieg und Fall der Stadt Mahagonny,'"
p. 1006.

81 Jarry is rarely mentioned in Brecht studies; but Klaus Völker ("Jarrys
Panoptikum des wissenschaftlichen Zeitalters," *Akzente*, 6, 1959: pp. 301–311;
here pp. 306–307) cites Brecht's use of the belly as a characteristic of plebeian
degradation in analogy to Ubu.

82 I cite *Mahagonny* from Brecht's *Gesammelte Werke*, vol. II, pp. 499–564. The
text differs slightly from that of the 1956 recording by the Norddeutscher
Radio-Chor und Orchester, featuring Lotte Lenya in her classic role as Jenny.
The names of the various figures also vary somewhat from performance to
performance.

83 Brecht, *Mahagonny*, p. 502.

84 See Schebera, *Kurt Weill*, p. 93; and Knopf, "Aufstieg und Fall," pp. 180–182.

85 The names, as well as parts of scenes, are changed from production to production, depending on local circumstances.

86 Brecht, *Mahagonny*, p. 507. Brecht is no doubt playing here on the recently
successful book by Brunold Springer, *Die genialen Syphilitiker* (Berlin-
Nicolassee: Neue Generation, 1926), which proclaimed that "civilization is
syphilization" (p. 2).

87 The phrase is Weill's; see his "Vorwort zum Regiebuch der Oper Aufstieg
und Fall der Stadt Mahagonny" in Hennenberg and Knopf, *Brecht/Weill
"Mahagonny,"* pp. 168–170; here p. 169.

88 Brecht, *Mahagonny*, p. 549.

89 Brecht, *Mahagonny*, p. 555.

90 Brecht, *Mahagonny*, p. 561.

91 Brecht, *Mahagonny*, p. 564.

92 The audiences would no doubt have been more profoundly offended if
they had noticed the many textual clues pointing to a parody of the Bible:
from Trinity Moses, who sets up the various laws established by the Widow
Begbick in her new city on the edge of the desert, where "gin and whisky"
flow, and the destructive floods that destroy other wicked pleasure cities, to
the passion of Jimmy Mahoney, who overthrows the old laws to establish
a new order of happiness and who is thrice denied by Jenny, and the final
apocalyptic conflagration that destroys Mahagonny (the biblical Magog?) as
his friends solemnly bear his reliquies in the final procession. (See Günter
G. Sehm, "Moses, Christus und Paul Ackermann: Brechts *Aufstieg und Fall der*

Stadt Mahagonny," in *Brecht-Jahrbuch 1976,* Frankfurt: Suhrkamp, 1976, pp. 83–100.) But there is no hint in the early reviews that the audience or the critics were aware of these parallels.

93 Klaus Pringsheim, "Mahagonny," *Weltbühne* 28 (March 18, 1930), pp. 432–434.

94 Pringsheim, "Mahagonny," p. 433.

95 Pringsheim, "Mahagonny," pp. 433–434.

96 Pringsheim, "Mahagonny," p. 434.

97 Pringsheim, "Mahagonny," p. 434.

98 Eberhard Preußner, in Arbeitsblätter für soziale Musikpflege und Musikpolitik, Musik und Gesellschaft; quoted in Schumacher, *Die dramatischen Versuche,* p. 275.

99 *Zeitschrift für Musik* 97 (April 1930), p. 292.

100 "Wird es endlich dämmern? Zur Mahagonny-Theaterschlacht, am 9. März im Neuen Theater zu Leipzig," *Zeitschrift für Musik* 97 (May 1930), pp. 392–395.

101 Heuss, "Wird es endlich dämmern?" p. 392.

102 Heuss, "Wird es endlich dämmern?" p. 393.

103 Heuss, "Wird es endlich dämmern?" p. 394.

104 Heuss, "Wird es endlich dämmern?" p. 395.

105 *Braunschweigerische Landeszeitung,* March 14, 1930; in Schebera, "Zur Wirkungsgeschichte," p. 231.

106 *Braunschweigerische Landeszeitung,* p. 231.

107 *Frankfurter Nachrichten,* March 17, 1930; in Hennenberg and Knopf, *Brecht/ Weill "Mahagonny,"* p. 236.

108 Walter Steinthal, *12-Uhr-Blatt* (Berlin), December 22, 1931; in Monika Wyss (ed.), *Brecht in der Kritik: Rezensionen aller Brecht-Aufführungen, sowie ausgewählter deutsch und fremdsprachiger Premieren: Ein Dokumentation* (Munich: Kindler, 1977), pp. 108–110, here p. 109.

109 Franz Körner, *Berliner Börsenzeitung,* December 22, 1931, in Monika Wyss (ed.), *Brecht in der Kritik: Rezensionen aller Brecht-Aufführungen, sowei ausgewählter deutsche und fremdsprachiger Premieren: Eine Dokumentation* (Munich: Kindler, 1977), p. 118.

110 Heinrich Strobel; in Schumacher, *Die dramatischen Versuche,* p. 276.

111 Friedrich Hussong, "Für die Größe des Schmutzes!," *Der Tag* (Berlin), December 28, 1931; in Hennenberg and Knopf, *Brecht/Weill "Mahagonny,"* pp. 242–243.

112 Hussong, "Für die Größe des Schmutzes!" pp. 242–243.

113 Paragraph 218 of the German penal code specified jail sentences for women who had abortions as well as their helpers. A heated debate raged about it in 1930–1931 in public and in the Reichstag.

114 Peter Panter, "Proteste gegen die Dreigroschenoper," *Weltbühne* 26 (April 8, 1930), pp. 557–558.

115 Schumacher, *Die dramatischen Versuche,* pp. 279. It should be pointed out, however, that the first revival in the German Democratic Republic at East Berlin's Komische Oper in 1977 enjoyed a huge popular success.

116 Schumacher, *Die dramatischen Versuche*, p. 273.

117 Schumacher, *Die dramatischen Versuche*, p. 273.

118 For further examples see Schebera, "Zur Wirkungsgeschichte."

119 *Berliner Tagesblatt*, March 10, 1930; in Hennenberg and Knopf, *Brecht/Weill "Mahagonny,"* p. 226.

120 "B.," *Die Reichspost* (Vienna), March 28, 1932; in Wyss, *Brecht in der Kritik*, p. 122.

121 Sächsische Arbeiterzeitung, March 3, 1930; in Hennenberg and Knopf, *Brecht/Weill "Mahagonny,"* p. 270.

122 Walter Trienes, "Neue Opern'kultur,'" *Nationalsozialistische Monatshefte*, March 1931; in Hennenberg and Knopf, *Brecht/Weill "Mahagonny,"* p. 238.

123 H. H. Stuckenschmidt, "Mahagonny," *Die Szene* 21 (1931), pp. 75–77.

124 Stuckenschmidt, "Mahagonny," p. 77.

125 Stuckenschmidt, "Mahagonny," p. 77.

126 Theodor W. Adorno, "Mahagonny," *Der Scheinwerfer. Blätter der städtischen Bühnen Essen* 3/14 (1930); rpt. in his *Gesammelte Schriften*, ed. by Rolf Tiedemann, 20 vols. (Frankfurt Suhrkamp, 2003), vol. XVII, pp. 114–122.

127 Adorno, "Mahagonny," p. 114.

128 Adorno, "Mahagonny," p. 116.

129 Adorno, "Mahagonny," p. 116.

130 Adorno, "Mahagonny," p. 118.

131 Adorno, "Mahagonny," p. 120.

132 Adorno, "Mahagonny," p. 120.

133 Adorno, "Mahagonny," p. 121. For a review of later musicological criticism see Knopf, "Aufstieg und Fall," pp. 192–194; and for a thorough musicological analysis Gottfried Wagner, *Weill und Brecht: Das musikalische Zeittheater* (Munich: Kindler, 1977), pp. 157–212 and passim.

134 These are gathered conveniently in Hennenberg and Knopf, *Brecht/Weill "Mahagonny,"* pp. 145–182, esp. pp. 168–174.

135 Weill, "Vorwort zum Regiebuch der Oper," in Hennenberg and Knopf, *Brecht/Weill "Mahagonny"*, pp. 168–170.

136 Hennenberg and Knopf, *Brecht/Weill "Mahagonny,"* p. 169.

137 Weill, "Zur Uraufführung der 'Mahagonny'-Oper," in Hennenberg and Knopf, *Brecht/Weill "Mahagonny"*, pp. 171–174, here p. 173.

138 Wagner, *Weill und Brecht*, pp. 93–95.

139 Eric Bentley, *The Brecht Commentaries 1943–1980* (New York: Grove, 1981), pp. 281–285, here p. 282, also mentions *The Waste Land*, without, however, pointing to the obvious stylistic analogy.

140 On the three phases of their relationship see Wagner, *Weill und Brecht*, pp. 61–73.

141 Kurt Weill, "Anmerkungen zu meiner Oper Mahagonny," *Die Musik*, 22 (1929/30), pp. 440–441; in Hennenberg and Knopf, *Brecht/Weill "Mahagonny"*, p. 171. Weill uses almost identical words in his later essay "Zur Aufführung der Mahagonny-Oper," *Leipziger Neueste Nachrichten*,

March 8, 1930; in Hennenberg and Knopf, *Brecht/Weill "Mahagonny,"* pp. 171–174.

142 In his pages on *Mahagonny* (*Performing Opposition*, pp. 157–165, 182–183), which do not assess Weill's contribution, Blackadder suggests that it was the failure of *Mahagonny* and his plays of the 1920s to change the audience that inspired Brecht to develop the subtler techniques of his later plays; and even (p. xiii) that his dismissive attitude toward his early rightwing audiences and critics contributed to—or, at least, did nothing to prevent—the rise of National Socialism.

143 See Ulrich Weisstein, "Von reitenden Boten und singenden Holzfällern: Bertolt Brecht und die Oper," in Walter Hinderer (ed.), *Brechts Dramen: Neue Interpretationen* (Stuttgart: Reclam, 1984), who ends his critical discussion by asking whether Brecht's libretto even belongs in his collected works.

144 Alex Ross, "Agit-Opera," *The New Yorker*, March 5, 2007, pp. 88–89.

145 *The New York Times*, August 12, 2008, E3.

6 OVERCOMING THE PAST

1 Reinhart Hoffmeister (ed.), *Rolf Hochhuth: Dokumente zur politischen Wirkung* (Munich: Kindler, 1980), p. 23.

2 Eric Bentley (ed.), *The Storm over the Deputy* (New York: Grove, 1964).

3 Fritz J. Raddatz (ed.), *Summa iniuria oder Durfte der Papst schweigen? Hochhuths "Stellvertreter" in der öffentlichen Kritik* (Reinbek bei Hamburg: Rowohlt, 1963). See the generous selection of reviews in Bernd Balzer, *Rolf Hochhuth: Der Stellvertreter* (Frankfurt: Diesterweg, 1986), pp. 50–58.

4 Reinhold Grimm, Willy Jäggi, and Hans Oesch (eds.), *Der Streit um Hochhuths "Stellvertreter"* (Basel: Basilius, 1963).

5 See the review of performances in Balzer, *Rolf Hochhuth*, pp. 59–60.

6 Report by Alfred Schüler, Sonntagsblatt (Hamburg), March 7, 1965; rpt. in Reinhart Hoffmeister (ed.), *Rolf Hochhuth: Dokumente zur politischen Wirkung* (Munich: Kindler, 1980), pp. 73–76.

7 Jacques Nobécourt, *"Le Vicaire" et l'histoire* (Paris: Éditions du Seuil, 1964).

8 Rosario F. Esposito, *Processo al Vicario: Pio 12 et gli ebrei secondo la testimonianza della storia* (Turin: SAIE, 1964); trans. by Father Eugène Hudon: *Procès au vicaire: Pie XII et le juifs selon le temoignage de l'histoire* (Sherbrooke, Canada: Apostolat de la Presse, 1965). I have seen only the Vatican-approved French translation by Father Eugène Hudon, which includes a useful survey of the reception in various countries (pp. 212–242).

9 In addition to Hoffmeister's Dokumente see, for instance, Jan Berg, *Hochhuths "Stellvertreter" und die Stellvertreter-Debatte: Vergangenheitsbewältigung in Theater und Presse der sechziger Jahre* (Kronberg: Scriptor, 1977); and Rudolf Wolff (ed.), *Rolf Hochhuth: Werk und Wirkung* (Bonn: Bouvier, 1987). These books also list dozens of articles.

10 Pieces by all of the mentioned figures are included in Bentley, *The Storm over the Deputy*. For the Bundestag statements see Balzer, *Rolf Hochhuth*, p. 47.

11 Hochhuth, to be sure, disclaims the term "moralist" as being a finger-pointer, preferring "non-partisan enlightener." See Barbara Fischer's piece on the premiere of *Der Stellvertreter* in www.kalendarblatt.de (January 30, 2007).

12 Patricia Marx, "Inteview with Rolf Hochhuth," *Partisan Review* 31 (Summer 1964); rpt. in Bentley, *The Storm over the Deputy*, pp. 52–65, here pp. 55–56.

13 *Der Spiegel*, February 27, 1963, p. 71.

14 Marx, "Interview," p. 54. See Léon Poliakov and Josef Wulf, *Das Dritte Reich und die Juden: Dokumente und Aufsätze* (Berlin: Arani, 1955). The documents relating to Kurt Gerstein appear on pp. 101–115, and those to Bernhard Lichtenberg on pp. 432–437. Maximilian Kolbe is not mentioned in this volume.

15 Marx, "Interview," p. 55.

16 Hochhuth's most extensive statement of his opposition to Adorno and his followers may be found in his Frankfurt Poetics Lectures: Rolf Hochhuth, *Die Geburt der Tragödie aus dem Krieg* (Frankfurt: Suhrkamp, 2001), pp. 56–63. See also Balzer, *Rolf Hochhuth*, pp. 39–42, who discusses Hochhuth's rejection of Marcuse's philosophy of history.

17 Rolf Hochhuth, "Soll das Theater die heutige Welt darstellen?" in *Die Hebamme: Erzählungen, Gedichte, Essays* (Reinbek bei Hamburg: Rowohlt, 1971), pp. 317–326, here p. 319.

18 Hochhuth, "Soll das Theater die heutige Welt darstellen?" p. 347.

19 Hochhuth, "Soll das Theater die heutige Welt darstellen?" p. 348.

20 Friedrich Dürrenmatt, "Theaterprobleme," in his *Das Dürrenmatt Lesebuch*, ed. by Daniel Keel, Afterword by Heinz Ludwig Arnold (Zurich: Diogenes, 1991), pp. 203–241, here p. 230.

21 Hochhuth's indebtedness to Schiller has been discussed by scholars and critics since Erwin Piscator's comments in his introduction to the first edition.

22 Marx, "Interview," p. 53. I cite the text in my own translation from: Rolf Hochhuth, *Der Stellvertreter: Ein christliches Trauerspiel* (Reinbek bei Hamburg: Rowohlt, 1967).

23 Hochhuth, *Der Stellvertreter*, p. 176.

24 See Hochhuth's stage directions, *Stellvertreter*, p. 32.

25 Hochhuth, *Der Stellvertreter*, p. 198.

26 See Piscator's account in the program brochure published for the 1963–1964 tour of his production through West German cities. It is available under the heading "Programmhefte" on the website www.erwin-piscator.de (accessed January 30, 2007).

27 "Berlin Sees Play Accusing Pius XII," *The New York Times*, February 23, 1963, p. 7.

28 *Der Spiegel*, September 30, 1963, pp. 84–88; and Nobécourt, "Le Vicaire," pp. 324–328.

29 See the report in *Der Spiegel*, December 25, 1963, p. 101.

30 *New York Herald Tribune*, March 3, 1964; rpt. in Bentley, *The Storm over the Deputy*, pp. 37–38.

31 Robert Brustein, "History as Drama," *New Republic*, March 14, 1964; rpt. in Bentley, *The Storm over the Deputy*, pp. 21–24.

32 See, for instance, Richard Gilman's review in *Commonweal*, March 20, 1964; rpt. in Bentley, *The Storm over the Deputy*, pp. 31–34; as well as other contemporary reviews reproduced there.

33 For a good overview of the situation see Balzer, *Rolf Hochhuth*, pp. 5–13.

34 This collective phenomenon—"the inability to mourn"—was famously described and analyzed by Alexander and Margarete Mitscherlich in *Die Unfähigkeit zu trauern. Grundlagen kollektiven Verhaltens* (Munich: Piper, 1967).

35 Rolf Zimmermann, "Drama or Pamphlet: Hochhuth's The Deputy and the Tradition of Polemical Literature"; originally in Reinhold Grimm, Willy Jäggi, and Hans Oesch (eds.), *Der Streit um Hochhuths "Stellvertreter"* (Basel: Basilius, 1963) and translated in Bentley, *The Storm over the Deputy*, pp. 123–148, here p. 138.

36 Lionel Abel, "Rolf Hochhuth's The Deputy," *Dissent* 11 (Spring 1964); rpt. in Bentley, *The Storm over the Deputy*, pp. 81–85, here p. 81.

37 On the historical significance of the subtitle see Balzer, *Rolf Hochhuth*, pp. 24–25.

38 Hochhuth, *Geburt der Tragödie aus dem Krieg*, p. 65. I have not seen the German translation; Hochhuth's statement actually conflates various passages from the opening chapter of the American original: Hannah Arendt, *Eichmann in Jerusalem: A Report on the Banality of Evil*, rev. edn. (New York: Viking, 1964), pp. 3–20, where Arendt compares the trial, its setting, and its participants to a play, the theater, the actors, and the audience. "In the center of a trial can only be the one who did—in this respect he is like the hero in the play" (p. 9); "an individual in the dock, a person of flesh and blood" (p. 20); "All the other questions of seemingly greater import [...] [must] be left in abeyance [...] On trial are his deeds, not the sufferings of the Jews, not the German people or mankind, not even anti-Semistism and racism" (p. 5).

39 Judy Stone, "Interview," in Bentley, *The Storm over the Deputy*, p. 43.

40 Arthur C. Cochrane, "Pius XII: a symbol," *Christianity and Crisis: A Christian Journal of Opinion*, March 30, 1964; rpt. in Bentley, *The Storm over the Deputy*, pp. 157–162, here p. 162.

41 Hochhuth, *Geburt der Tragödie aus dem Krieg*, pp. 53–54.

42 See, for instance, the contributions to the commemorative volume published for Henze's eightieth birthday: Michael Kerstan and Clemens Wolken (eds.), *Hans Werner Henze: Komponist der Gegenwart* (Berlin: Henschel, 2006).

43 Don Michael Randel (ed.), *The New Harvard Dictionary of Music* (Cambridge, Mass.: Belknap Press of the Harvard University Press, 1986), pp. 570–572.

44 I take the facts in this paragraph from Schnabel's account in his afterword to *Das Floss der Medusa* (Munich: Piper, 1969)., pp. 70–71; Schnabel, in turn, bases his account on the firsthand report by two survivors, the ship's surgeon Henri Savigny and the surveyor Alexandre Corréard. The little book was

initially published in 1817 in Paris but was immediately prohibited and confiscated by the police; a few copies were smuggled abroad, and the work was soon translated into five different languages, including German: *Schiffbruch der Fregatte Medusa auf ihrer Fahrt nach dem Senegal im Jahr 1816* (Leipzig: Kummer, 1818). See also Julian Barnes's lively account in his *History of the World in 10½ Chapters* (London: Jonathan Cape, 1989), pp. 115–124; and Jonathan Miles, *Medusa: The Shipwreck, the Scandal, the Masterpiece* (London: Cape, 2007).

45 Schnabel, *Floss der Medusa*, p. 51.

46 In her novel *The Raft* (London: Picador, 2007), Arabella Edge has provided a lively account of Géricault's creation of his great painting.

47 I base this paragraph on Schnabel's account in *Floss der Medusa*, pp. 49–50, which reproduces the text of the oratorio. For an exhaustive analysis of the work, see Kay-Uwe Kirchert, "Das Floss der Medusa: Reale und bildnerische Hintergründe in Hans Werner Henzes Oratorio," *Archiv für Musikwissenschaft*, 57 (2000), pp. 264–285.

48 Quoted from his autobiography, Hans Werner Henze, *Bohemian Fifths*, trans. by Stewart Spencer (London: Faber & Faber, 1998), p. 230.

49 Schnabel, *Floss der Medusa*, pp. 11–12.

50 Schnabel, *Floss der Medusa*, p. 44.

51 (Anonymous), "Henze: Kindliches Entzücken," *Der Spiegel*, December 2, 1968, p. 182.

52 See Henze's website at www.schott-henze.de (accessed January 4, 2007). I rely for most of the biographical information on *Bohemian Fifths*.

53 Henze, *Bohemian Fifths*, pp. 146, 173, and passim.

54 Henze, *Bohemian Fifths*, p. 116.

55 From a conversation in 1971, quoted by Wolfgang Stähr, "Konzertskandal und Straßenkampf: Hans Werner Henze und die Weltrevolution," *Berliner Philharmoniker—das magazin* (November/December 2006), pp. 4–8.

56 Cited by Stähr, "Konzertskandal und Straßenkampf."

57 Henze, *Bohemian Fifths*, p. 229.

58 For example, Henze, *Bohemian Fifths*, p. 241; Porter, *Financial Times*, December 11, 1968, p. 3; *Der Spiegel*, December 16, 1968, p. 152.

59 *Der Spiegel*, December 2, 1968, p. 182.

60 Rudi Dutschke, "Es kracht an allen Ecken und Enden," *Der Spiegel*, December 9, 1968, p. 50.

61 Henze, *Bohemian Fifths*, p. 244.

62 Schnabel, *Floss der Medea*, p. 48.

63 Schnabel, *Floss der Medea*, p. 67.

64 A recording of the dress rehearsal was produced in 1970 by the Deutsche Grammaphon Gesellschaft. I base my account of the evening on the first-hand reports by Henze in *Bohemian Fifths*, pp. 245–248, and Schnabel in *Floss der Medusa*, pp. 65–79. There were also innumerable newspaper accounts, among which the most thorough and objective is that by Andrew Porter in *The Financial Times*, December 11, 1968, p. 3.

65 The firsthand reports are confusing and inconsistent; I follow the accounts by Henze, Schnabel, and Andrew Porter.

66 As reported by Rudolf Augstein, "Apropos Henze," in *Der Spiegel*, December 16, 1968, p. 154.

67 Henze, *Bohemian Fifths*, p. 235.

68 *Der Spiegel*, December 16, 1968, p. 153.

69 *Financial Times*, December 11, 1968, p. 3.

70 Henze, *Bohemian Fifths*, pp. 262–263.

7 CONCLUSION

1 Both are fully treated in Blackadder, *Performing Opposition*, pp. 69–108, 109–130. See also Regina Standun, "John Millington Synges 'The Playboy of the Western World': Wie aus einem Theaterskandal die dramaturgische Nationalhymne Irlands wurde," in Stefan Neuhaus and Johann Holzner (eds), *Literatur als Skandal: Fälle—Funktionen—Folgen* (Göttingen: Vandenhoeck & Ruprecht, 2007), pp. 257–265; and Eoin Bourke, "Von 'The Plough and the Stars' zu 'The Drums of Father Ned': Sean O'Casey und die irische Moral," in Stefan Neuhaus and Johann Holzner (eds), *Literatur als Skandal: Fälle—Funktionen—Folgen* (Göttingen: Vandenhoeck & Ruprecht, 2007), pp. 289–298.

2 Michael Benedikt, "Introduction," in *Modern French Theatre: An Anthology of Plays*, ed. and trans. by Michael Benedikt and George E. Wellwarth (New York: Dutton, 1964), pp. ix–xxxv; here p. xxii.

3 I am indebted for this reference to Wolfgang Stähr's piece for the concert program of the Munich Philharmonic, March 20/22, 2003: pp. 13–17. For further examples see Walter Panofsky, *Protest in der Oper: Das provokative Musiktheater der zwanziger Jahre* (Munich: Laokoon, 1966).

4 See Gitta Honegger, *Thomas Bernhard: The Making of an Austrian* (New Haven, Conn.: Yale University Press, 2001), pp. 270–304.

5 See Günter Berghaus, *Theatre, Performance, and the Historical Avant-garde* (New York: Palgrave Macmillan, 2005), pp. 105–111.

6 Interview with Corinna Harfouch in *Der Spiegel*, June 18, 2007, pp. 184–186, here p. 184.

7 Thomas Mann, "Versuch über das Theater," in his *Gesammelte Werke in zwölf Bänden* (Frankfurt: Fischer, 1960), vol. X, pp. 23–62, here p. 41.

8 I take the example and the quotation from Adolf Dresen's essay, "Betreibt das Regietheter die Hinrichtung der Klassiker," in Thomas Zabka and Adolf Dresen, *Dichter und Regisseure: Bemerkungen über das Regie-Theater* (Göttingen: Wallstein, 1995), pp. 59–123; here p. 59.

9 Zabka and Dresen, *Dichter und Regisseure*, p. 59.

10 Thomas Mann, *Doktor Faustus*, in *Gesammelte Werke*, vol. VI, p. 349.

11 Romain Rolland, *Jean-Christophe*, trans. by Gilbert Cannen, 3 vols. (New York: Modern Library, 1938), vol. II, p. 140.

12 Thomas Mann, "Ist Schiller noch lebendig?," in *Gesammelte Werke*, vol. X, pp. 909–910.

13 Otto Brahm, "Der Naturalismus und das Theater," in *Kritiken und Essays*, ed. Fritz Martini (Zurich: Artemis, 1964), p. 402.

14 Jost Nolte, "Gespräch mit Rolf Hochhuth über 'Judith,'" *Penthouse* (German edn.), February 1985; rpt. in *"Ich bin Judith: Texte und Bilder zur Rezeption eines mythischen Stoffes,"* ed. Marion Kobelt-Groch (Leipzig: Leipziger Universitätsverlag, 2003), pp. 136–147; here p. 139.

15 Peter Sprengel, *Gerhart Hauptmann: Epoche—Werk—Wirkung* (Munich: Beck, 1984), p. 56. See in this connection Hans Robert Jauss, *Toward an Aesthetic of Reception*, trans. by Timothy Bahti (Minneapolis, Minn.: University of Minnesota Press, 1982).

16 Otto Brahm, *Theater. Dramatiker: Schauspieler*, ed. by Hugo Fetting (Berlin: Henschel, 1961), p. 402.

17 Marcel Proust, *Within a Budding Grove, in Remembrance of Things Past*, trans. by C. K. Scott Moncrieff and Terence Kilmartin, 2 vols. (New York: Random House, 1981), vol. I, p. 572.

18 Blackadder, *Performing Opposition*, p. xi, calls these decades "a key transitional phase in the evolution of normative audience response."

19 Blackadder, *Performing Opposition*, pp. 185–189, attributes the decline of scandal in most countries outside Germany to various factors: the accommodation of like-minded audiences to director's theater, the rise of film and television, the new and more intimate configuration of theater spaces, and the effort of directors to involve the spectators as participants.

20 Stephen Labaton, "Decency Ruling Thwarts F.C.C. on Vulgarities," *The New York Times*, June 5, 2007, p. 1.

21 Berghaus, *Theatre, Performance, and the Historical Avant-garde*, pp. 236–237.

22 Friedrich Dürrenmatt, "Das Theater als moralische Anstalt heute," in *Das Dürrenmatt Lesebuch*, pp. 257–267, here p. 263.

23 Dürrenmatt, "Das Theater als moralische Anstalt heute," p. 261.

Bibliography

Adelung, Johann Christoph, *Grammatisch-kritisches Wörterbuch der Hochdeutschen Mundart*, 2nd edn., 4 vols. (Leipzig: Breitkopf, 1793–1801).

Adorno, Theodor, *Gesammelte Schriften*, ed. Rolf Tiedemann, 20 vols. (Frankfurt: Suhrkamp, 2003).

Affron, Charles, *A Stage for Poets: Studies in the Theatre of Hugo and Musset* (Princeton, NJ: Princeton University Press, 1971).

Alberti, Conrad, "Die 'Freie Bühne:' Ein Nekrolog," *Die Gesellschaft*, 6 (August 1890), pp. 1104–1112.

Alcandre, Jean-Jacques, *Écriture dramatique et pratique scénique: Le "Brigands" sur la scène allemande des XVIIIe et XIXe siècles*, 2 vols. (Berne: Lang, 1986).

Arendt, Hannah, *Eichmann in Jerusalem: A Report on the Banality of Evil*, rev. edn. (New York: Viking, 1964).

Arnaud, Noël, *Alfred Jarry d'Ubu Roi au Docteur Faustroll* (Paris: La Table Ronde, 1974).

Arnold, Heinz Ludwig, "Der falsch gewonnene Prozess," *Text + Kritik* **138/139** (1998), pp. 114–122.

Augstein, Rudolf, "Apropos Henze," *Der Spiegel*, December 16, 1968, p. 154.

Bahr, Hermann, *Mit Gerhart Hauptmann: Erinnerungen und Bekenntnisse aus seinem Freundeskreis*, ed. Walter Heynen (Berlin: Stilke, 1922).

Balzer, Bernd, *Rolf Hochhuth: Der Stellvertreter* (Frankfurt: Diesterweg, 1986).

Barnes, Julian, *History of the World in 10½ Chapters* (London: Jonathan Cape, 1989).

Bax, Arnold, *Farewell, My Youth, and Other Writings*, ed. Lewis Foreman (Aldershot: Scolar, 1992).

Beaumont, Keith, *Alfred Jarry: A Critical and Biographical Study* (New York: St. Martin's, 1984).

Ubu Roi, Critical Guides to French Texts, 69 (London: Grant & Cutler, 1987).

Becker, Marie Luise, "Gertrud Eysoldt," *Bühne und Welt*, **5** (1903), pp. 635–641.

Beecham, Sir Thomas, *A Mingled Chime: An Autobiography* (New York: Putnam, 1943).

Ben Chaim, Daphna, *Distance in the Theatre: The Aesthetics of Audience Response* (Ann Arbor, Mich.: UMI Research Press, 1984).

Benedikt, Michael, "Introduction," in Michael Benedikt and George E. Wellwarth (ed. and trans.), *Modern French Theatre: An Anthology of Plays* (New York: Dutton, 1964), pp. ix–xxxv.

Bennett, Susan, *Theatre Audiences: A Theory of Production and Reception* (London: Routledge, 1990).

Bentley, Eric, *The Brecht Commentaries, 1943–1980* (New York: Grove, 1981).

The Storm over the Deputy (New York: Grove, 1964).

Berg, Jan, *Hochhuths "Stellvertreter" und die Stellvertreter-Debatte: Vergangen-heitsbewältigung in Theater und Presse der sechziger Jahre* (Kronberg: Scriptor, 1977).

Berghaus, Günter, *Theatre, Performance, and the Historical Avant-Garde* (New York: Palgrave Macmillan, 2005).

Blackadder, Neil, *Performing Opposition: Modern Theater and the Scandalized Audience* (Westport, Conn.: Praeger, 2003).

Brahm, Otto, *Kritiken und Essays*, ed. Fritz Martini (Zurich: Artemis, 1964).

Theater; Dramatiker; Schauspieler, ed. Hugo Fetting (Berlin: Henschel, 1961).

Braque, Georges, *Illustrated Notebooks, 1917–1955* (New York: Dover, 1971).

Brecht, Bertolt, *Gesammelte Werke in 20 Bänden* (Frankfurt: Suhrkamp, 1970).

Broder, Henryk, *Hurra, wir kapitulieren! Von der Lust am Einknicken* (Berlin: WJS, 2006).

Burda, Wolfgang, *Strawinsky: Leben, Werk, Dokumente* (Munich: Piper, 1993).

Caradec, François, *À la Recherche de Alfred Jarry* (Paris: Seghers, 1974).

Carl, Carl, and Margaretha Carl, *"Kann man also Honoriger seyn als ich es bin?" Briefe des Theaterdirektors Carl Carl und seiner Frau Margaretha Carl an Charlotte Birch-Pfeiffer*, ed. Birgit Pargner and W. Edgar Yates, Quodlibet, 6 (Vienna: Lehner, 2004).

Carlson, Marvin, *The German Stage in the Nineteenth Century* (Metuchen, NJ: Scarecrow, 1972).

"Theater audiences and the reading of performances," in Thomas Postlewait and Bruce A. McConadrie (eds.), *Interpreting the Theatrical Past: Essays in the Historiography of Performance* (Iowa City, Iowa: University of Iowa Press, 1989), pp. 82–98.

Chassé, Charles, *Sous le masque d'Alfred Jarry (?): Les Sources d'Ubu Roi* (Paris: Floury, 1921).

Chauveau, Paul, *Alfred Jarry, ou la naissance, la vie et la mort du Père Ubu* (Paris: Mercure de France, 1932).

Civardi, Jean-Marc (ed.), *La Querelle du Cid (1637–1638)* (Paris: Champion, 2004).

Connolly, Cyril, *Ideas and Places* (London: Weidenfeld & Nicolson, 1953).

Cooper, Judith, *Ubu Roi: An Analytical Study*, Tulane Studies in Romance Languages and Literatures, 6 (New Orleans, LA: Department of French and Italian, Tulane University, 1974).

Coupe, W. A., "An ambiguous hero: in defense of Alfred Loth," *German Life and Letters*, 31 (1977/1978), pp. 13–22.

Cowen, Roy C., *Hauptmann-Kommentar zum dramatischen Werk* (Munich: Winkler, 1980).

Naturalismus: Kommentar zu einer Epoche (Munich: Winkler, 1973).

Crosland, Margaret (ed.), *Cocteau's World: An Anthology of Writings by Jean Cocteau* (London: Owen, 1972).

Daffner, Hugo, *Salome: Ihre Gestalt in Geschichte und Kunst, Dichtung, bildende Kunst, Musik* (Munich: Schmidt, 1912).

Danto, Arthur C., *Encounters and Reflections: Art in the Historical Present* (New York: Farrar, 1990).

Del Mar, Norman, *Richard Strauss: A Critical Commentary on His Life and Works*, 2 vols. (London: Barrie & Rockliff, 1962).

Detering, Heinrich, "Kunstreligion und Künstlerkult: Bemerkungen zu einem Konflikt von Schleiermacher bis zur Moderne," in Günter Meckenstock (ed.), *Schleiermacher-Tag 2005: Eine Vortragsreihe*, Nachrichten der Akademie der Wissenschaften zu Göttingen, I. Philologisch-Historische Klasse 2006, Nr. 4 (Göttingen: Vandenhoeck & Ruprecht, 2006), pp. 179–200.

Dettelbach, Hans von, *Breviarum Musicae: Probleme, Werke, Gestalten* (Darmstadt: Wissenschaftliche Buchgesellschaft, 1958).

Dombois, Johanna, and Richard Klein, "Das lied der unreinen gattung: zum Regietheater in der oper," *Merkur*, **61** (2007), pp. 928–937.

Dottin, Mireille (ed.), *Salomé dans les collections françaises* (Saint-Denis: Musée d'Art et d'Histoire, 1988).

Dürrenmatt, Friedrich, *Das Dürrenmatt Lesebuch*, ed. Daniel Keel, Afterword by Heinz Ludwig Arnold (Zurich: Diogenes, 1991).

Edge, Arabella, *The Raft* (London: Picador, 2007).

Eksteins, Modris, *Rites of Spring: The Great War and the Birth of the Modern Age* (Boston, Mass.: Houghton Mifflin, 2000).

Ellmann, Richard, *Oscar Wilde* (New York: Knopf, 1988).

"Overtures to Wilde's Salomé," *Tri-Quarterly*, 5 (1969), pp. 45–64.

Esposito, Rosario F., *Processo al Vicario. Pio 12 et gli ebrei secondo la testimonianza della storia* (Turin: SAIE, 1964); trans. by Father Eugène Hudon: *Procès au vicaire: Pie XII et le juifs selon le temoignage de l'histoire* (Sherbrooke, Canada: Apostolat de la Presse, 1965).

Esslin, Martin, *Theatre of the Absurd*, rev. edn. (Garden City, NY: Doubleday, 1969).

Finck, Henry T., *Richard Strauss: The Man and His Works* (Boston, Mass.: Little, Brown, 1917).

Fischer, Jens Malte, "Oper wohin?," *Merkur*, 60 (2006), pp. 1067–1072.

Fontane, Theodor, *Aufsätze, Kritiken, Erinnerungen*, part 3, vol. II of *Sämtliche Werke*, ed. Walter Keitel (Munich: Hanser, 1962).

Frenzel, Elisabeth, *Stoffe der Weltliteratur: Ein Lexikon dichtungsgeschichtlicher Längsschnitte*, 9th edn. (Stuttgart: Kröner, 1998).

Gautier, Théophile, *Histoire du romantisme suivie de notices romantiques et d'une étude sur la poésie française, 1830–68* (Paris: Librairie des Bibliophiles, 1870).

Victor Hugo (Paris: Charpentier, 1902).

Gay, Peter, *Schnitzler's Century* (New York: Norton, 2002).

Gilliam, Bryan (ed.), *Richard Strauss and His World* (Princeton, NJ: Princeton University Press, 1992).

Gilman, Lawrence, *Strauss' "Salome": A Guide to the Opera* (London: Lane, 1907).

Gilman, Sander, "Salome, syphilis, Sarah Bernhardt, and the 'modern Jewess,'" *The German Quarterly*, **66** (1993), pp. 195–211.

Grimm, Reinhold, Willy Jäggi, and Hans Oesch (eds.), *Der Streit um Hochhuths "Stellvertreter"* (Basel: Basilius, 1963).

Haacke, Hans, "Museums, managers of consciousness," in Brian Wallis (ed.), *Hans Haacke: Unfinished Business* (Cambridge, Mass.: MIT Press, 1986).

Habermas, Jürgen, *Strukturwandel der Öffentlichkeit: Untersuchungen zu einer Kategorie der bürgerlichen Gesellschaft* (Frankfurt: Suhrkamp, 1990).

Halbwachs, Pierre, "Apropos de la 'Bataille d'Hernani,'" *Romantisme et politique, 1815–1851.* Colloque de l'École Normale Supérieure de Saint-Cloud, 1966 (Paris: Colin, 1969), pp. 99–109.

Hamann, Richard, and Jost Hermand, *Gründerzeit* (Berlin: Akademie, 1965).

Hauptmann, Gerhart, *Die großen Beichten* (Berlin: Propyläen, 1966).

Die Kunst des Dramas. Über Schauspiel und Theater, ed. Martin Machatzke (Frankfurt: Ullstein, 1963).

Notiz-Kalender 1889 bis 1891, ed. Martin Machatzke (Vienna: Propyläen, 1982).

Hawthorne, Don, "Does the public want public sculpture?," *ART News*, 81 (May 1982), p. 61.

Hecker, Max (ed.), *Schillers Persönlichkeit: Urtheile der Zeitgenossen und Documente*, 3 vols. (Weimar: Gesellschaft der Bibliophilen, 1904).

Hegel, Georg, *Werke*, ed. Eva Moldenhauer and Karl Markus Michel, 21 vols. (Frankfurt: Suhrkamp, 1970).

Heine, Wolfgang (ed.), *Kampf um den Reigen: Vollständiger Bericht über die sechstägige Verhandlung gegen Direktion und Darsteller des Kleinen Schauspielhauses Berlin* (Berlin: Rowohlt, 1922).

Hennenberg, Fritz, and Jan Knopf (eds), *Brecht/Weill "Mahagonny"* (Frankfurt: Suhrkamp, 2006).

Henze, Hans Werner, *Bohemian Fifths*, trans. by Stewart Spencer (London: Faber & Faber, 1998).

Heuss, Alfred, "Wird es endlich dämmern? Zur Mahagonny-Theaterschlacht, am 9. März im Neuen Theater zu Leipzig," *Zeitschrift für Musik*, **97** (1930), pp. 392–95.

Heynen, Walter, *Mit Gerhart Hauptmann: Erinnerungen und Bekenntnisse aus seinem Freundeskreis* (Berlin: Stilke, 1922).

Hochhuth, Rolf, *Die Geburt der Tragödie aus dem Krieg* (Frankfurt: Suhrkamp, 2001).

Die Hebamme: Erzählungen, Gedichte, Essays (Reinbek bei Hamburg: Rowohlt, 1971).

Räuber-Rede: Drei deutsche Vorwürfe: Schiller, Lessing, Geschwister Scholl (Reinbek bei Hamburg: Rowohlt, 1982).

Der Stellvertreter: Ein christliches Trauerspiel (Reinbek bei Hamburg: Rowohlt, 1967).

Hoffmeister, Reinhart (ed.), *Rolf Hochhuth: Dokumente zur politischen Wirkung* (Munich: Kindler, 1980).

Holt, Elizabeth Gilmore (ed.), *The Triumph of Art for the Public: The Emerging Role of Exhibitions and Critics, 1785–1848* (Garden City, NY: Anchor Doubleday, 1979).

Honegger, Gitta, *Thomas Bernhard: The Making of an Austrian* (New Haven, Conn.: Yale University Press, 2001).

Hovasse, Jean-Marc, *Victor Hugo, vol. I: Avant l'exil (1802–1851)* (Paris: Fayard, 2001).

Hugo, Adèle, *Victor Hugo raconté par Adèle Hugo; texte intégral*, ed. Evelyne Blewer (Paris: Plon, 1985).

Hugo, Victor, *Oeuvres complètes*, ed. Jean-Pierre Reyaud, 14 vols. (Paris: Laffont, 1985).

Victor Hugo: Hernani, ed. Anne Ubersfeld (Paris: Librairie Générale Française, 1987).

Irailh, Augustin Simon, *Querelles littéraires, ou Mémoires pour servir à l'Histoire des Révolutions de la République des Lettres, depuis Homere jusqu'à nos jours* (Paris: Durand, 1761).

Jarry, Alfred, *Tout Ubu*, ed. Maurice Saillet (Paris: Le Livre de Poche, 1962).

Ubu: Publiés sur les textes définitifs, ed. Noël Arnaud and Henri Bordillon (Paris: Gallimard, 1978).

Jauss, Hans Robert, *Toward an Aesthetic of Reception*, trans. by Timothy Bahti (Minneapolis, Minn.: University of Minnesota Press. 1982).

Johnson, James H., *Listening in Paris: A Cultural History* (Berkeley, Calif.: University of California Press, 1995).

Kammen, Michael G., *Visual Shock: A History of Art Controversies in American Culture* (New York: Knopf, 2006).

Kelly, Thomas Forrest, *First Nights: Five Musical Premieres* (New Haven, Conn.: Yale University Press, 2000).

Kerr, Alfred, *Gesammelte Schriften*, 7 vols. (Berlin: Fischer, 1917–1920).

Kerstan, Michael and Clemens Wolken (eds.), *Hans Werner Henze: Komponist der Gegenwart* (Berlin: Henschel, 2006).

Kessler, Marni Reva, *Sheer Presence: The Veil in Manet's Paris* (Minneapolis, Minn.: University of Minnesota Press, 2006).

Kirchert, Kay-Uwe, "Das Floss der Medusa: Reale und bildnerische Hintergründe in Hans Werner Henzes Oratorio," *Archiv für Musikwissenschaft*, **57** (2000), pp. 264–285.

Kirchmeyer, Helmut, *Strawinskys russische Ballette* (Stuttgart: Reclam, 1974).

Knopf, Jan, "Aufstieg und Fall der Stadt Mahagonny," in Jan Knopf (ed.), *Brecht Handbuch*, 5 vols. (Stuttgart: Metzler, 2001), vol. I, pp. 178–197.

Koebner, Thomas, *Arthur Schnitzler: Reigen – Erläuterungen und Dokumente* (Stuttgart: Reclam, 1997).

Kohlmayer, Rainer, "Oscar Wildes Einakter *Salome* und die deutsche Rezeption," in Winfried Herget and Brigitte Schultze (eds.), *Kurzformen des Dramas* (Tübingen: Francke, 1990), pp. 159–186.

Korngold, Julius, *Deutsches Opernschaffen der Gegenwart: Kritische Aufsätze* (Leipzig: Leonhardt, 1921).

Koselleck, Reinhart, *Kritik und Krise: Ein Beitrag zur Pathogenese der bürgerlichen Welt* (Freiburg: Alber, 1954).

Lawton, David A., *Blasphemy* (Hemel Hampstead: Harvester Wheatsheaf, 1993).

Lecke, Bodo (ed.), *Dichter über ihre Dichtungen: Friedrich Schiller von den Anfängen bis 1795* (Munich: Heimeran, 1969).

Leppmann, Wolfgang, *Gerhart Hauptmann: Leben, Werk und Zeit* (Berne: Scherz, 1986).

Lesure, François (ed.), *Igor Stravinsky, Le sacre du printemps: dossier de presse/press-book* (Geneva: Minkoff, 1980).

Lorenz, Dagmar (ed.), *A Companion to the Works of Arthur Schnitzler* (Rochester, NY: Camden House, 2003).

Louis, Rudolf, "Die erlöste Salome," *Süddeutsche Monatshefte*, **4** (1907), pp. 246–49.

Luhmann, Niklas, *The Reality of the Mass Media* (1994), trans. (from 2nd edn.) by Kathleen Cross (Cambridge: Polity, 2000).

Luserke-Jacqui, Matthias (ed.), *Schiller-Handbuch: Leben – Werk – Wirkung* (Stuttgart: Metzler, 2005).

Lusztig, J. C., "Richard Strauss' Musikdrama Salome," *Bühne und Welt*, **8** (1906), pp. 298–300.

Mahler, Alma, *Gustav Mahler: Memories and Letters*, ed. Donald Mitchell and trans. by Basil Creighton, 3rd edn. (Seattle, Wash.: University of Washington Press, 1975).

Mallarmé, Stéphane, *Correspondance*, ed. Henri Modor and Lloyd James Austin, 11 vols. (Paris: Gallimard, 1959–1985).

Mann, Thomas, *Gesammelte Werke in zwölf Bänden* (Frankfurt: Fischer, 1960).

Marcuse, Ludwig, *Obszön: Geschichte einer Entrüstung* (Munich: List, 1962).

Marinetti, Filippo Tommaso, *Selected Writings*, ed. R. W. Flint (London: Secker, 1972).

Matthus, Siegfried, "Die Kunst ist nie frei gewesen," *Berliner Morgenpost*, October 1, 2006.

Mendès, Catulle, *L'Art du théâtre*, 3 vols. (Paris: Fasquelle, 1897–1900).

Merkel, Karstin, *Salome: Ikonographie im Wandel* (Frankfurt: Lang, 1990).

Miles, Jonathan, *Medusa: The Shipwreck, the Scandal, the Masterpiece* (London: Cape, 2007).

Mitscherlich, Alexander and Margarete, *Die Unfähigkeit zu trauern. Grundlage kollektiven Verhaltens* (München: Piper, 1967).

Molière, *Oeuvres complètes*, ed. Robert Jouanny, 2 vols. (Paris: Garnier, 1962).

Molinari, Danielle, *Voir des étoiles: Le Theater de Victor Hugo mis en scene*, Catalogue of an exhibition at the Maison de Victor Hugo, April 12–July 28, 2002 (Paris: Paris-Musées, 2002).

Monteux, Doris, *It's All in the Music: The Life and Work of Pierre Monteux* (London: Kimber, 1965).

Neuhaus, Stefan and Johann Holzner (eds), *Literatur als Skandal: Fälle – Funktionen – Folgen* (Göttingen: Vandenhoeck & Ruprecht, 2007).

Neuse, Erna, "Die Funktion von Motiven und stereotypen Wendungen in Schnitzlers *Reigen*," *Monatshefte für deutschen Unterricht*, **64** (1972), pp. 359–367.

Nobécourt, Jacques, *"Le Vicaire" et l'histoire* (Paris: Éditions du Seuil, 1964).

Nolte, Jost, "Gespräch mit Rolf Hochhuth über 'Judith,'" *Penthouse* (German edn.), February 1985; rpt. in *"Ich bin Judith." Texte und Bilder zur Rezeption eines mythischen Stoffes*, ed. Marion Kobelt-Groch (Leipzig: Leipziger Universitätsverlag, 2003), pp. 136–147.

Oellers, Norbert (ed.), *Schiller: Zeitgenosse aller Epochen – Dokumente zur Wirkungsgeschichte*, 3 vols. (Frankfurt: Athenäum, 1970).

Panofsky, Walter, *Protest in der Oper: Das provokative Musiktheater der zwanziger Jahre* (Munich: Laokoon, 1966).

Richard Strauss: Partitur eines Lebens (Berlin: Deutsche Buch-Gemeinschaft, 1967).

Panter, Peter, "Proteste gegen die Dreigroschenoper," *Weltbühne*, **26** (April 8, 1930), pp. 55–58.

Poe, Edgar Allan, *Complete Works* (New York: Putnam, 1900).

Polgar, Alfred, *Kleine Schriften*, ed. Marcel Reich-Ranicki and Ulrich Weinzierl, 6 vols. (Reinbek bei Hamburg: Rowohlt, 1982–1986).

Poliakov, Léon and Josef Wulf, *Das Dritte Reich und die Juden: Dokumente und Aufsätze* (Berlin: Arani, 1955).

Porter, Andrew, "Raft of the Medusa," *The Financial Times*, December 11, 1968, p. 3.

Praz, Mario, *The Romantic Agony*, trans. by Angus Davidson (New York: Meridian, 1956).

Pringsheim, Klaus, "Mahagonny," *Weltbühne*, **26** (March 18, 1930), pp. 432–34.

Proust, Marcel, *Remembrance of Things Past*, trans. by C. K. Scott Moncrieff and Terence Kilmartin, 2 vols. (New York: Random House, 1981).

Puccini, Giacomo, *Letters*, ed. Giuseppe Adami and trans. Ena Makin, rev. edn. (London: Harrap, 1974).

Puffett, Derrick (ed.), *Richard Strauss: Salome* (Cambridge: Cambridge University Press, 1989).

Rachilde (pseud. of Marguérite Vallette), *Alfred Jarry ou le surmâle de lettres* (Paris: Grasset, 1928).

Raddatz, Fritz J. (ed.), *Summa iniuria oder Durfte der Papst schweigen? Hochhuths "Stellvertreter" in der öffentlichen Kritik* (Reinbek bei Hamburg: Rowohlt, 1963).

Randel, Don Michael (ed.), *The New Harvard Dictionary of Music* (Cambridge: Belknap Press of Harvard University Press, 1986).

Reimarus Secundus, *Geschichte der Salome von Cato bis Oscar Wilde, gemeinverständlich dargestellt* (Leipzig: Wigand, 1907–1908).

Renan, Ernest, *The Life of Jesus* (Garden City, NY: Dolphin Books [n.d.]). Reprint of earlier edition trans. Charles Edwin Wilbur (New York: Carleton, 1984).

Requardt, Walter, *Gerhart Hauptmann Bibliographie: Eine Zusammenstellung der von und über Gerhart Hauptmann im In und Auslande erschienenen Werke*, 3 vols. (Berlin: Selbstverlag, 1931).

Riedel, Wolfgang, *Die Anthropologie des jungen Schiller: Zur Ideengeschichte der medizinischen Schriften und der "Philosophischen Briefe"* (Würzburg: Königshausen & Neumann, 1985).

Robillot, Henri, "La Presse d'Ubu Roi," *Cahiers du Collège de 'Pataphysique*, **3–4** (1950), pp. 73–88.

Röder, Adam, *Salome* (Wiesbaden: Berend, 1907).

Rohde, Thomas (ed.), *Mythos Salome: Vom Markusevangelium bis Djuna Barnes* (Leipzig: Reclam, 2000).

Rolland, Romain, *Jean-Christophe*, trans. by Gilbert Cannen, 3 vols. (New York: Modern Library, 1938).

Ross, Alex, "Agit-Opera," *The New Yorker*, March 5, 2007, pp. 88–89.

The Rest is Noise: Listening to the Twentieth Century (New York: Farrar, Straus & Giroux, 2007).

Royce, Anya Peterson, *Anthropology of the Performing Arts: Artistry, Virtuosity, and Interpretation in a Cross-Cultural Perspective* (Walnut Creek, Calif.: AltaMira, 2004).

Rudloff-Hille, Gertrud, *Schiller auf der Bühne seiner Zeit* (Berlin: Aufbau, 1969).

Sanders, Ronald, *The Days Grow Short: The Life and Music of Kurt Weill* (New York: Holt, 1980).

Sautermeister, Gert, "Die Räuber: Ein Schauspiel," in Matthias Luserke-Jacqui (ed.), *Schiller-Handbuch* (Stuttgart: Metzler, 2005), pp. 1–45.

Schebera, Jürgen, *Kurt Weill: An Illustrated Life*, trans. by Caroline Murphy (New Haven, Conn.: Yale University Press, 1995).

"Zur Wirkungsgeschichte bis 1933," in Fritz Hennenberg and Jan Knopf, eds., *Brecht/Weill Mahagonny* (Frankfurt: Suhrkamp, 2006), pp. 219–246.

Schiller, Friedrich, *Die Räuber: Texte und Zeugnisse zur Entstehungs und Wirkungsgeschichte*, ed. Herbert Kraft and Harald Steinhagen (Frankfurt: Insel, 1967).

Sämtliche Werke, ed. Gerhart Fricke and Herbert G. Göpfert, 5 vols. (Munich: Hanser, 1967).

Schläder, Jürgen (ed.), *OperMachtTheaterBilder: Neue Wirklichkeiten des Regietheaters* (Leipzig: Henschel, 2006).

Schlenther, Paul, *Gerhart Hauptmann: Sein Lebensgang und seine Dichtung* (Berlin: Fischer, 1898).

Wozu der Lärm? Genesis der Freien Bühne (Berlin: Fischer, 1889).

Schmidt, Otto, "Die Uraufführung der 'Räuber' – ein theatergeschichtliches Ereignis," in Herbert Stubenrauch and Günter Schulz, *Mannheimer Soufflierbuch* (Mannheim: Bibliographisches Institut, 1959), pp. 151–180.

Schnabel, Ernst, *Das Floss der Medusa* (Munich: Piper, 1969).

Schneider, Gerd K., *Die Rezeption von Arthur Schnitzlers "Reigen," 1897–1994. Text, Aufführungen, Verfilmungen, Pressespiegel und andere zeitgenössische Kommentare* (Riverside, Calif.: Ariadne, 1995).

"Ich will jeden Tag einen Haufen Sternschnuppen auf mich niederregnen sehen." Zur künstlerischen Rezeption von Arthur Schnitzlers "Reigen" in Österreich, Deutschland und den USA (Vienna: Praesens Verlag, 2008).

"The social and political context of Arthur Schnitzler's Reigen in Berlin, Vienna, and New York: 1900–1933," in Dagmar Lorenz (ed.), *A Companion to the Works of Arthur Schnitzler* (Rochester, NY: Camden House, 2003), pp. 27–57.

Schneider, Gerd K, and Peter Michael Braunwarth (eds), *Ringel-Ringel-Reigen: Parodien von Arthur Schnitzlers "Reigen"* (Vienna: Sonderzehl, 2005).

Schnitzler, Arthur, *Briefe 1875–1931*, ed. Therese Nickl, Heinrich Schnitzler, Peter Michael Braunwart *et al.*, 2 vols. (Frankfurt: Suhrkamp, 1981–1984).

Ein Liebesreigen: Die Urfassung der "Reigen," ed. Gabriella Rovagnati (Frankfurt: Fischer, 2004).

Schnitzlers "Reigen," ed. Alfred Pfoser, Kristina Pfoser-Schewig, and Gerhard Renner, 2 vols. (Frankfurt: Fischer, 1993).

Tagebuch, ed. Kommission für Literarische Gebrauchsformen (Werner Welzig, Peter Michael Braunwarth *et al.*), 10 vols. (Vienna: Österreichische Akademie der Wissenschaften, 1981–2000).

Schorske, Carl E., *Fin-de-Siècle Vienna: Politics and Culture* (New York: Knopf, 1980).

Schuch, Friedrich von, *Richard Strauss, Ernst von Schuch und Dresdens Oper*, 2nd edn. (Leipzig: Breitkopf, 1953).

Schumacher, Ernst, *Die dramatischen Versuche Bertolt Brechts 1918–1933* (Berlin: Rütten, 1955).

Sehm, Günter G., "Moses, Christus und Paul Ackermann: Brechts *Aufstieg und Fall der Stadt Mahagonny*," in *Brecht-Jahrbuch 1976* (Frankfurt: Suhrkamp, 1976), pp. 83–100.

Sharpe, Lesley, *Friedrich Schiller: Drama, Thought and Politics* (Cambridge: Cambridge University Press, 1991).

Shattuck, Roger, *The Banquet Years: The Arts in France 1885–1918* (New York: Harcourt, 1958).

Showalter, Elaine, *Sexual Anarchy: Gender and Culture at the Fin de Siècle* (New York: Viking, 1990).

Sinfield, Alan, "The theater and its audience," in Alan Sinfield (ed.), *Society and Literature 1945–1970*, (London: Holmes, 1983).

Solomon, Maynard, *Mozart* (London: Hutchinson, 1995).

Sontag, Susan, *Against Interpretation and Other Essays* (New York: Noonday, 1966).

Sprengel, Peter, *Gerhart Hauptmann: Epoche – Werk – Wirkung* (Munich: Beck, 1984).

Springer, Brunold, *Die genialen Syphilitiker*, 2nd–4th edn. (Berlin-Nicolassee: Neue Generation, 1926).

Stähr, Wolfgang, "Konzertskandal und Straßenkampf: Hans Werner Henze und die Weltrevolution," *Berliner Philharmoniker – das magazin* (November/December 2006), pp. 4–8.

Steiner, George, *The Death of Tragedy* (New York: Knopf, 1963).

Strauss, Richard, *Betrachtungen und Erinnerungen*, ed. Willi Schuh (Zurich: Atlantis, 1981).

Stravinsky, Igor, *Autobiography* (1936) (London: Calder, 1975).

Stravinsky, Igor and Robert Craft, *Memories and Commentaries* (London: Faber & Faber, 2002).

Stubenrauch, Herbert and Günter Schulz (eds.), *Schillers Räuber: Urtext des Mannheimer Soufflierbuches* (Mannheim: Bibliographisches Institut, 1959).

Stuckenschmidt, H. H., "Mahagonny," *Die Szene*, **21** (1931), pp. 75–77.

Symons, Arthur, *Studies in Seven Arts* (London: Constable, 1906).

Tenschert, Roland, "Richard Strauss' Opernfassung der deutschen Übersetzung von Oscar Wildes *Salome*," in Willi Schuh (ed.), *Richard Strauss Jahrbuch 1959–60* (Bonn: Bossey, 1960), pp. 99–106; English trans. in Puffet (ed.), *Salome*, pp. 36–50.

Ther, Philipp, *In der Mitte der Gesellschaft: Operntheater in Zentraleuropa 1815–1914* (Vienna: Oldenbourg, 2006).

Thilo, Georg and Hermann Hagen (eds.), *Servii Grammatici qui feruntur in Vergilii carmina commentarii*, vol. I (Leipzig: Teubner, 1881).

Thomé, Horst, "Arthur Schnitzlers 'Reigen' und die Sexualanthropologie der Jahrhundertwende," *Text + Kritik*, **138/139** (1998), pp. 102–113.

Turnbull, Michael T. R. B., *Mary Garden* (Portland, Oreg.: Amadeus, 1997).

Van Vechten, Carl, *Music after the Great War* (New York: Schirmer, 1915).

Voigt, Felix, *Hauptmann-Studien: Untersuchungen über Leben und Schaffen Gerhart Hauptmanns*, vol. I: *1880 bis 1900* (Breslau: Maruschke, 1936).

Völker, Klaus, "Jarrys Panoptikum des wissenschaftlichen Zeitalters," *Akzente*, **6** (1959), pp. 301–311.

Wagner, Gottfried, *Weill und Brecht: Das musikalische Zeittheater* (Munich: Kindler, 1977).

Walsh, Stephen, *Stravinsky: A Creative Spring: Russia and France, 1882–1934* (London: Cape, 2000).

Weisstein, Ulrich, "Von reitenden Boten und singenden Holzfällern: Bertolt Brecht und die Oper," in Walter Hinderer (ed.), *Brechts Dramen: Neue Interpretationen* (Stuttgart: Reclam, 1984).

Wellek, René, *A History of Modern Criticism 1750–1950*, 7 vols. (New Haven, Conn.: Yale University Press, 1955–1991).

Wellek, René and Austin Warren, *Theory of Literature* (New York: Harcourt, 1956).

Wellwarth, George, *The Theater of Protest and Paradox: Developments in the Avant-Garde Drama* (New York: University Press, 1964).

Wolff, Rudolf (ed.), *Rolf Hochhuth: Werk und Wirkung* (Bonn: Bouvier, 1987).

Wyss, Monika (ed.), *Brecht in der Kritik: Rezensionen aller Brecht-Aufführungen, sowei ausgewählter deutsche und fremdsprachiger Premieren: Eine Dokumentation* (Munich: Kindler, 1977).

Yeats, W. B., *Autobiographies* (New York: Macmillan, 1938).

Zabka, Thomas, and Adolf Dresen, *Dichter und Regisseure: Bemerkungen über das Regie-Theater* (Göttingen: Wallstein, 1995).

Zagona, Helen G., *The Legend of Salome and the Principle of Art for Art's Sake* (Geneva: Droz, 1960).

Zelle, Carsten, "Die Schaubühne als moralische Anstalt betrachtet," in Matthias Luserke-Jacqui (ed.), *Schiller-Handbuch: Leben – Werk – Wirkung* (Stuttgart: Metzler, 2005), pp. 343–357.

Zeller, Bernhard (ed.), *Gerhart Hauptmann: Leben und Werk*, Catalogue for the Memorial Exhibition at the Deutsches Literatur-Archiv of the Schiller-Nationalmuseum Marbach, May–October 1962 (Stuttgart 1962).

Ziolkowski, Margaret, *Hagiography and Modern Russian Literature* (Princeton, NJ: Princeton University Press, 1988).

trans. and ed., *Tale of Boiarynia Morozova: A Seventeeth-Century Religious Life* (Lanham, Md.: Lexington, 2000).

Ziolkowski, Theodore, *Fictional Transfigurations of Jesus* (Princeton, NJ: Princeton University Press, 1972).

German Romanticism and its Institutions (Princeton, NJ: Princeton University Press, 1990).

Index